The Last Mazurka

The Last Mazurka

A TALE OF WAR, PASSION AND LOSS

Andrew Tarnowski

Aurum

First published 2006 by Aurum Press Limited,
25 Bedford Avenue,
London WCIB 3AT

Copyright © 2006 by Andrew Tarnowski

The moral right of Andrew Tarnowski to be identified as the
author of this work has been asserted by him in accordance with
the Copyright, Designs and Patents Act 1988.

A catalogue record for this book is available from the British Library.

ISBN 1 84513 139 8

1 3 5 7 9 10 8 6 4 2
2006 2008 2010 2009 2007

The author and publishers would like to thank Oxford University Press for
permission to quote the poem by Edward Slonski on pp. 22–3, translated by
Norman Davies in *God's Playground: A History of Poland*, vol. 2,
first published in 1982.

Every effort has been made to trace the copyright holders of material
quoted in this book. Please contact the publishers in the case of any
omission, which will then be corrected in future editions.

Text design by Peter Ward
Typeset in Adobe Garamond by SX Composing DTP, Rayleigh, Essex
Printed and bound in Great Britain by MPG Books, Bodmin

For Wafa', who encouraged me over the years,
and for Sophie, Marcos, Daisy and Stefan.
Darlings, this is where we come from.
Unbelievable!

Contents

Contents

A note on pronunciation

For the sake of clarity, Polish accents, which are numerous and potentially confusing for those unused to them, have been omitted from the text. For readers who want to know how the names of the principal characters and places in the book are pronounced, there is a basic guide below, with accents where appropriate.

Note that 'w' in Polish is pronounced 'v' at the beginning of a word and 'f' in the middle or end, and that 'c' is pronounced 'ts'.

People		Places	
Elżbieta	*Elzhbeeyeta*	Dzików	*Jeekoof*
Jaś	*Jash*	Kraków	*Krakoof*
Róża	*Roozha*	Łańcut	*Winesoot*
Stanisław	*Staneeswaff*	mały domek	*mawee domek*
Staś	*Stash*	Rzeszów	*Zheshoof*
Tadeusz	*Tadayoosh*	Szlak	*Shlak*
Tarnowski	*Tarnofskee*	Załęże	*Zawenzhay*
Wacek	*Vatsek*		
Wacław	*Vatswaff*		
Władysław	*Vwadiswaff*		
Zdzisław	*Zdjeeswaff*		

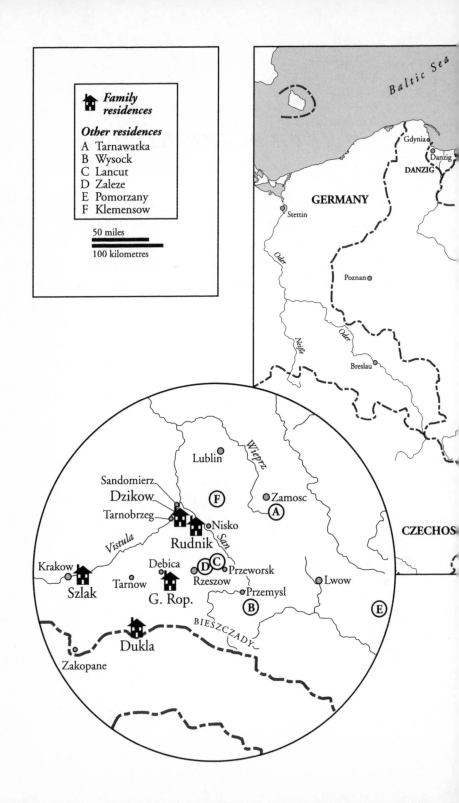

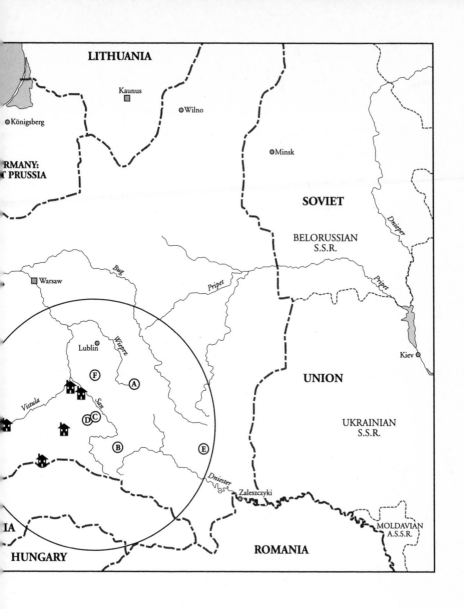

Poland 1919-39

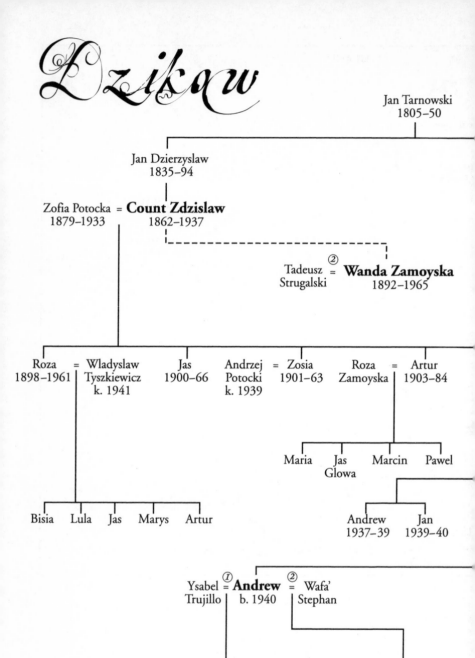

Dzikow

Jan Tarnowski
1805–50

Jan Dzierzyslaw
1835–94

Zofia Potocka = **Count Zdzislaw**
1879–1933   1862–1937

Tadeusz ② = **Wanda Zamoyska**
Strugalski   1892–1965

Roza = Wladyslaw   Jas   Andrzej = Zosia   Roza = Artur
1898–1961   Tyszkiewicz   1900–66   Potocki   1901–63   Zamoyska   1903–84
      k. 1941   k. 1939

Maria   Jas   Marcin   Pawel
     Glowa

Bisia   Lula   Jas   Marys   Artur

Andrew   Jan
1937–39   1939–40

Ysabel ① = **Andrew** ② = Wafa'
Trujillo   b. 1940   Stephan

Sophie   Maxi   Marcos   Daisy   Stefan
b. 1972   b/d. 1974   b. 1976   b. 1986   b. 1987

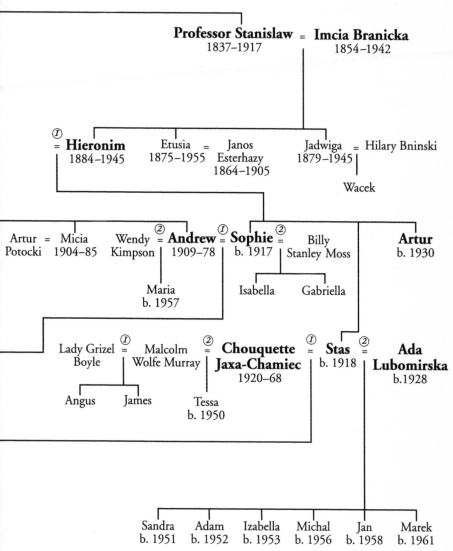

Professor Stanislaw = Imcia Branicka
1837–1917   1854–1942

(1) = **Hieronim**   Etusia = Janos   Jadwiga = Hilary Bninski
1884–1945   1875–1955   Esterhazy   1879–1945
                     1864–1905

Wacek

Artur = Micia   Wendy (2)= **Andrew** (1)= **Sophie** (2)= Billy   **Artur**
Potocki   1904–85   Kimpson   1909–78   b. 1917   Stanley Moss   b. 1930

Maria   Isabella   Gabriella
b. 1957

Lady Grizel (1)= Malcolm (2)= **Chouquette** (1)= **Stas** (2)= **Ada**
Boyle   Wolfe Murray   **Jaxa-Chamiec**   b. 1918   **Lubomirska**
                       1920–68   b.1928

Angus   James   Tessa
                   b. 1950

Sandra   Adam   Izabella   Michal   Jan   Marek
b. 1951   b. 1952   b. 1953   b. 1956   b. 1958   b. 1961

'I describe a world which, for me, has not died. I lived with those people. I feel as if I had seen them yesterday. Writing is a form of struggle against the death of a cause, it is the salvation of entire generations from oblivion. In literature, the dead live on, as if in a dream.'

Isaac Bashevis Singer, chronicler
of the lives of Poland's vanished Jews,
1978 Nobel Laureate for Literature.

The Rose of Tobruk

*O*ne of my most treasured possessions is a wallet so fragile and scuffed with age that the leather has faded to grey and the pockets come apart and fall out if it is not delicately handled. It is stamped 'Tobrouk 1941', a souvenir from long ago. When I hold it I feel I am holding history in my hands; I am touching the past.

In one of the pockets are the dry, brown remains of flower petals, and tucked behind another is a small black-and-white photograph, cracked with age and stained around the edges. It shows a beautiful young woman with a joyful smile and sunshine on her face. Her dark hair is parted in the middle and gathered at the ears in the fashion of an Italian Renaissance portrait. A child sits sideways on her lap, blond hair escaping from his bonnet, his mouth open in something between a smile and a cry.

My father gave me the wallet in Warsaw a few years ago on his eightieth birthday. He told me my mother sent it to him as a Christmas present in 1941 when he was serving as a corporal in the Carpathian Rifle Brigade, a Polish Army unit fighting alongside the Australians and British at Tobruk in one of the famous battles of the Second World War. The young woman in the photograph is my mother, Sophie, who was known as Chouquette, and the child is me at about fifteen months. The crumbled petals are the remains of a rose she gave my father Stas as he lay in hospital after the siege of Tobruk was lifted.

My heart swelled for a moment at the thought that these faded things were perhaps mementoes of unsuspected happy times between my parents. It filled me with gladness that Stas had kept the wallet, the photograph and the crumbled rose petals for more than half a lifetime, although he and Chouquette had divorced after the war and she had been dead many years. Perhaps, despite everything, he had retained some trace of affection for her.

But that was an illusion. Chouquette did not give him the rose for love, for they were estranged by then. It was her tribute to a brave soldier, one of the victors of Fortress Tobruk that had delivered the first check of the war to Hitler's land armies. Nor had Stas kept the rose and the wallet and photograph in memory of love between him and Chouquette, but as a reminder of the halcyon days and grand adventures he had lived through when he was young and brave and fighting Hitler in the war that destroyed his country and his world. War breeds actions and feelings so intense that many prefer to forget them, but Stas embraced every detail of his war with elation. Even at eighty, in his drab little box house in post-communist Warsaw, half blind and nearly helpless with age, he remembered it as the time of his life: 'Oh yes, those were the days,' he drawled in his upper-class English accent, a smile lighting up his hawk-like old face, 'Oh, they were wonderful times.' And he regaled me with tales of adventures and battles, and of his many love affairs, including one while my mother was giving birth to me. He spoke of just about everything with nostalgia, except Chouquette.

It was painful to hear, and I sometimes had to restrain myself, but my conversations with Stas were part of my search for the past. I needed his memories, because after Chouquette remarried my childhood and youth were spent in Scotland

and England, cut off from my Polish heritage. Even as I was being raised as a Briton I was drawn by echoes, some near, some far, of my parents' pre-war lives in Poland and their wartime adventures. By the time Stas was eighty I had long been delving into my unknown Polish past. Conversations with him and other family members, and long, magical talks with his sister, Aunt Sophie, in her absurdly untidy kitchen in Putney, had opened up a past that was utterly foreign to my life in Britain. As the lives of my parents, grandparents and great-grandparents unfolded I felt I was finding my own family, my own lost identity, and the almost Tolstoyan world from which I came.

But the story turned out to be more painful and tragic than I could ever have imagined. When Chouquette sent Stas the wallet they had only been married for two years, after fleeing Poland during Hitler's invasion. But the marriage was already broken by violence and betrayal that involved not only them but close friends and family with whom they had fled. They had left Poland in a convoy of cars packed with aristocratic relatives, and travelled on to the Middle East with Stas's sister Sophie, and her husband and cousin Andrew, who was Stas's best friend. Despite the strains that developed between the four of them as the marriage soured they had clung together through the Balkans and Palestine, penniless refugees with only each other to rely on. It helped that Stas, Sophie and Andrew came from an ancient aristocratic caste back in Poland and had been raised according to archaic traditions and rigid perceptions of correct behaviour. Their family had given great men to Poland and had once held great power in the land. They were proud of their heritage, even inordinately proud, and held each other in special esteem as members of the same historic clan.

They had learned in the spacious hallways of their ancestral homes that one never discussed personal difficulties between family members. One respected the older generation absolutely, one never argued within the family, one behaved with perfect manners in every circumstance and maintained the appearance of family unity at all costs. Although they had lost everything when they left Poland, parents, homes, wealth and estates, they had carried the family code of behaviour into exile, and it had helped them stick together despite the strains between them. Only Chouquette, the daughter of a brilliant and charming Warsaw financier and entrepreneur, was not an aristocrat. But alone, far from her family with no one else to turn to, she could only fall in with the rules of behaviour set by her companions.

Sophie, Stas and Andrew had grown up in the privileged world of a semi-feudal landowning aristocracy. Even though southern Poland in the 1920s and 1930s was one of the poorest regions of Europe, they were raised by foreign nannies and governesses and waited on by liveried retainers in mansions and castles, on country estates inhabited by peasants who were sometimes barefoot and greeted their lord by kissing his hand or stooping to embrace his knees in an ancient gesture of submission.

Their world was cocooned by wealth and tradition and populated by faithful retainers and a vast network of relatives and connections. Andrew's home had been the seat of the senior branch of the family for nearly four hundred years. Its library was bursting with priceless archives, its walls hung with fine paintings, including one of Rembrandt's most famous works, *The Polish Rider*. Its stables had been home to a famous stud farm, and its forests teemed with game. The cream of the Polish aristocracy came for hunts that lasted two or three days, and they shot wild boar, bear, buck, stags, wolves, foxes, hare, badgers and even eagles. The estate on which Sophie and Stas grew up was not far away, and they, too, could gallop endlessly through forests and meadows and hunt the finest roe buck in the land.

The world in which the two couples had fallen in love was idyllic, but their fate once the war broke out mirrored the tragedy of their country. Neither marriage survived the war, although they might not have survived anyway. Stas and Sophie were themselves children of a disastrous marriage which had poisoned their parents and themselves and bestowed a crippling lovelessness on their family. When their own turn came to marry they had no way of recognising love, and little understanding of how to give it.

Stas and Chouquette were already refugees when they married in Belgrade just after the war began, but Sophie and Andrew had married in Poland two years earlier. Their romance began in the snow during a mid-winter wolf hunt, and early in 1937 Sophie and Andrew were married in a little wooden chapel beside her father's mansion. It was a gloomy winter's day. The trees were bare, the sky was grey and snow lay on the ground, but the mansion was decorated with flowers and winding garlands adorned the pillars of the portico. Dozens of relatives came to stay and overflowed into neighbouring castles and mansions. People from the estate and the nearby town crowded up to the mansion to watch the wedding party, the ladies sparkling with jewels and the lords strutting in the traditional silks and furs of the Polish nobility, with peacock feathers in their hats and sabres at their sides.

Sophie's wedding was the last joyful family gathering before the war swept them all away, and they celebrated through the night. After the speeches in praise of the young couple came the toasts, and champagne, vodka and home-brewed mead flowed freely. They feasted on caviar and carp cooked in aspic, with roast pork, beef and pheasant, venison and home-cured wild boar hams, followed by home-made sweets and fruit preserves and cheeses matured in the sandy soil of the estate.

A gypsy band played and the party grew boisterous. They danced on the polished parquet floor beneath dark larch beams spanning the ceilings of the mansion. On and on they danced to the gypsy violins: waltzes, tangos and two-steps, sambas, mambas and Charlestons, and for old time's sake a last mazurka, that most patriotic of ancient Polish dances. The couples whirled around the room in a lively and elegant stream, heads high, heels stamping and clicking, hands gesturing gracefully.

As dawn broke they were served hot, clear beetroot soup and pasties stuffed with wild mushrooms. It was Sunday morning and as the guests were driven home they could hear the bells of the church in the nearby town ringing to call the faithful to early Mass. Although none of them knew it, the bells would soon be tolling for their country and for the noble caste from which they came.

CHAPTER I

Secrets and Forebodings

Sophie's wedding was not the first in the family to take place in times heavy with foreboding. War had loomed more threateningly on 8 July 1914, the day her parents were married. The Archduke Franz Ferdinand, heir to the throne of the Austro-Hungarian Empire, had been assassinated in Sarajevo ten days earlier, raising the spectre of a great conflict between Germany, Austria-Hungary and Russia, the three empires that had ruled the divided Polish lands since slicing up the country between them at the end of the eighteenth century. The outbreak of hostilities was so imminent that close relatives of the bride and groom who lived in the Russian-ruled region of Poland stayed away from the wedding in Habsburg-ruled Krakow in case the war should catch them on the wrong side of the border.

They were married in the Gothic gloom of the Mariacki church, the cavernous Basilica of the Most Holy Virgin Mary which stands on a corner of the vast market square in Krakow, Poland's ancient royal capital. A crowd of princes, counts and notables and their ladies watched as my grandfather Hieronim Tarnowski exchanged vows with the beautiful Wanda Zamoyska beneath Wit Stwosz's huge polyptych, a marvel of high medieval sculpture that towers above the high altar, its tortured wooden figures depicting scenes from the life and death of Christ and the Virgin.

Afterwards, the wedding party paraded across the square beneath the elegant mansions and palaces of lords and burghers, the ladies in tiaras and long dresses, the gentlemen in silk overcoats trimmed with fur, trousers tucked into calf-length boots, sabres dangling at their sides and peacock feathers waving from their fur hats. The reception was held in the Palace *pod Baranami* or 'Under the Rams', a magnificent mansion on the square named for the carved stone rams' heads supporting the balcony above the entrance. The signatures of more than a hundred guests and the wise and joyous speeches given for the occasion were inscribed in the opening pages of a large, leather-bound volume embossed with the star and crescent moon of Leliwa, the armorial crest of the Tarnowski family, which Hieronim's parents presented to the young couple as the visitors' book for their future home.

The wedding guests did not know, as they celebrated the union of cadet branches of two historic families, that Hieronim's cousin Karol Tarnowski had felt Wanda pulling back on his arm as he led her to the altar to give her away. Neither he nor any of the other guests could have had any inkling of the drama that would take place that night, when Hieronim rushed weeping from the bridal chamber in a Krakow mansion to seize a pistol, point it at his heart and fire. The bullet entered the left side of his chest but missed his heart and Wanda rushed to his side as he fell to the floor. The wound turned out not to be too serious, but the implications for the marriage of Hieronim's desperate act were grave and he would have many problems before he eventually consummated the union. Relatives had to coach him delicately in the bedroom arts, and there were whispers of minor surgery.

The family wrapped the shooting in impenetrable silence to avoid a scandal, and it was nearly eighty years before word of it leaked out. It was Uncle Tomasz Zamoyski, a nephew of

Wanda, who revealed the secret to me on a grey April afternoon in the early 1990s at his apartment on a quiet Warsaw back street. Old, frail and almost blind, Uncle Tomek, as he was known, relayed the astonishing anecdote for the first time, adding that it should not be repeated. He had no doubt that the reason for Hieronim's despair was the damage his male pride suffered on the wedding night as a result of Wanda's reluctance to marry him and his own inexperience in the bedroom.

Everyone who knew them said Hieronim and Wanda were so ill matched that they should never have married. The marriage had been arranged by the mothers of the bride and groom, who were close friends. But while Hieronim was much taken by Wanda's beauty, and may have loved her, she was not in the least interested in him. He was nine years older than her, rather small and a bit eccentric and unpredictable. Although he was quite nice looking there were far more handsome young men to be found in Krakow high society, and he generally tended to be serious, although he was not without his moments of humour. He was, however, the son of one of the most distinguished couples in Krakow society and heir to a substantial fortune, an important consideration for Wanda's widowed mother whose family fortunes were not in the best condition.

As the youngest child of ageing parents, Hieronim had been brought up almost as an only child, mainly by his devoted but rather eccentric mother. She had raised him in the most conservative tradition of nineteenth-century Roman Catholicism, in which purity and piety were high ideals and chastity a supreme virtue. Although he was thirty when he married, he was completely ignorant of women and throughout his life he never knew a woman other than Wanda.

He had dark, wavy hair, a high forehead, a big bony nose and a handlebar moustache. As a young man he had a genial look, though it changed to an air of sadness in later life. He was a true gentleman, good-natured, honourable and sincere. He was selfless and highly principled, and had a touch of real holiness. He liked to attend Mass most mornings, and some of those who knew him thought he might have been better suited to being a Catholic priest than a husband and father.

Hieronim was highly educated, well read and knowledge-able in Polish and foreign literature and in ancient and modern history, and he spoke fluent German, French, English, Latin, Greek, Italian and Spanish. He wrote to his closest friends in Latin all his life and loved to settle down over coffee after dinner for a Latin conversation. He had an extraordinary memory. He remembered a page of text after reading it twice, and could recite from memory long passages of poetry and chapters of prose by Polish and foreign authors – Schiller was a favourite. He was a Wagner enthusiast and used to sing the Swan Song from *Lohengrin* in his bath in a rich baritone. He was almost laughably old-fashioned, and his cousins considered him a *dziwak*, an eccentric. He hated motor cars and telephones and refused to own or use them, and he would never start a journey on a Monday or do anything important on the thirteenth of the month.

But Hieronim also had a choleric streak. He could explode with anger, raising his voice and waving his arms. His rages passed quickly and without serious consequences, but his opinions were dogmatic and narrow and he was rigid in argument and unable to compromise, sometimes taking his argument to the point of absurdity. An ardent monarchist, he was once heard discussing the merits of monarchy and democracy with a nephew. The discussion grew heated, and when Hieronim ran out of arguments he said in desperation, 'But Roman, don't forget that Jesus said "Thy kingdom come", not "May democracy come".' He argued violently with his mother, who liked to discuss politics and social issues but was unbending and accepted nothing that contradicted her husband's ultra-conservative beliefs. His older sisters blamed their mother for fostering intolerance and narrow opinions that made him inflexible in handling people and problems.

Wanda, on the other hand, was a formidable woman, immensely strong-willed and self-assured. She believed in absolute self-discipline and would not tolerate weakness in any form, in herself or in others. Her iron self-control and unbreakable courage would help her surmount every trial the twentieth century was to throw at her. But she was also self-centred and there was a hardness in her heart. The youngest of six children, whose father had died when she was seven, she did what she liked and did not care what others felt or thought. She was always convinced of her own rightness, no matter what, and careless of the trouble and pain she caused. Admirable in some ways, but impossibly bold and self-willed, Wanda was far from being the loving, reassuring companion that Hieronim needed for a wife.

When they married in 1914 Wanda was every inch an aristocratic beauty: tall, willowy, auburn-haired, with fine features and a delicate complexion, she had great charm and wit, and a love of art and beauty. She loved glamour and high society. Nothing could have suited her less than being tucked away on a distant country estate with a serious, highly strung and devoutly religious man like Hieronim, who was happiest out and about on horseback in his forests or on his farm, in comfortable tweeds and sensible shoes. Wanda had, in fact, already been in love with a young man named Adam Szembek, and had wanted to marry him. But her mother considered Szembek insufficiently well off to make a match with her daughter.

Hieronim's family enjoyed great prestige in Krakow and throughout Galicia, the province annexed by the Austrian Empire in the eighteenth century, which included Krakow, southern Poland and part of what is today western Ukraine but had for centuries been part of Poland. Not only had his ancestors been immensely powerful Krakow lords who had played an important role in Polish history during the golden age of the kingdom between the fourteenth and sixteenth centuries, but his father was a figure of great eminence in his own right and his mother came from an immensely rich princely family.

Unusually for an aristocrat, Hieronim's father Professor Stanislaw Tarnowski was a renowned academic and one of the most prominent political and intellectual figures in pre-1914 Galicia. The professor was a cult figure among the Krakow conservative intelligentsia. At the turn of the century many fellow intellectuals and academics attended a lunch each Thursday in his honour at the *Resursa Krakowska* or Krakow Club. He was an historian of Polish literature, a prolific writer of *belles lettres*, a political thinker and co-founder of an influential group known as *Stanczycy*, and a fine public speaker known for his patriotism and moving perorations that made the ladies sigh. He had first-class patriotic credentials, having been imprisoned for a year by the Austrian authorities as a young man for his role in helping to finance and arm a doomed nationalist uprising in Russian Poland in 1863.

Great honours had since been showered upon him. His eminence was witnessed by the fact that in 1900 he was the first man to be elected to a second term as Rector Magnificus of the Jagiellonian University in Krakow, Poland's most ancient seat of learning. His ancestors' signatures were on the university's founding charter, and in 1900 he had presided over the university's 500th anniversary celebrations. He was also President of the Polish Academy of Sciences, a member of the Galician Diet in Lwow and of the imperial House of Lords in Vienna, and he was a secret counsellor to the Emperor Franz Jozef.

The professor had a large head with a fine, classical profile, plenty of long white hair and a bushy beard, but his head was set on a small body, which gave him an unusual appearance. The air of self-importance he affected and his florid literary and speaking styles made him an easy target for satirists and cartoonists. Humourless, taciturn and jealous of his dignity, he was easily offended and could be ruthless in trying to destroy his critics and publications that dared to publish their lampoons.

His wife, who was born Princess Roza Maria Branicka, had inherited some of the great riches that the Russian Empress Catherine II had heaped upon her family for their political services at the end of the eighteenth century. She was known as Imcia, and she was a well-meaning and affectionate woman. She was sixteen years younger than her husband, but their relationship was close and loving; she worshipped him, and in her eyes he could do nothing wrong.

Imcia was scatter-brained, a figure of fun to contemporaries, and Hieronim must have inherited his eccentricity from her. She was always so late for everything that it was said that when she was invited to her first grandchild's christening in Hungary she arrived in time for the christening of the second. She had such an odd way of walking – bouncing up and down from heel to toe in a sort of floating motion, her head in the air, a seraphic smile on her face – that Austrian friends mockingly called her the dancing kangaroo. She had been known in her youth for her beautiful profile resembling that of the ill-fated French Queen Marie Antoinette, but by 1914 she had lost her looks and settled into middle age, and wore the shapeless old black dresses favoured by Krakow matrons.

The couple's Krakow residence was an historic mansion known as the Szlak or 'Track', which had been built in the sixteenth century as the first head office of Poland's royal mail. It took its name from an old track along which the bodies of Polish kings who died outside the ancient royal capital were brought into the city. By tradition, the king's body had laid for a night in the mansion before being carried within the city walls for the funeral.

The Szlak buzzed with high society in the years leading up to the turn of the twentieth century, thanks to the professor's eminence and lineage, Imcia's wealth and the fact that they had two daughters to marry off. Invitations were keenly sought in Krakow society and by visitors from all over Poland, particularly during the pre-Lenten Carnival when Krakow gave itself over to a month of nightly balls and merry-making. Whenever the professor and Imcia gave a party they showed their philanthropic piety by donating a sum equalling its cost to their friend Brother Albert Chmielowski, who set up the Albertinian Order that cared for the region's poor and homeless, and was later raised to sainthood by the Polish Pope John Paul II.

Imcia kept an easygoing household, and no one ever knew how many people would sit down to dinner at the Szlak. Despite her wealth, the couple let the mansion become run down and dilapidated and never bothered to install central heating, although it sometimes got so cold in winter that they moved to the Grand Hotel in town. But normally the house was full of relatives, children and guests, and family wedding receptions and other celebrations were often held in its immense gardens that extended over two hectares.

The professor was nearly fifty when Hieronim was born, and he had no idea how to develop an intimate relationship with his youngest child and only son. He was extremely busy with his many duties outside the house, and like most aristocratic parents in those days he and Imcia left Hieronim with nannies and governesses in his infancy and childhood. The best attempt the professor made at intimacy was when Hieronim received his First Holy Communion aged twelve, when he wrote him an affectionately couched thirty-page letter commending to him the beliefs and sacraments of the Roman Catholic Church with an orthodox zeal worthy of a Cardinal of the Holy Office.

Receive this Sacrament, my dear little son with a gratitude commensurate with all that God has given you since birth and for what he is giving you now, with piety as lively and ardent as you are able to muster and with a constant and certain will never to turn away from God, but rather to remain faithful and obedient to Him until death. May you diligently and with all your strength guard your faith, your love of God and fellow man, your purity of mind, heart and life, and may truth and honesty be reflected in all your words and deeds. Take this to heart that the older you get and the more grace you receive from God, the greater will be your responsibility before God and man. Promise yourself that whatever difficulties, sorrows, penance or struggle you encounter in later life, you will always seek help from God and only in His Most Blessed Sacrament against these difficulties, and comfort for these sorrows, and light and strength for this penance and struggle . . .

The professor was fifty-nine when he wrote this letter, and it was as close to intimacy and paternal affection as he could get.

When the time came for Hieronim to marry, the professor was already retired and in his late seventies and he left the match-making to Imcia, having learned his lesson twenty years earlier when he intervened disastrously in the affairs of his oldest daughter Elzbieta. Etusia, as she was affectionately known, lost her heart during the Krakow Carnival of 1895 to Janos Esterhazy, a cavalry officer in the Austro-Hungarian army who came from a famous Hungarian family. But when Esterhazy asked the professor for her hand, he replied in a fit of self-importance that he would never permit his daughter to marry a soldier of the occupying army.

Esterhazy left Krakow, and Etusia went into deep depression. She refused to eat and fell seriously ill. After two years the professor consulted a doctor, who told him she was likely to die if she was not reunited with her love. So for once the professor swallowed his pride, went to Vienna to find Esterhazy and asked him to marry his daughter. Etusia and Janos were married at last in 1898, but they had only seven years together before Janos died of a heart attack. The professor was so full of remorse at what he had done that when he died he left an apology to Etusia in his will.

Wanda's and Hieronim's betrothal was an easier matter than Etusia's. They had known each other since childhood. Their parents' country estates in southern Poland were not far from each other, and they had danced together at Wanda's coming-out dance in Krakow in 1911 when she was eighteen. Waclaw Lednicki, a young man newly arrived in Krakow for the pre-Lenten Carnival, wrote a vivid account of the evening in his memoirs.

> In great excitement, we tied white ties and put on tail coats for the first time. Madame Zamoyska's house was small and surrounded by gardens, but very beautiful inside. I was introduced to ladies and gentlemen of the greatest Polish families and I noticed that there was no lack of good looks among them. Among the gentlemen I noticed after a short while a slim, dark-haired young man who could play perfectly the role of an aristocrat in a play by d'Annunzio. He had black, silky, wavy hair, a black moustache and energetic movements, and he spoke freely and joked, knowing everybody. This was Imus, son of Professor Stanislaw Tarnowski.

Imus, the diminutive by which Hieronim was known, had won a waltzing competition in Vienna and he led the opening waltz with Wanda. Lednicki's account captures the joyous spirit of the occasion.

> It is difficult to re-create the excitement provoked in all of us young people by the lively and at the same time fluent and rapturous rhythm of the waltz. We stood like horses before the race, nervously awaiting the moment when we would be free to sail up with a brisk step to the chosen lady.

Next came the mazurka, danced as a dashing, intricate series of changing patterns and figures demanding great skill and stamina. Wanda's brothers Adam and Zygmunt were renowned as the best mazurka dancers in Krakow. They were tall, handsome and athletic, and when they took the floor with their partners everyone moved to the ballroom to watch.

Even the old ladies and gentlemen paused in their conversations or card games in the neighbouring salon, or their involvement at the cold buffet, and went in to admire. At the climax of the mazurka the dancers slid on their knees into the centre of the ballroom to form stars, and rose in pairs, joining hands and whirling faster and faster until it seemed that arms and legs would give way.

Despite their families' closeness and the friendship between their mothers, however, there was a very good reason why Wanda and Hieronim should not have married. Unknown to them, Wanda was probably the illegitimate daughter of Hieronim's first cousin, Count Zdzislaw Tarnowski of Dzikow, the patriarch of the extended family who was believed to have had an adulterous fling with her mother when he was a young man. For reasons known only to herself, Wanda's mother had arranged a marriage between her former lover's illegitimate daughter and his first cousin. Hieronim and Wanda were first cousins once removed, a relationship seen in Poland as equivalent to that of uncle and niece.

It is strange that the marriage was allowed to go ahead, because the family knew all about the relationship. Michal Marczak, the archivist and librarian at Dzikow castle, Count Zdzislaw's country estate, wrote in his diary in 1914 that when the extended family gathered at Dzikow that year to celebrate Count Zdzislaw's saint's day* the talk was all about the impending marriage: 'They whispered quietly about this Wanda, a very handsome girl, that she is the daughter of Count Zdzislaw of Dzikow, because her mother was not distinguished by virtue.'

The blood tie should have been enough to arouse fears of all

---

*Saint's days are traditionally celebrated in Poland rather than birthdays.

sorts of complexities in their relationship and in their off-spring, but the family raised no objections. It may have been that the other members of the family feared Count Zdzislaw, who was something of a tyrant, and found it too daunting to raise the issue of his youthful affair. Or perhaps the family did not consider the issue worth raising, since such affairs were common among the Polish aristocracy. They were routinely covered up by the wronged husband, who gave the child his name and accepted him into the family. It was something of a joke that the youngest child of aristocratic marriages was often fathered by another man from an equally aristocratic house.

Whatever the reason for the family's silence about Hieronim's and Wanda's blood relationship, their marriage was disastrous from the start and turned out to be miserable. The misery did not end with them but affected those who came after, because they passed down to their children all the characteristics that had made them incompatible with each other. The misery they suffered lived on in the disunity that plagued their descendants down through the twentieth century. The shot that Hieronim fired so dramatically on that summer night in Krakow was not only a tocsin sounding a grim warning of the wars and revolutions ahead; the misery it heralded for Hieronim and Wanda would also be echoed down the years from generation to generation in the loveless-ness and unhappiness that has haunted their descendants until today.

CHAPTER TWO

The Old World Passes

When Hieronim and Wanda married, his parents decided to give the young couple their country estate at Rudnik beside the River San, which Imcia had bought in 1898 from a widowed Austrian baroness.

Rudnik became Hieronim and Wanda's married home, and as soon as Hieronim was able to travel after the wedding-night drama they went there to set up their household. From there they made the traditional newly-weds' visit to Count Zdzislaw, Hieronim's cousin and quite possibly Wanda's father, at Dzikow castle, about fifty kilometres north-west of Rudnik. He invited a family house party to welcome them and they spent several days at Dzikow, joining the household each afternoon on leisurely cavalcades that wound through the copses along the banks of the River Vistula.

Soon after the couple returned to Rudnik war broke out. They had barely unpacked the wedding gifts and settled into the mansion with its crenellated towers and mock battlements when on 1 August 1914, Austria-Hungary ordered general mobilisation in preparation for war with Russia and Serbia. Hieronim was called up to his regiment, and so he and Wanda were unable to settle down amid the forests at Rudnik, where they might perhaps have begun to overcome the trauma they had suffered.

They hurried back to Krakow, where Hieronim reported for duty as a reserve lieutenant of cavalry. On 6 August, the day the war began, he rode out with his regiment, Prince Schwarzenberg's Second Lancers of the Austro-Hungarian imperial army, to fight the Russians. Wanda did not return to Rudnik, which lay on the border of Austrian and Russian Poland, in the path of a Russian advance into Galicia. But her mother hurried over to Rudnik from her nearby estate and had the wedding presents re-packed and sent back to Krakow. The estate manager at Rudnik buried some of the family's most precious possessions as a precaution against looting or destruction.

As the war got under way Wanda noted down in the Rudnik visitors' book some of Hieronim's experiences at the front, among the signatures and thanks of their guests. Her notes were sparse and occasional, but Hieronim's mother Imcia lovingly recorded his war experiences in an older visitors' book that she and the professor had kept since buying Rudnik in 1898. Imcia covered ten pages in her small, spidery handwriting after the Germans and Austrians had beaten back the Russian offensives of 1914 and 1915, and her opening words ring with the drama of the times:

> This Guest Book lay buried, hidden in the earth, during the Russian invasion, and this is why it looks so damaged. We thought it had perished or been destroyed, like most things at Rudnik, so we were very happy that it has been saved. I want to write in it a little bit of what happened to Imus and Rudnik, our house, which now stands empty, looted, damaged by machine-gun fire and shells, without doors and windows, with its rooms gutted.

The war on the eastern front was more mobile than the trench-bound attrition in the West, where the British and

French fought the Germans to a bloody standstill. But the Polish lands were laid waste amid terrible carnage as the Russian, German and Austro-Hungarian armies fought back and forth over the entire country. Millions of men died in battle on the eastern front, and millions of civilians died, too. Tragically, each of the three armies conscripted Poles from the Polish territories they controlled. Nearly two million Poles ended up fighting, although the war had little to do with them, and they suffered more than 1.35 million casualties. Polish soldiers often heard Polish songs coming from the enemy trenches, and many of the 450,000 Poles who died were killed by other Poles. The pointless fratricidal slaughter was poignantly commemorated in a wartime poem by Edward Slonski:

> We're kept apart, my brother,
> By a fate we can't deny.
> From our two opposing dug-outs
> We're staring death in the eye.
>
> In the trenches filled with groaning
> Alert to the shellfire's whine,
> We stand and confront each other.
> I'm your enemy: and you are mine.
>
> So when you catch me in your sights
> I beg you, play your part,
> And sink your Muscovite bullet
> Deep in my Polish heart.
>
> Now I see the vision clearly,
> Caring not that we'll both be dead;

For *that which has not perished*^{*}
Shall rise from the blood that we shed.[1]

The Russians threw millions of men into their opening offensives in German and Austrian Poland, and bloody battles were fought as soon as the war began. At the very start, in August 1914, the Germans in the north trapped a Russian army advancing through the forests and lakes of East Prussia and destroyed it in the Battle of Tannenberg. It was a famous encounter in the age-old conflict between Germans and Slavs, hailed by the Germans as vengeance for a Polish-Lithuanian victory over the Teutonic Knights in 1410 at the nearby field of Grunwald. By the end of September the Germans had won a second battle at the Mazurian Lakes, completing the destruction of the Russian armies that had pushed into East Prussia.

But in the south the Russians made deep inroads into Austrian-ruled Galicia. Hieronim was in the thick of the fighting, but appears not to have been an outstanding soldier. 'A loveable eccentric,' wrote Prince Alfons Clary, an Austrian friend in his regiment, 'an indifferent soldier, although his superiors, appreciating his good qualities, overlooked this point. At least he was a good horseman, and that in a cavalry regiment was an important skill.'[2]

But within days of riding off to war Hieronim returned to Krakow after apparently twisting a leg in a heavy fall from his horse. After resting for a week he went back to the front, and on 23 August he came under fire for the first time at Ilza, a Polish town 150 kilometres north-east of Krakow. In the next four months he was in twenty battles and skirmishes. From

---

^{*}A reference to the opening lines of the Polish national anthem: 'Poland has not perished yet / So long as we still live'.

Ilza he took part in an Austro-Hungarian offensive eastwards into Russian Poland which was intended to take the city of Lublin. But it was beaten back. 'Then began a horrendous retreat through swamps and sands,' Imcia wrote.

> They crossed the River San into Galicia and later passed through Dzikow [Count Zdzislaw's residence]. Imus stopped there for a while, asking for a clean shirt (he hadn't changed his for weeks!) and for something to eat, since for the previous few days he had hardly eaten at all. He soon marched on with sorrow and distress in his heart that Dzikow would fall into the power of the Muscovites who were closing in on it.

It was 11 September 1914, when Hieronim visited Dzikow. Michal Marczak, the Dzikow librarian, recorded in his diary that Hieronim's regiment was involved in the defence of a nearby crossing of the River Vistula against the pursuing Russians. During the fighting he and a fellow officer rode over to Dzikow for dinner with Count Zdzislaw. 'They talked about the battle and then they had to go back,' Marczak wrote. Five days later the Russians forced the Vistula, took the neighbouring town of Tarnobrzeg, and reached the castle.

The Russians advanced into western Galicia, forcing the Austro-Hungarian army back towards Krakow. Many people fled the city, and in early September Wanda, her mother and grandmother were evacuated by train to Vienna, the Austrian capital. By late September the Russians were in sight of Krakow, but before they could take the city the Germans sent troops to reinforce the Austro-Hungarians and their combined forces halted the Russians and mounted a counter-offensive that drove them northwards towards Warsaw.

Hieronim was appalled by the devastation he saw as the

army pursued the Russians through central Poland. 'All along the way, everywhere around them,' wrote Imcia, 'were raging fires and looting caused by the retreating Russian army, an immemorial tactic of defence by destruction.'

The Austro-Hungarian army came within sight of the outskirts of Warsaw, and Hieronim hoped to take part in the capture of the city. But the Russians checked them before they could reach it and began to push them westwards. At Sochaczew, fifty kilometres from Warsaw, the Russians defeated them and forced them to retreat further west. Imcia wrote:

> They retreated under worse conditions than the previous retreat from Lublin, amid constant skirmishes, with the enemy army pressing on the rearguard where Imus was. He remained under fire all the time from the defeat at Sochaczew until past the River Warta [more than 100 kilometres west]. With despair in his heart Imus looked around him at the increasingly widespread destruction of historical places and houses and at the abysmal destitution of the civilian population who were begging the army for bread.

After retreating across the Warta, the Austro-Hungarians again linked up with the Germans and together they drove the Russians back to Warsaw. By then it was mid-November, winter was closing in and Hieronim was exhausted after four months of constant campaigning. He fell ill with a high fever and was unable to speak, but carried on with his duties until a general saw the condition he was in and ordered him to hospital. While he was waiting for transport to the rear, he lived in a hut with a peasant family. 'He stayed there for a few days and tried to save from requisition the last cow of that peasant family whose father was away at the front,' Imcia wrote. 'All through the campaign he had tried to save what he could for the people from requisition or looting.'

He was invalided back to Krakow, and as the train passed through German Silesia he looked with wonder at the countryside untouched by war, the people working in the fields, the cattle and horses, and the children playing among geese and chickens. It was such a long time since he had seen normal life, Imcia explained, and his heart ached with the contrast.

When Hieronim reached Krakow at the end of November he found that Wanda was away in Vienna, and he travelled on to join her in the small apartment she had taken at 10 Rauhensteingasse. He was still sick, and Imcia wrote that he was very changed by the experience of war. Wanda noted that he was suffering from inflammation of the lungs, or tuberculosis. She took him to a sanatorium at Baden near Vienna where he spent several weeks. He remained on sick leave for six months and underwent surgery in the Loew Sanatorium in Vienna on 11 April 1915.

Wanda gives no explanation of the operation in the visitors' book. The only ailment she mentions is inflammation of the lungs. Imcia, however, implies that the surgery had nothing to do with Hieronim's lungs. 'After a few months he needed an operation – the fall from his horse at the beginning of the war left him with some complications,' she wrote. 'The operation was successful.'

Perhaps the operation was connected with complications from the wedding-night shooting and Imcia did not want to mention it. Or perhaps it was a delicate matter connected with Hieronim's difficulties in the marriage bed. Whatever the facts, he saw no more action during the war. He remained with Wanda, convalescing in Vienna while the Russians and Austro-Hungarians fought the decisive struggle in 1915 for western Galicia.

During the months of waiting in Vienna they asked anxiously for news of Rudnik, their home. Wounded men and officers who had fought in a battle at Rudnik early in the war told them of terrible bloodshed and destruction. At last, by early July 1915, the Russian army had been thrown back far to the east and the fighting in western Galicia ended. They were able to return to Krakow, where Hieronim was promoted to Oberleutnant and appointed commandant of two military hospitals. But Wanda was anxious to learn what had happened to Rudnik, and she set off on her own to find out.

Leaving Krakow by train on 29 July 1915, she travelled 150 kilometres east to the city of Rzeszow and then rode alone all day to reach Rudnik. 'I spent the night in Rzeszow, from where at seven in the morning I went on horseback via Sokolow to Rudnik, where I arrived at six in the evening,' she wrote later in the visitors' book. She had ridden alone through seventy kilometres of devastated countryside, and when she got to Rudnik she was horrified by what she saw. 'I found terrible destruction, the house completely stripped by looters and riddled with gunfire, the garden criss-crossed with trenches and mostly destroyed by shelling, the woods in the countryside burned, the people living in dugouts and lean-tos.'

Beneath Wanda's brief account of her journey Hieronim wrote: 'Ten shell holes in the house, the home farm burned, about 3,000 *morgi* (4,000 acres) of woods burned and laid waste.'

The battle for Rudnik had lasted more than three weeks from 10 October to 4 November 1914, as the Russian Third Army smashed westwards across the River San into Galicia, driving the Austrians from earthworks high on the river banks and battling through the forests, park and gardens around Hieronim's mansion. When Hieronim and Wanda eventually returned home in the autumn of 1915 they found dozens of mass graves in the gardens and park, and strange mushrooms growing in the park that seeped something like blood when they were knocked over. When the graves were dug up in December, 3,600 bodies were found. Hieronim had them reburied in a single grave on a hillock not far from the house, where he erected a cross with a plaque requesting prayers for the fallen.

Although the fighting was over, there was terrible misery all around. So many homes had been destroyed that peasants were living in the fields in dirt dugouts. Hunger, smallpox, typhus and cholera were raging in the small town of Rudnik two kilometres from Hieronim's ruined mansion, and the bodies of the dead were still being carried to the cemetery every night. Of the town's 615 houses, 367 had been burned down and the rest wrecked by shelling. The wooden church built in 1791, the presbytery, the synagogue, the railway station, the pharmacy and the town hall had all been burned down. The courthouse and most of the houses on the square were gutted. Many townspeople had been killed. Photographs show crowds of townspeople digging graves for piles of bodies, handkerchiefs clutched to their faces against the stench of death.

'Tears spring to the eyes at the sight of thousands of wretched and destitute people, widows and orphans, men and women in rags,' Father Feliks Senkiewicz, the parish priest of Rudnik, wrote to his sister.[3] 'The whole town is in ruins. In the whole of Rudnik, except for a few houses, only chimneys remain. The woods, the gardens and the plots of the townspeople are full of graves. Apart from the war cemetery, there are dozens of graves under the window of the vicar's house. In the middle of the square there is a big grave of the fallen.'

Wanda, along with her former French governess who was now her companion, settled into *maly domek,* a little wooden house in the park which had been the home of the estate manager before the war. At first there were no servants and only a few old farmhands and horses, but with the help of an old man and his wife the two women prepared for winter, chopping firewood, storing food and laying mattresses on the floor and against the windows for protection.

While the graves around Hieronim's mansion were being dug up, a Hungarian lady came to look for the body of her son. They tried to find him, but dug in vain for days until Wanda had a strange dream. She dreamed that she was walking in the small garden near *maly domek* when she noticed a small acacia tree. It had huge bunches of flowers, not white flowers as the acacia has in Poland, but pink and much bigger. They were so beautiful that she knelt and held out the apron she was wearing, and the flowers dropped into it like tears. When she woke she went into the garden and saw that there was indeed a small acacia tree there, although it had miserable little white flowers. Remembering the Hungarian lady, she asked the men to dig at the spot, and they found the body of the lady's son.

The grieving mother signed the visitors' book on 10 December 1915, as Marie Polony from Szynesvanalja in Hungary. Hieronim wrote beneath her signature: 'During the exhumation of the dead in the garden she looked for several days for the body of her son – she recognised it from the monograph on his shirt.'

Normality slowly returned and by early 1916 Hieronim was

coming from Krakow for long stays and they were receiving a steady flow of visitors. At last, early in the autumn of 1916, Wanda realised she was pregnant, and on 16 March 1917, her first child, my Aunt Sophie, was born. The christening ceremony was held in a little wooden chapel among the trees in front of the mansion, which the previous owners of Rudnik had built in the ornate style of Zakopane in the Tatra mountains. She received a string of names in accordance with the aristocratic practice of the time: Zofia Roza Jadwiga Elzbieta Katarzyna Amelia.

Hieronim's father the professor died on the last day of 1917, aged eighty, passing away with the old order of which he had been a luminary. The old Emperor Franz Josef had died in 1916. His successor Karl was to abdicate in November 1918, bringing the Habsburg Empire to an end. The Russian revolution had despatched Tsar Nicholas in 1917, and the defeat of the Central Powers in the war also brought the downfall of the German Kaiser.

The three empires that had partitioned Poland since the late eighteenth century had collapsed. It was time for Poland to be reborn and reclaim its place on the map of Europe.

CHAPTER THREE

The Pet Wild Boar Has Gone

*E*ighteen months after Sophie's birth, when the Great War was ending and the family was enjoying their only period of domestic tranquillity, Stas was born in the little wooden house beside the ruined mansion on the estate at Rudnik. The two births no doubt caused satisfaction in the extended family after the concerns the couple's difficulties had aroused, and may have raised hopes for the future of the mariage. But the circumstances of Stas's arrival in the world were far from tranquil.

He used to say it was not surprising that he turned out to be wild, not because of the signs and wonders arising from the political turbulence that accompanied his birth, but because Wanda continued riding until she was six months pregnant. In fact, he arrived in the world at a time of immense upheaval in Central and Eastern Europe and of great turbulence in Poland. The three empires which had ruled the partitioned Polish lands since 1795 collapsed as the war neared its end, and anarchy raged for a while before a new Polish state emerged.

Hieronim noted in the Rudnik visitors' book that his son was born on 16 September 1918, and the christening was to take place a month later in the wooden chapel in front of the mansion. The ceremony was postponed when Sophie fell ill with the Spanish influenza that killed tens of millions of people around the world in 1918, and when she recovered Hieronim set 7 November as the new date.

But by the time the day approached the great events surrounding Poland's rebirth were rumbling to their climax. As the Central Powers crumbled, cities all over the Polish lands liberated themselves of their various occupiers. The Austro-Hungarian army pulled out of Galicia in October and went home, and the civil administration and police of the province vanished with it. Bands of armed deserters from the disintegrating army roamed the Galician countryside, attacking mansions and estates, pillaging and murdering. In Tarnobrzeg, the small town beside the family castle at Dzikow, a renegade Catholic priest helped to set up a short-lived socialist mini-republic. In Warsaw, still occupied by the German army despite the German collapse on the Western front, there was confusion bordering on chaos.

The Polish state was reborn in November 1918 after Jozef Pilsudski, a former socialist activist and anti-tsarist conspirator, arrived in Warsaw and took over from the Germans. Pilsudski had led a volunteer Polish Legion against the Russians during the war, but when he refused to put his men under German command in 1917, he was arrested. As the war neared its end he was released from Magdeburg Castle and allowed to travel to Warsaw. On 11 November, the day the armistice that ended the war in the West was signed, a Polish Regency Council hurriedly named Pilsudski Commander-in-Chief, and national independence was proclaimed. The German garrison agreed to disarm and left Warsaw. Three days later Pilsudski was made Chief of State of the Polish Republic.

While Polish flags were raised throughout the country and euphoria gripped the land, armed bands continued to roam

Galicia and an outbreak of violence at Rudnik forced
Hieronim and his family to flee for their lives. 'When God
allowed Poland to be resurrected, uproar began!' he wrote in
the visitors' book. 'Twice attacks on the house were repulsed
by the militia from Kopki and our people. On November 12
I took my wife and the children to Krakow.'

The militia that had defended Rudnik was in reality just
another band of brigands whom Wanda, in one of her many
courageous acts, had persuaded to protect her family. She and
her French lady companion had been alone when the anarchy
began. When they heard that an armed band had occupied
the village of Kopki, a few kilometres away on Hieronim's
estate, and was about to attack Rudnik itself, Wanda decided
to appeal to them personally. She had a carriage harnessed and
was driven to the village. But the old driver stopped in the
forest a few hundred metres before they reached Kopki.

'My lady countess, I'm terribly sorry, I won't go any
further,' he told her. 'I have a wife and children and I'm just
afraid of these people.'

Asking him to wait there, she got down and walked on
alone. As she entered the village she told the armed men
milling around: 'I want to see your commanding officer.'
They hurried to obey.

'What, did you come here on your own?' the bandit leader
exclaimed as she was brought into the house in which he was
staying.

She was twenty-five and utterly fearless, and she had an
easy way with people. 'Yes,' she replied, 'I have come here on
my own because I have heard that bands of brigands, who are
killing and looting, are coming here. I am alone at Rudnik
with my babies and I have come to ask for your protection.'

Her courage won the day. The brigands promised to

protect Rudnik. They kissed her hand as she left, and they kept their promise.

Stas was baptised in the chapel of the archbishop of Krakow the day after they arrived there. He received a string of names: Stanislaw-Kostka Stefan Jan Juliusz Krzysztof Jerzy Hubert Gustaw. He used to joke that the first seven names each had some family significance but he never understood why he was named Gustaw.

The anarchy in the countryside was overcome soon enough after the transfer of power in Warsaw. As Pilsudski organised the new state an army was created from soldiers of the three former occupying armies, and police forces were formed throughout the country. Hieronim took his family back to Rudnik; farmhands, foresters and servants began to return, and as the whole of Europe subsided into peace work on rebuilding the home farm, the town and the church got under way again. The mass grave of the victims of the 1914 battle was dug up and the bodies were sent home to Hungary or re-buried in the town cemetery, and Hieronim hired an architect to rebuild his shattered mansion.

He must have hoped, like every Pole, for years of peace to raise his family and nurse his ruined property to prosperity. But once again he and Wanda had no chance to settle down. As soon as the Polish Republic was reborn it was drawn into a series of mini-wars and wars to establish its borders.

The Great Powers at the Versailles peace conference of 1919, which had endorsed Polish independence, failed to pronounce definitively on its borders. It was left to Poland and her neighbours to settle them. Threatened by Germany and the Soviet Union, the new state fought in the north, south, east and west between 1918 and 1921. By mid-1919 Polish troops had taken the ancient Polish city of Lwow and parts of eastern Galicia from Ukrainian nationalists. In the north, they took the predominantly Polish city of Vilno from the Lithuanians in 1919–20. In the west, the Poznanian war with Germany was settled by the Treaty of Versailles in June 1919. The Silesian war, fought in three uprisings against the Germans, was settled by agreement in 1922. The Czechoslovak war in the south, which followed a Czechoslovak invasion of Cieszyn in early 1919, was settled by Allied arbitration in 1920. But the fighting with Bolshevik Russia, which began as another territorial dispute in February 1919, grew into a major conflict. By the spring of 1920 Poland was locked in a struggle with the Red Army that threatened the very existence of the young republic.

Poles flocked to the colours. Landowners like Hieronim, whose class the Bolsheviks had slaughtered in Russia and the Ukraine in 1917, took down their rifles and swords and rode off to the war. On his estate at Dzikow, the seat of the senior branch of the family, Count Zdzislaw Tarnowski equipped and uniformed fifty men for Prince Jozef Poniatowski's Eighth Lancers, the most aristocratic cavalry regiment in the new Polish army, including his seventeen-year-old son Artur and the gamekeeper Roman Sarnek. His oldest son Jas was already fighting with the 'Young Eagles' defending Lwow against the Ukrainians. Count Zdzislaw also gave six million crowns to the war effort and gave over a mansion on the estate, part of the castle at Dzikow and part of his large Krakow residence for military hospitals.

As in 1914, Wanda accompanied Hieronim when he went to Krakow to answer the call of duty. He joined Poniatowski's Lancers and was appointed aide de camp to General Maxime Weygand, the head of a small French military mission. Weygand had arrived uninvited in Warsaw, expecting to help direct operations against the Red Army. But he was largely ignored by the Polish high command, which was angered by the refusal of the western Allies to help protect Poland from the Bolsheviks. President Woodrow Wilson of the United States had declared in his Fourteen Points in 1917 that Poland had the right to exist as an independent and autonomous state, and Britain and France had followed suit. The Paris peace conference had confirmed Poland's right to exist, so the Poles were incensed that the Allies sent no troops and the French cut off military credits, while a 'Hands off Russia' propaganda campaign in the West stirred up anti-Polish sentiments.

In the summer of 1920 the war raged in the east and Poland's survival hung in the balance. More than a million men fought along a front stretching hundreds of kilometres from north to south through the forests, steppes and marshlands of the *kresy* or borderlands, as the Poles called their historic eastern marches. The fighting went well at first for Pilsudski's makeshift armies, but the Russians assembled a strike force of 700,000 men and in June the Cossacks of Marshal Semion Budyenny's First Cavalry Army smashed through the southern end of the Polish line and poured westwards. In the north, the Soviet General Mikhail Tukhachevsky broke through on 4 July and marched westwards, proclaiming: 'To the West. Over the corpse of White Poland lies the road to worldwide conflagration. On our bayonets we bring happiness and peace to the people toiling by the sweat of their brow. To the West! Our time has come. To Wilno, Minsk and Warsaw! March!'

By early August, five Soviet armies were converging on Warsaw. Salvation was only achieved, according to popular myth, by the 'Miracle of the Vistula', when the Black

Madonna of Czestochowa, an icon of the Virgin Mary revered as Queen of Poland, is said to have appeared in the skies above Warsaw and guided Pilsudski's armies to victory. In more military terms, Pilsudski rapidly regrouped his exhausted divisions before Warsaw in the space of a few days, covertly redeployed them and sprung a trap on Tukhachevsky, slicing through the rear of his over-extended forces and encircling them outside the city. The Poles took a hundred thousand prisoners and forty thousand Russians fled north into East Prussia where the Germans disarmed them. Three Soviet armies were annihilated and the Poles chased the rest back to the east. After several more successes, the Poles seemed about to march on Moscow when Lenin sued for peace in October and an armistice was signed. The eastern borders of the republic were finally secured.

The Battle of Warsaw was a famous victory in a campaign that saw the last great cavalry battle in Europe. There was relief in the West that the Bolsheviks had been stopped before they could reach Germany, which was bubbling with pre-revolutionary ferment in the aftermath of defeat. So decisive was Poland's victory that the Soviet Union quietly withdrew upon itself during the 1920s and abandoned the cause of international revolution. Lord d'Abernon, who headed the InterAllied Mission to Poland, believed it was one of the decisive battles of world history.

'Had Pilsudski and Weygand failed to arrest the triumphant advance of the Soviet Army at the Battle of Warsaw, not only would Christianity have experienced a dangerous reverse, but the very existence of western civilisation would have been imperilled,' d'Abernon wrote.[1] 'The Battle of Tours [against the Saracens, in 732] saved our ancestors from the yoke of the Koran; it is probable that the Battle of Warsaw saved Central and parts of Western Europe from a more subversive danger – the fanatical tyranny of the Soviet.'

Sophie's earliest childhood memory was of fleeing Rudnik that summer as the Bolshevik armies advanced into southern Poland. Although she was only three, she remembered travelling in a strange railway wagon without seats apart from an armchair from the wooden house at Rudnik in which a strange man sat, and a potted palm tree from the hall, which swayed with the carriage. A cow was tethered in the wagon behind a wooden partition, and its fresh dung splashed on the suitcase in which the infant Stas lay.

The family returned home in autumn 1920 to find that this time the Russians had not reached Rudnik. But tragedy greeted them. Lucza the pet wild boar was gone. Ah Lucza! Of all the tales from the southern Polish forest, few are stranger than the story of the pet boar. Luzca was a 200 kilo, one metre tall tusked beast from a species that could charge human beings like a torpedo, and unzip a man with their tusks like a can opener.

But Lucza was house-trained and as tame as a dog, and he was dearly loved. He slept indoors, he carried the children on his back and there are photographs of him up on his hind legs with his front trotters planted on Wanda's chest. Sometimes he put them on the dining table and got his snout into the food.

Lucza had come into the family after Hieronim and Wanda returned to Rudnik in 1915. A peasant woman came to Wanda and asked if she would take in a boar, explaining that some time before boars had been rooting in her potatoes and when they were chased away her children had caught a tiny baby. They raised him lovingly in their home, but he grew rapidly. 'Now we are so short of food that we can't go on feeding him,' she lamented. 'Maybe you have enough food to feed him, Madame Countess.'

When they returned again in the autumn of 1920 to find Lucza gone the family feared hungry local people had made a meal of him. They always wanted another pet boar and kept one that was fairly tame in an enclosure near the house. But Lucza was never really replaced, although there was no lack of half-tame animals thanks to the fires caused by sparks sent out by the trains that ran through Hieronim's forests. His forest rangers were forever rescuing singed red deer, roe deer, rabbits, hare, badgers, foxes and owls, which were kept in a little menagerie. There was also a tame deer that would go out into the fields with the cows and return with them three times a day for the milking.

Despite the alarms that kept interrupting their young lives, and their parents' troubled relationship, Sophie and Stas always remembered Rudnik as a childhood paradise. Relations between Hieronim and Wanda grew steadily worse as the 1920s advanced, and Sophie and Stas began to understand the deep unhappiness around them as they emerged from childhood. But they saw their parents only briefly each day, and spent most of their time with governesses whom they loved dearly and retainers who treated them as little lords. Cocooned from their parents' misery by the affection of those around them, they were free to enjoy the life of a country estate in southern Poland that in the 1920s still had a timeless, almost Tolstoyan quality. There was the large house at the centre of a busy estate; the close, lifelong relationships with governesses, servants, gamekeepers, grooms and other retainers;

there were patriarchal relationships with the farm workers and peasants; and the lifestyle was close to nature, governed by the changing seasons and punctuated by the spring and harvest festivals and the great religious vigils and feasts – Advent, Christmas, Lent, Easter, Corpus Christi and the Assumption of the Blessed Virgin Mary. It was a slow-moving, traditional world in which church bells rang for the Angelus at noon and six p.m. and the peasants stopped work in the fields to pray: 'The angel of the Lord declared unto Mary and she conceived by the Holy Ghost . . .'

The children's lives were ruled by governesses. They were educated at home and made to study hard. There was no respite even on Sundays, when the parish priest came from the town to give them religious instruction and lunch with Hieronim and Wanda.

But outside lessons life was wonderful. They played in the garden and the park, in the cherry orchard beside the stables with its delicious red and white cherries. They played with the half-tame animals in the menagerie, and in summer they roamed the forests in search of wild strawberries, raspberries, blueberries, hazelnuts and mushrooms, or went for rides on their pony. On summer afternoons they were driven in a trap to the River San, about a kilometre from the house, for a swim, or they went for long drives along forest roads, perhaps catching sight of deer and buck among the trees. As they grew older they learned to gallop along the forest roads and across the beautiful water meadows, always carrying large blankets under their saddles, which they were to spread out over the ground for safety if their horse got bogged down in swampy ground and they were in danger of sinking. Sophie developed such close relationships with people on the estate, and loved the house, the park and the estate so much, that when she eventually left Rudnik she felt she could remember every blade of grass in the park and forests.

By 1926 the mansion had been redesigned and the rebuilding was completed. Sophie and Stas, then aged nine and eight, were sad to leave the cosiness of *maly domek,* the little wooden house where they had been born, but they soon grew to love the mansion. The nineteenth-century turrets and battlements had gone, a new wing had been added, and it had been converted to the simple, semi-classical style that Poles favoured. It was now an elegant two-storey building, the exterior finished in a sand-coloured plaster that gave it a warm and homely look, and the entrance adorned with four pillars set forward in pairs and topped with a Palladian-style pediment to form an elegant portico. Inside, high ceilings and tall doors and windows emphasised the fine proportions, and the parquet floors and great larch beams supporting the ceilings of the two drawing rooms and the dining room gave an austere, almost Castilian elegance.

The top of the five broad steps leading up to the front door created a veranda under the portico where Hieronim and Wanda would sit with their guests, looking out over an oval lawn towards the trees that partially hid the wooden chapel in which Sophie had been christened. Down beyond the chapel to the right were two ornamental lakes, on the far banks of which stood a fine old granary and a large and beautiful stables block surrounded by gardens and orchards, with the estate office and employees' cottages nearby. Before the Great War the stables had housed fourteen riding and carriage horses and nine carriages, including large four-wheel coaches, a landau, a long hunting cart, a pony trap and a horse-drawn sled for winter. Some of the carriages were still in use, thanks to Hieronim's dislike of cars. On the left side of the house, the

French windows of the little drawing room gave onto another veranda that looked over parkland towards the flower garden Wanda cultivated beside a large vegetable garden. Further to the left, leading away from the back of the house, was an avenue of roses and cherry trees that led towards the River San.

After they installed themselves in the big house Hieronim and Wanda began to receive a constant stream of guests. Many relatives came, and since the forests of the estate offered superb hunting the visitors' book in the 1920s is packed with notes of thanks from guests who shot buck, stag, boar, fox, hare, badgers and eagles. 'Thank you for the splendid hunting, such as there has never been,' wrote Hieronim's cousin Count Zdzislaw of Dzikow on 7 August 1926. 'Yesterday evening and today we killed eight fine buck.'

Hieronim's estate was a substantial property of several thousand hectares, mostly forest, but including a few hundred hectares of arable land. The family lived comfortably, though in simple style, and the domestic establishment was unpretentious compared with some of the palaces maintained by the Polish aristocracy.

Wojciech Hass, the butler, supervised four or five manservants, and Pani Katarzyna Sarnecka, the housekeeper, was in charge of three or four maids who helped the fat, bad-tempered female cook and kept the house spotless. Pani Sarnecka's cellars were always neatly stocked with home-grown provisions. Rows of jars held fruit preserves, honey and pickled wild mushrooms; there were barrels of pickled cucumbers and cabbage; cheeses matured in the sandy Rudnik soil that tasted like Camembert, and garlic sausages and wild boar hams that were a local speciality.

Like any Polish landed estate, the mansion was at the centre of an agro-industrial complex. The 500-hectare home farm raised beef and dairy cattle and grains, and there were extensive market gardens, greenhouses, orchards and beehives, a vodka distillery and commercial fishponds for breeding carp, that essential ingredient in Polish cuisine. The beautiful forests of fir, larch, spruce and birch, oak, beech and elm were carefully nursed and harvested under the management of a head forester, and were divided into four districts, each of which had a director and teams of rangers. Thanks to the previous owner, the water drained from the forest water-meadows for which Rudnik was renowned flowed along canals to a hydro-electric plant that powered the estate and the town of Rudnik.

Hieronim took the management of the estate seriously. During the week he liked to consult with his estate manager, the head forester and the forest directors, as well as with the manager of the wicker factory which gave employment to the townspeople, and with Laurencjusz, the market gardener. Living the life of a country gentleman, he took his recreation by hunting game, and he was a fine shot, and by riding on his estate or driving a horse-drawn carriage through the forests.

But he had to struggle to survive during the inter-war period. The new Polish Republic faced a huge task of creating a unified economy from the three formerly partitioned areas, and southern Poland had long been the poorest region. For over a hundred years Galicia had been a distant and neglected province of the Austro-Hungarian Empire and a byword for backwardness and misery, sending vast numbers of indigent emigrants to the New World, many of them Jews. Beset by a rapidly expanding population in the 1920s and '30s, Poland was almost crushed by the cycle of recession, inflation, depression and hyperinflation.

Hieronim, whose fortune had been much reduced by war and rebuilding, found himself at the mercy of falling world prices for grain and wood, the chief products of the estate, and during the 1930s he had to raise money by leasing the buck hunting at Rudnik to Count Zdzislaw. He also sold off parts of the estate and some building lots from the two-hectare garden at the Szlak, his Krakow mansion, and some of the artistic treasures that his father the professor had collected. By the time the Second World War began the estate had shrunk by about one-third, and he had sold Count Zdzislaw his greatest artistic treasure, the manuscript of *Pan Tadeusz*, Adam Mickiewicz's nineteenth-century epic poem beloved by every Pole, which the professor had bought in Paris from the poet's indigent son.

About 250 people were on the estate payroll, including pensioners who received a retirement home on the estate, a small cash allowance, and free basic supplies of milk, meat and firewood. Although peasants in southern Poland still greeted the landowner by kissing his hand or stooping to clasp him below the knee, Hieronim discouraged servility and would not permit such gestures. But he took very seriously the traditional patriarchal approach in his dealings with people on his estate.

Wacek Bninski, the son of his older sister Jadzia, who often stayed at Rudnik as a boy and a young man, remembered that Hieronim was always ready to help people. 'If a farmhand or a villager went to Hieronim to ask for advice and help, he got it,' Wacek recalled. When a peasant's house burned down or his cow died, Hieronim gave timber for rebuilding or an animal as a replacement. If a beggar came to the door, he took him to the estate office and asked the cashiers to give him a few zloties. The estate office also issued permits for local people to gather free firewood in the forests. Hieronim gave a house in the town as an orphanage and paid for the upkeep of the orphans. After the Great War he gave timber and thirteen acres of land to build a new church in the town to replace the eighteenth-century wooden church destroyed in 1914.

Zofia Sabok, daughter of the chief groom at Rudnik who was Hieronim's batman during the Great War and the Polish-Soviet war, recalled that he and Wanda set up a co-operative to help his workers. 'A shop was opened on the estate where the workers could buy different kinds of groceries and also textiles,' Zofia explained. 'The shop was run by Mr Cetera and the goods were cheaper than in the Jewish shops in the town.'[2] Wanda also bought sewing machines for local women and organised a sewing and embroidery school for children from the estate.

'Countess Tarnowska often visited sick children of estate workers and sent them food and nourishing things from the mansion's kitchen,' Zofia recalled. 'In years when there were poor harvests the workers always received, no matter what, their wages and payment in kind although sometimes the Count himself felt scarcity.'

On Christmas Eve, which is the main day of celebration during Christmas in Poland, Wanda gave a party for the children of the estate. Dozens of children gathered at two p.m. in the hall of the mansion beside the winding wooden staircase, where a large Christmas tree stood with a pile of presents beneath. They were practical gifts like shoes, sweaters, shawls, stockings and hats, and a few nuts, apples and sweets. Wanda handed a package to each child, and afterwards joined them and their parents singing Christmas carols for a long time before everyone wished each other Happy Christmas and went home happily through the snow.

CHAPTER FOUR

Scandal

*I*t was no secret among friends and family that Hieronim and Wanda grew increasingly miserable during the 1920s. 'Fortune did not shine on that marriage,' wrote Waclaw Lednicki, who had seen them waltzing together at Wanda's coming-out party in 1911. He had later become Hieronim's friend and they often lunched together at the Grand Hotel in Krakow, where he learned of Hieronim's domestic troubles. 'Poor Imus Tarnowski, who was orderly, infinitely upright and held strongly to religious and moral principles, suffered greatly,' Lednicki wrote in his memoirs.

When Wanda took a lover in the mid-1920s her choice was so flamboyant that it looked like the action of a woman past caring about appearances. He was Count Alfred Potocki, lord of Lancut, one of Poland's most magnificent stately homes at the centre of a large landed estate, about seventy kilometres south of Rudnik, near the southern city of Rzeszow. Alfred was renowned throughout Europe for the ostentatious hospitality he dispensed at his vast seventeenth-century palace, where he welcomed kings, princes and archdukes as well as more dubious guests like Hitler's foreign minister Joachim von Ribbentrop.[1]

Alfred was short and a little chubby, with thinning fair hair, a round face and a snub nose, but he was a great showman and he worked his way with gusto through at least two fortunes. The entertainments he put on for his guests were so extravagant that some Poles of his own class considered him vulgar and shunned Lancut, scandalised by a lifestyle that in their view had nothing to do with country life and the stewardship of a great landed estate.

When the Duke and Duchess of Kent came for a weekend in 1937, Alfred's green-liveried orchestra marched from the palace to the little town of Lancut and struck up 'God Save the Queen' at the railway station. He invited enormous house parties, waited upon by platoons of uniformed servants. The palace had eleven dining rooms and dinner was served in a different one each night with two or three servants standing behind each chair. It was followed by dancing in the great ballroom or film shows, or plays performed by the guests in the Louis XVI theatre. Sometimes they spent the late-night hours under the stars with Chinese lanterns flickering in the trees and distant trumpeters sounding Wagnerian fanfares from the surrounding forest. During the day there was polo, riding or fox-hunting on Alfred's English hunters, fishing, pheasant shooting, deer stalking, roebuck and wild boar hunting, or golf at the private course at Julin, Alfred's hunting lodge. It was said that butlers doubled as ball boys at the tennis court and presented the balls on silver salvers. 'Good God, I couldn't possibly afford to live like this,' King Karol of Romania remarked during a weekend at Lancut.

Alfred loved to pack his guests into his four-in-hand mail coach and drive it at top speed through the great doors of the palace, thundering through the hallway and clattering into the courtyard beyond to fanfares from the trumpeters of the Potocki Orchestra. On Sundays, barefoot girls in colourful national dress swept the avenues of the park before him and his rather grand mother, who was born Princess Elizabeth Radziwill, as they processed to Mass with their guests. At the church in the town they sat upstairs in a private gallery behind a glass partition. 'They say the smell from the peasants made this imperative,' explained Agnes de Stoeckl, a Russian aristocrat who visited in the 1930s.[2]

After Mass, beggars crowded around Alfred and his mother outside the church and fought for the coins they handed out, before the orchestra led the procession back to the palace playing a tune, its big drum pulled on wheels by a Shetland pony. When they reached the palace, the guests took aperitifs in a courtyard while the orchestra played on.

'Life in Lancut ever reminded me of what it must have been like in one of the great French chateaux in the eighteenth century, but with all the modern luxury imaginable,' wrote de Stoeckl. Her grandson Vincent Poklewski remembered that when he stayed at Lancut as a small boy, a toy electric Rolls Royce was brought from the stables and he drove it slowly around the park, followed by a butler with a broom who swept the avenues behind him to cover up the tyre tracks.

Alfred probably met Wanda in Paris, on one of the visits she used to make to manage Imcia and Hieronim's investments. The visitors' book shows that he visited Rudnik as a family friend for the first time in April 1925, which probably indicated the start of his relationship with Wanda, and he returned ten times in the next four years. He was a charming and witty man with a zest for living. His sense of fun soon made him a favourite uncle for little Sophie and Stas, who were eight and seven when he first visited.

Although the affair became a public secret, Wanda did not move out of Rudnik to join Alfred at Lancut. It was said that his mother, who was known as Betka, did not favour the idea. A formidable lady raised at the Kaiser's court in Berlin, she did not want a rival or any unseemly behaviour at Lancut. Divorce was almost unknown in those days in Catholic

Poland, and there was virtually no chance of Wanda and Alfred marrying. But by staying at Rudnik while continuing the affair Wanda caused great tension and created an unpleasant environment in the home that scarred Sophie and Stas for life. Uncle Tomek Zamoyski, Wanda's nephew who visited Rudnik as a young man, found there was no family atmosphere: 'Since the parents were so far apart it was impossible that they could bring the children up well.'

The unhappiness Sophie and Stas felt around them was intensified by family customs which isolated them. They spent most of their time with governesses, whom they loved, and only saw Wanda and Hieronim briefly twice a day. Just before lunch they trotted into the little drawing room, where their parents were drinking an aperitif, and kissed their hands in greeting. They received a pat on the cheek from their father and perhaps a caress from their mother. Maybe they chatted for a moment, but then they left, walking back over the dark red carpet beneath the forest of hunting trophies – buck and stag antlers and wild boar tusks – adorning the walls. They repeated the hand-kissing ritual before bedtime, after which Hieronim took them upstairs to say their prayers.

There were no open rows between Hieronim and Wanda. Despite his choleric nature, Hieronim was too much of a gentleman for that. But Wanda often wept and made unpleasant remarks about him to the children. Her sister-in-law and confidante, Wanda Zamoyska *née* Badeni, told them their father was treating their mother badly. Sophie and Stas thoroughly disliked their Aunt Wanda as a meddler, but they could not help sympathising with their mother's tears and accusations against their father. Hieronim never took them into his confidence or tried to explain the situation and defend himself to them. He had had such a distant relationship with his own father that he had no idea how to become close to his own children. And he was so upright that he believed one just did not discuss troubles in the family. So during years of misery he never spoke to Sophie and Stas about the marriage or his own difficulties. He never explained the situation, nor attempted to comfort them, even when they began to show signs of distress and alienation from him.

When Stas was still a small boy the whole household was shocked by the discovery that he had drawn a series of pigs and had written in French beside the biggest of them: '*C'est mon père.*' That marked the beginning of an uneasy and rebellious relationship between Stas and his father. Sophie also had an outburst against him when she was quite small. 'I'm ashamed of you, you make my mother cry,' she shouted after one of her mother's weeping fits. 'Perhaps one day you will understand,' was his only reply.

The children grew wild as a result of the unhappiness and distress around them. Sophie was a quiet and easy child when she was small, but she changed suddenly and deliberately into a troublemaker. She came to the conclusion she would never be as beautiful as her mother, so she decided that since she could not compete as a woman, she would rather be a boy. One day she stuck her needle into the sewing she was doing, put it down and said loudly: 'From now on I will be naughty.' She had nothing more to do with girlish things or good behaviour. She wanted to hunt and shoot and think up pranks. She became so bold that Stas called her 'Lion' while she called him 'Hare'. She was the strong-willed one, the leader, and Stas was her brave and eager follower. Together they drove the household to distraction.

When they heard the servants at Rudnik gossiping that the estate manager was stealing from Hieronim they decided to give him a fright. They got up very early one morning, took a shotgun from the gun cabinet in their father's study, and ran to *maly domek,* where the manager now lived. Crouching under his bedroom window, they fired both barrels in the air and raced back to the mansion through the trees. The estate manager reported the incident to the police and Wojciech Hass, the butler, locked Hieronim's study to hide the guns. But they were determined to pursue the manager. By chance they met a man in town who had just got out of jail. They persuaded him to break into the study and steal them a shotgun. Once again they ran over to *maly domek* early in the morning and fired both barrels under the manager's window. This time they unleashed an enormous row which again involved the police.

One of their worst escapades was a cruel trick Stas played on one of the governesses. One May morning he and Sophie were out riding in the forest when they came across a nest of vipers. Stas was quite fearless. He jumped off his horse and killed one of the snakes, squashing its head with his riding crop and then picked it up and took it back to the mansion. Dead vipers carry on wriggling for ages, and it was still wriggling when Stas placed it under the pillow of Pani Wrzeszinska, Sophie's piano teacher. When the poor woman lay down for her afternoon nap and found a snake wriggling in her bed she had a screaming fit.

Hieronim ordered Stas to come to the large drawing room to be punished at noon next day. But he and Sophie got up very early next morning, saddled their horses and rode off into the forest. They roamed for three days and nights, sleeping in foresters' houses, before sneaking back to Rudnik. But as soon as Hieronim learned of their return, he summoned Stas and thrashed him before the whole household.

Stas remembered the beating all his life, although it had no effect on his behaviour.

He also learned as he grew older to dislike and distrust his mother. He realised as he became a teenager that he had hated her severity towards him and Sophie when they were children. He hated the fear she instilled in them when they misbehaved, never punishing them on the spot but always making them wait for hours before she beat them with a belt or a horsewhip on their bare behinds. Whereas Sophie learned to admire and imitate Wanda's intolerance of weakness and her insistence on strength of will at all times, Stas found her cold and forbidding. Above all, he resented her for a deep wound she inflicted on him when he was a small boy by suddenly dismissing his favourite governess, whom he dearly loved, and ignoring his tears and pleas for her return. As he grew up he learned to blame his mother, not Hieronim, for the family break-up.

Stas had been a happy baby and a cheerful, good-natured child, so sweet that when they were infants their governesses used to urge Sophie to be like him. But as he grew older amid the strains and unhappiness surrounding him and Sophie, he became not only wild but arrogant and violent, and he developed an uncontrollable temper that often got him into trouble.

Sophie, however, developed close relationships with people on the estate, again imitating Wanda who would always visit the sick and take food, clothes and medicine to people in need. Although Sophie played a leading role in the mischief that she and Stas caused, she followed her parents' example in taking care of their people. She knew that when her mother was twenty she had risked her life to help the sick during a cholera epidemic at the Zamoyski estate at Wysock, where she had been brought up. Although large numbers of people were dying from the disease, Wanda had ridden from house to house, taking food and medicines to the sick while other people stayed away. Sophie admired her mother's actions, and as she emerged from childhood she came to realise how privileged she was to be a landowner's daughter. She was still quite small when she began to feel that she was duty bound to take part in the life of the estate and take responsibility for those who were dependent on her family. 'I decided I wanted to be a banner to my class,' she explained. 'I felt I was a *proporczyk*, a standard-bearer. I decided that whatever I did, I would do it in the right way.'

One morning when Sophie was about eleven she went to the stables and saw men unharnessing horses from a trap and asked where they had been. They told her they had been to fetch the doctor to attend to a farm worker's baby girl who was having fits, but he had refused to come. 'Put the horses back into harness and I will go to see the doctor,' Sophie said imperiously. When she reached the doctor he told her he had already seen the sick baby and had given her every possible medical attention. 'There is no sense in me going there again because there are other patients who need me,' he told Sophie. 'If the child has another fit, put her in a warm bath until it's over.'

Back at Rudnik Sophie found the baby asleep, but the mother was beside herself with worry. Somewhat precociously for an eleven-year-old, she advised her to relax. 'If you are in such a state and your baby drinks your milk, she will catch your tension and misery. So try to relax for her sake and I am sure this will pass. Have hot water ready all the time to give the baby a warm bath if she has a fit, as the doctor said.' Then Sophie sat down, rested one hand on the baby to calm her, and chatted with the mother until a servant came to fetch her to lunch at the mansion. While she was eating, men came and told her the baby was having another fit and the mother, who now believed Sophie had healing hands, wanted her to come back. Sophie returned many times in the following days until the infant recovered. The mother was so grateful that she promised Sophie the baby girl would one day be her personal maid.

'You can see the sort of relationship I had with those people,' Sophie explained. 'I don't know if it was the same on every estate in those days, but certainly in Rudnik and at Dzikow [the estate of the senior branch of the Tarnowski family] one felt such deep duties towards the people. If you go to an estate like Rudnik or Dzikow you will find that the orphanage or the church were built and looked after by the family. When anybody was sick we made sure they got the right attention from the doctors and the hospitals.'

But things were to change at Rudnik. The carefree life of childish pranks and adventures in the forests came to an end in 1929 when the situation between Wanda and Hieronim reached a climax. Stas always remembered the day. It was probably in August, during Alfred Potocki's last visit to Rudnik. Stas and Hieronim had just said night prayers in his bedroom, which looked out over the lawn in front of the mansion, when Hieronim said: 'Look, Stas, don't be so very nice to Uncle Alfred.'

'Oh, why not, Papa? I like him a lot.'

'Well, because Uncle Alfred has done me the worst wrong that a man can do to another man.' Hieronim did not explain and he never spoke of it again, but the comment seems to have marked the final breakdown of his marriage.

A month later Stas was sent away to boarding school in England, suddenly cut off from his home and family and sent to live in a strange country. He left home on the day after his eleventh birthday and travelled across Europe with his last governess, a pleasant Scotswoman who told him his father was the noblest man she had ever known. She delivered Stas to the Benedictine monks of Downside School in southern England, where he was a pupil for the next five years. Downside was a popular destination for the sons of the Polish aristocracy in those days, so he found comfort in the presence of several cousins.

At the end of his first term, Hieronim made an unexpected visit. 'I've come because your mother is having a child,' he said. Artur was born at Rudnik on 7 January 1930. Hieronim and Wanda parted soon afterwards, and by 1933 they were formally separated. Wanda took Artur to live at Dukla, a lovely old mansion with a small estate in the foothills of the Carpathian Mountains near the Czechoslovakian border that had recently been bequeathed to Stas. Sophie, who was not yet thirteen when Artur was born, was given the choice of staying at Rudnik with her father or leaving with her mother. She chose to leave, and Hieronim was left alone with only his mother Imcia, who was seventy-six in 1930, for company.

The mansion took on a desolate air. Wanda took away carpets, furniture and curtains when she left, and Sophie was shocked by the bareness of the rooms when she returned on a visit. Visitors said Hieronim looked absolutely destroyed. He was forty-six and his life had collapsed about him. His once genial face took on an air of sadness. 'He was terribly unhappy. He started to become a hermit at Rudnik,' his nephew Wacek Bninski remembered. 'He avoided people. He avoided his cousins.' His sisters Etusia Esterhazy and Jadzia Bninska rallied round, staying at Rudnik as often as they could. Jadzia also sent her three daughters, and her teenaged son Wacek and his tutor spent a whole winter. The lonely Hieronim and Wacek became fast friends.

It was two or three years before Hieronim began to emerge from his shell. Although he and a group of friends had been involved in politics during the 1920s, playing a role in small conservative and monarchist parties, he dropped his political activities after his marriage break-up and during the 1930s he threw himself into the scientific management of his forests. He had studied forestry at Munich as a young man, and he now developed new forestation techniques in collaboration with Poland's only forestry school at Lwow University and his neighbour Prince Piotr Czartoryski. By the end of the 1930s the Rudnik forests were among the best managed in Poland. But all Hieronim's hard work was to be in vain.

CHAPTER 5

Rites of Passage

*I*nstalled in her new home, Wanda entertained a stream of relatives, bishops, generals, writers and lords. Alfred Potocki was a frequent guest and Artur remembered sitting contentedly in bed between him and Wanda, a Tintoretto painting of the Virgin on the wall above them. But Sophie, who had come to understand Alfred's role in the break-up of her family, went away whenever he was about to arrive and stayed with a friend. Many years later Stas also showed his anger against Alfred by ripping out handfuls of pages from the Dukla visitors' book that Alfred had signed.

The house was a jewel packed with artistic treasures, and a more congenial home than Rudnik for a woman of Wanda's taste. Set in the foothills of the Carpathian Mountains on the edge of the small town of Dukla, it was surrounded by a park and gardens with ornamental lakes and avenues that stretched for 1,500 metres lined with millennial oaks, great linden trees and hornbeam. The eighteenth-century central block was an empty ruin, gutted by shelling during the Great War; but set apart on either side of it were two fourteenth-century wings, unusually shaped like long, narrow triangles, with steep roofs, small windows and walls two metres thick. Inside were narrow passageways, spiralling stone staircases and rooms crammed with the ancestral portraits and treasures collected by previous owners during grand tours: paintings by Rembrandt, Rubens, Ribera, Angelica Kaufmann and Tintoretto, Flemish tapestries, oriental carpets, marble busts, crystal and Chinese porcelain.

Beneath one of the ancient hornbeam trees, which still stood in the 1960s, ten-year-old Princess Jadwiga, heiress to the Polish crown, was said to have rested in 1384 on a fateful journey from Hungary to Krakow, where Hieronim's ancestors and other great lords forced her to abandon her betrothal to Wilhelm of Habsburg. They married her off instead to Grand Duke Jagiello of heathen Lithuania, creating a dynasty that united Poland and Lithuania into one of the most powerful realms in Europe during the fifteenth and sixteenth centuries.

Wanda created a beautiful home at Dukla. Artur remembered proudly showing the French writer Rosa Bailly round the house and gardens, and treasuring her comments: 'This is like entering a carefree world from *A Thousand and One Nights* . . . a world from which all trace of ugliness and decay has been banished,' she said. Later she wrote: 'In the same manner as she maintains the park, the countess adorns the walls, decorates and beautifies her rooms. There is nothing around her untouched by the charm of her genius. Having enclosed life in the castle, she transmogrified a medieval fortress into a jewel where everything is harmony and beauty – luxury, quietude and bliss.'

Wanda was in her element as lady of the manor although as a woman living alone she relied on charm as well as courage to confront unexpected situations. She and Alfred were being driven one evening to a reception when the chauffeur braked sharply with a cry of alarm and armed men surrounded the car in the forest.

'It's Panicz and his gang,' said the chauffeur. Panicz, or the Lordling, was a bandit chief who terrorised the countryside round Dukla in the early 1930s. He had a price on his head for murder and highway robbery, but he laughed at the police and sent them notes every now and then suggesting that they increase the reward for his capture. Now he strode to the car, a handsome, stocky man with a drooping moustache, and opened the rear door where Wanda was sitting in her evening gown and jewellery with a tiara on her head. She was unconcerned.

'Oh Panicz! What an unexpected pleasure,' she said coolly. 'I always wanted to meet you.'

'Oh, it's you, Countess. Good evening. I wanted to meet you, too.'

'Splendid. Now we have both had our wish granted, you must step in for a chat.'

Wanda told the chauffeur to fetch brandy from the boot of the car and they drank and chatted, Panicz relating some of his exploits while his men gathered and roasted wild mushrooms from the surrounding forest. Alfred looked on in angry silence. After a couple of hours Panicz took his leave, kissing Wanda's hand as he departed. 'Countess, if ever you need anything, let me know,' he promised. 'You can always travel through my forests in complete safety.'

'Thank you, Panicz,' she replied, smiling. 'These forests are actually mine, so I'll feel doubly safe.'

Sophie came to love Dukla, but she was homesick for Rudnik at first. She was lonely and depressed without Stas, so Wanda and Hieronim decided to send her to a boarding school run by Sacred Heart nuns at Zbilitowska Gora near the southern city of Tarnow. She and Wanda visited the school in the summer of 1930. It was a massive grey stone, square building on a hilltop that called to mind a nineteenth-century house of correction rather than a school for the daughters of the wealthy. The huge neo-Romanesque church squatting beside the school added to the sense of oppression.

The visit did not go well. As Wanda chatted with the Mother Superior in her study, Sophie asked to go to the toilet. A nun led her down long corridors and showed her in. But inside the toilet a picture of Jesus looked down from the wall, showing his bleeding heart. Sophie recoiled. 'I can't do it here,' she told the nun. She went back to the Mother Superior's study almost bursting and sat fidgeting until the visit ended and she and her mother were driven to a hotel in Tarnow.

Sophie had been sceptical about religion ever since she and Stas made their first Confession and Holy Communion a year earlier. A photograph of them on the day shows two unhappy children standing side by side – Stas unsmiling and aloof, a beautiful boy in grey shorts, jacket and an open-necked white shirt, and Sophie in a white dress and veil. She looks boldly out at the camera, her mouth curled in a hint of mischief.

She thought the priest who heard her First Confession was nosy, and when he absolved her of her childhood peccadilloes she did not feel cleansed and happy as everyone had promised. She had confessed with deep remorse to accidentally killing a ladybird while she and Stas were playing in the forest at Rudnik. They had squabbled over a rare mushroom they found, and when Stas grabbed it from her she had swatted angrily at a passing ladybird with her wooden spade and unintentionally killed it. Horrified, the two children knelt to scratch out a tiny grave, and from then on Sophie believed that killing in anger was the biggest sin of all.

'But when I told the priest about killing the ladybird,' she remembered, 'he said it was no sin. He didn't understand.'

She decided there and then that she could not identify with such a religion.

She became a boarder at the Sacred Heart school in September 1930, and the discipline was a shock. Getting up in her dormitory cubicle on her first morning she had twenty minutes to wash, dress, make her bed, brush her hair, clean her shoes and get downstairs to the chapel for Mass before breakfast. At home all those things were done for her, and she had no idea even how to brush and plait her long brown hair. She was almost weeping by the time a nun bustled in to help her.

Next day a nun swept into her cubicle in the morning as Sophie was washing in a tin basin with only a towel round her waist. 'Oh my child, how could you? You are naked!' the nun exclaimed in a horrified whisper.

'Yes, mother, I am washing,' Sophie replied.

'You must learn to wash in your nightie.' After that a nun poked her head in every morning to check that she was washing without exposing any part of her body.

The first time she saw her name on the weekly bath rota, she hopped straight into the tub. Soon afterwards, a nun's coiffe poked through the curtain, and again came a shocked whisper. 'Oh my child, you are naked.'

'Yes, mother, I'm having a bath.'

'Didn't you notice there is something on the chair which you have to wear when you're having a bath?' It was a Mother Hubbard, a voluminous gown reaching to the ankles that the girls had to wear to avoid seeing their own body in the bath.

Sophie also found the strict silences hard to bear: silence while dressing and undressing, silence when washing and bathing, silence while moving between classrooms, and silence or hymn-singing while filing into the dining room and sitting down to meals. She rebelled very quickly. One morning during her first term she washed quickly and picked up her basin of dirty water and waited. As she heard a nun approaching her cubicle she rushed out and collided with her, tipping the water over her. 'Oh, mother, I'm so sorry,' she gasped. 'I didn't know you were there. I was just going to throw away the water.'

One mealtime when the school was served a tough red jelly for dessert that all the girls hated, Sophie took the dish of jelly from her table, put it on the floor and stood up and put one foot in it. A hush fell over the dining room. A nun rang a bell and hurried over, demanding in a hysterical whisper, 'What on earth are you doing?'

'Well, mother, I am trying to see if the jelly will support my weight, because it's usually so tough that we can hardly eat it.'

Sophie wrote to her parents, pleading to be taken away from the school, and making rude comments about the Mother Superior's body odour. The nuns read the letter and called her in for an explanation.

At the end of her first term the family spent the Christmas holidays together at Rudnik for the last time. Sophie begged her parents to take her away from school, but Hieronim said it could not be done because it might take two or three years to find a governess able to teach her all the subjects she would need to take the Matura examination, the Polish baccalaureat.

'Oh God,' Sophie thought, 'I won't wait. I'll run away from school.' She prepared her escape during the holidays by sewing money she received at Christmas into the lining of her overcoat and finding a warm hat to cover her ears from the bitter cold when she made her dash for freedom.

'Good luck,' said Stas, whom she had told about her plan, when she left Rudnik at the end of the holidays.

Back at school she decided to act quickly, and told her cousins Jadzia Bninska and Bisia Tyszkiewicz what she was planning.

'You can't do it,' Jadzia protested.

'But there's no way I can stay here,' she replied.

'What will you do?'

'The day after tomorrow we are going skating and I will jump into the forest and run to Tarnow. I'll take a train and that'll be it.'

'But you've never travelled on your own in a train,' Jadzia argued. 'You don't know what may happen to you.'

'Don't be silly!' Sophie retorted. 'A train is for people to travel from A to B. What do you think might happen?'

'Promise me you'll go first class.'

On 18 January 1931, she went into her empty classroom, wrote 'Goodbye – Sophie' on the blackboard, and walked out to the main gate carrying a small bag of her possessions. 'I'm very late. I have my skates with me and I want to join the skaters,' she told the nun at the gate, and quickly walked past her out of the school grounds. Once out of sight she dashed into the forest and ran to the road to Tarnow.

She walked into the town freezing and frightened of being spotted. At the railway station she bought a first-class ticket to Krakow, eighty kilometres to the west, where she knew her parents were seeing Stas off to Downside. As she waited for a train she saw a teacher from the school walk onto the platform, and she hid behind a pillar until the teacher met a friend off a train and left with her. After that Sophie jumped onto the first train that pulled in. Luckily it was heading for Krakow.

The thirteen-year-old runaway was comfortably settled in an empty first class compartment when an army officer got in at the first stop. He looked at her curiously. 'It's unusual to see a young lady like you travelling on your own,' he commented. 'I have a feeling that you've come from the school at Zbilitowska Gora. I feel like stopping at the next station and ringing them up.'

'You may do that, but if you do I will lose all my trust in the Polish army,' Sophie replied. The officer laughed, and didn't fulfil his threat.

In Krakow Sophie took a *dorozka* or horse-drawn cab to the Grand Hotel where her parents were staying. When they arrived, she gave all the money she had left to the cab driver, telling him to buy carrots for his horse, and walked into the lobby where she got a big smile from the hall porter. But Wanda fainted when she saw her, and Hieronim was so angry that he refused to talk to her. Instead of being given a bedroom, she had to sleep alone on a chaise longue in a cold room. Instead of the usual treats in Krakow, like going to the cinema and nice restaurants, she was left alone in her room for days with nothing to do.

Wanda took her back to Dukla after telling her that three other girls had tried to run away from the school, and the nuns would not take her back. Hieronim tried to get her into Sacred Heart schools in Belgium and Switzerland, but they rejected her. He eventually found a governess, but Sophie's relations with both her parents had been seriously damaged, and they would remain strained for years.

If Sophie was headstrong, Stas grew wild. The beautiful boy sent to Downside when he was barely eleven was growing into a handsome young man by the time he returned from

England. But the disturbed child was becoming an arrogant and violent tearaway. Five years of English discipline had failed to tame him, and he left under a cloud after throwing a schoolmaster over a fence. He had passed the School Certificate examination, but his chief boast was that he had lost his virginity behind the cricket pavilion as soon as he arrived to a beefy Italian maid named Carnero.

He was nearly sixteen when he returned to Poland in the summer of 1934, and he was beginning to be the picture of a dashing young East European nobleman. Slim and tall, he walked with a lithe tread, ramrod straight, head high. His receding forehead, dark hair, broad cheekbones and hawklike nose gave him a predatory air. His high spirits and graceful manners matched his looks, but they thinly veiled a touchy, quarrelsome nature, and his grey-green eyes carried more than a hint of violence.

Like Hieronim, he was inflexible in argument and choleric, but he lacked the gentlemanly moderation that tempered Hieronim's outbursts and let them pass like summer storms. Instead, he had inherited Wanda's wilfulness, fearlessness and carelessness for the feelings of others, and the result was a man lacking in all restraint. He was arrogant, impatient and petulant, always ready to react with his fists. Unusually strong for a man of his slender build, when he fought he gave himself over completely to a bellowing rage, unleashing all the bitterness of a loveless childhood and lost home and family. When he lost control only the whites of his eyes could be seen, and afterwards he remembered nothing and never apologised for what he had done.

Hieronim sent him to boarding school with the Piarist monks at Rakowice on the edge of Krakow, to study for the Matura. But he considered the school a step down from

65

Downside, and the Polish monks managed him no better than the English Benedictines. He had been at the school a short while when a monk told him: 'Milord count, the prince has arrived.'

'Prince? What prince?' asked Stas, disdainful of anyone who addressed him deferentially. It was Prince Roman Sanguszko, his favourite uncle, who had come to take him out. Stas stayed away three days, and, since the monks made no objection, he began to make a habit of slipping away to Krakow to enjoy the nightlife. But the monks grew tired of his absences, his rages and his fights and asked him to leave. Hieronim sent him to another boarding school in Zakopane, a ski resort in the Tatra Mountains south of Krakow, but he was quickly expelled for punching a boy in the face. Hieronim then settled him at the Szlak, his Krakow mansion, to study under the supervision of an older cousin for the Matura, which he passed at seventeen.

He had his first fight in public in the Grand Hotel in Krakow. When a man entered the dining room wearing a hat Stas got up from his table, went up to him and demanded that he remove his hat. The man refused and Stas punched him in the face. Around the same time, the Szlak gatekeeper stopped a young woman leaving the mansion early one morning with a bundle of bed linen. She explained that the young count had no money and had given her the sheets in payment for her services. Hieronim was outraged and banned Stas from sleeping at the Szlak. The incident brought relations between Stas and Hieronim close to breaking point, although later Stas denied it and said he was banned for having kissed a girl in the professor's study. 'I was just a brat, after girls' skirts, which to my father was unthinkable,' Stas explained, adding, 'Well, I was rather good looking, you know.'

He had wreaked havoc already among housemaids and village girls, and he had gone about it with energy. At Rudnik he lifted Salomea, a peasant girl, onto his horse and carried her off into *Czarny Las* or Black Wood, a stretch of primeval forest on the estate, where they stripped and made love at a gallop. Among his conquests at Dukla were the maids Karolcia and Michalina, and he was infatuated with the beautiful Dzidka, niece of the head forester of the bishop of Przemysl, who owned the neighbouring estate. He sat holding hands with her on a park bench in the snow. He once showed off by forcing his horse to jump a barrier, but it balked and fell, rolling onto him and breaking a bone in his knee that stuck out through the skin. He showed Dzidka his bravery by remounting and clearing the barrier.

But Stas's youthful years were not all misadventure. There were the rites of passage of his class, like shooting his first roebuck at Rudnik, and his first stag at Dzikow when he was sixteen after his return from Downside. It was just after dawn on 13 November 1934, the feast of St Stanislaw, Stas's patron saint, and he was taken up to the beast in the forest by Roman Sarnek, the tall, gangling Dzikow gamekeeper. There is a photograph of them on the lawn in front of the castle with the stag lying at their feet, a smile of triumph on Stas's face. Next day he wrote in the Dzikow visitors' book: 'On July 7, 1892, my father killed his first duck and rabbit here. Now, 42 years later, I have killed my first duck and partridge, and yesterday my first stag (a 12-pointer). Thank you so very much, uncle, I am so happy with my first stay at Dzikow.'

Stas admired Sarnek, who could take a hunter up to any beast in the forest. He was descended from a petty Tartar khan captured centuries before in one of Poland's interminable wars and settled in the nearby forests. Sarnek was proud of his Tartar ancestry, and his organising abilities and integrity won him great respect in hunting circles. Stas learned from Sarnek never to abandon a chase. If the hunter wounded a stag, Sarnek never left it to die but tracked it down and completed the kill, no matter how long it took.

Stas often went out hunting roebuck at Rudnik. He would be woken at four a.m. by Antoni Podstawek, the second butler, or Franek Vrager the pantry boy. He dressed hurriedly and ate a hunter's breakfast of sausage, eggs and coffee, and before sunrise one of Hieronim's rangers drove him in a carriage to a sector of the forest where good buck had been sighted on the previous evening. Sometimes he hunted the broad meadows of the high forest at Groble, the most beautiful part of his father's estate. With the first rays of the sun fingering through the mist they drove silently along forest roads until they neared the spot where buck were feeding at the edge of a meadow. The ranger stopped the carriage and Stas quietly jumped down with his rifle and began working his way towards the beasts, creeping up for the shot. He inched his way forward, picked the best prize and fired a single shot that startled the silent forest. They gutted the animal on the spot and loaded the carcass onto the back of the carriage. By half-past eight Stas was back home. He took a bath, changed his clothes and went downstairs for a second breakfast of home-made sausages, wild boar ham and Rudnik cheese. In summer he would head down to the River San for a swim.

When a full-scale hunt took place at Rudnik, usually on the day before Christmas Eve, the house awoke early in uproar while it was still dark. Servants rushed about on errands as the guests breakfasted. Stable boys muffled up warmly against the cold saddled horses, harnessed carriages and carts and drove them past the frozen lakes to the front of the mansion, the horses' breath hanging on the air. The head stable boy drove the *linijka*, a long, open wagon pulled by two horses. The hunters climbed on and sat back-to-back in two rows facing outwards, with their guns between their knees. They shouted cheerful farewells to the ladies waving from the steps of the mansion, and the *linijka* drove off into the dark forest, the horses' hooves muffled, the sled runners hissing over the snow. Behind came a cart carrying big pots of *bigos*, a hunters' stew of meat, cabbage and wild mushrooms that the fat old cook had been simmering for three or four days. There were loaves of freshly baked rye bread, tables, chairs and table-cloths, cutlery, mugs and solid silver plates that Hieronim always used for hunts because they were unbreakable. An empty cart to carry the game trundled along behind, and the ladies mounted their horses and trotted off in pursuit to watch the sport, escorted by the head groom.

When they reached the spot where the hunt was to begin, the hunters climbed down from the *linijka* and spread out silently along the edge of a section of the forest. Far away a horn sounded over the crisp morning air and a crowd of stable boys, rangers and peasants began beating their way slowly through the trees, shouting and banging sticks against the tree trunks to drive the game towards the hunters. If it was a boar hunt, the first shot that was fired at each stand had to be at a wild boar, no matter what other game charged out from the trees. After that, the hunters could shoot whatever animals or birds came at them. The drives were repeated in three or four sections of the forest until early afternoon, when the short mid winter days began to draw in, the last shot was fired and the hunters and their ladies gathered for lunch

The pots of stew were simmering over a fire in the forest, until the shooting ended. While rangers loaded the game onto a cart and drove it back to the mansion, the party wolfed platefuls of *bigos* in the dusk by a blazing fire, washing down the delicious stew with vodka and beer, talking excitedly about the day's sport. By the time they were driven back to the mansion it was dark. While the guests were bathing, the game was laid out in a great circle on the lawn in front of the mansion and before going in to dinner the hunters and their ladies came out with their aperitifs in their hands to inspect the trophies by the light of blazing torches. A stag with a fine set of antlers might lie in the place of honour in the centre, surrounded by circles of roebuck, wild boar, foxes, badgers and pheasant, all ringed by a garland of hares.

There were many other important family events during Stas's youth. Weddings, anniversaries and festivals were often celebrated with his cousins at Dzikow or the Szlak. But family events and entertainments were only pleasant interludes in Stas's life. His behaviour got no better as he grew older. By late 1935, when he was seventeen, Hieronim was so tired of his endless rows and fights, the sexual scandals, and the debts he was accumulating that he decided to take decisive action. 'You can take your choice,' he told Stas, 'you can join either the French Foreign Legion or the Polish Merchant Navy.'

Stas naturally chose the Polish Merchant Navy School at the Baltic port of Gdynia and spent months sailing around the world on the tall-masted training ship *Dar Pomorze*, going as far as Buenos Aires. But even naval discipline failed to tame him, and while he was on holiday after nearly a year at the school, the director wrote to Hieronim, suggesting that since the young count had no intention of becoming a naval officer there was little point in his returning.

Hieronim was at his wits' end. Angry and frustrated, he was on the brink of disowning his son, so that he would no longer be able to use his credit or inherit his wealth. It took firm intervention from his sisters Etusia and Jadzia to dissuade him. Instead, Hieronim had Stas admitted to a sanatorium in southern Poland that was in reality a psychiatric clinic for the wealthy. He stayed for several months, but when he emerged he cockily remarked that he had enjoyed himself and had a long affair with an attractive nurse.

Hieronim enrolled Stas as a law student at the Jagiellonian University in Krakow, but he did not study and treated professors with arrogant contempt when they behaved respectfully towards him as the grandson of the former Rector Magnificus of the university. When Stas discovered that his name gave him unlimited credit in Krakow, Hieronim was so deluged with bills that he moved him to Poznan University in western Poland, hoping he would be unable to spend so much money there. Hieronim was a wealthy man, largely thanks to the fortune his mother Imcia had brought into the family, but the destruction of his property during the wars, the cost of rebuilding and the economic crises of the 1920s and 1930s had eaten into his fortune. Unfortunately, Stas found that the family's credit was just as high in Poznan as in Krakow, and he carried on spending freely and ignoring his studies.

Stas had no interest in education. He did not want to make anything of himself. He knew that when he came of age in September 1939 he would become the outright owner of Dukla and a rich man. The art treasures that Dukla housed were worth millions in any currency, and he planned to use them for a life of leisure and luxury. For a start, he would buy an ocean-going yacht and start wandering the world. As for Dukla, he would leave the estate in the hands of a manager.

But in the winter of 1938, when he was twenty, Stas fell in love and everything changed. He was on a skiing holiday in

Zakopane in the Tatra Mountains in southern Poland and was sitting one afternoon with a group of friends in the lobby of a hotel when two beautiful young ladies walked past. One of his friends pointed to one of them, who was wearing ear muffs like rabbit ears. 'Look Stas,' he said, 'that's the girl you should marry.'

Stas looked at her. 'Yes,' he replied. 'Yes. I will marry her.'

The girl was Sophie Jaxa-Chamiec, but she was known as Chouquette, nicknamed by her adoring parents after a sweet, delicate little French pastry. She was nineteen, a tall, slender, green-eyed brunette with fine-boned, delicate features and a softly radiant smile, said to be the most beautiful young woman in Warsaw. They met that evening, and within a week Chouquette had fallen in love with Stas and agreed to marry him.

Although she was no aristocrat, her parents came from landowning families. Her father Zygmunt was a brilliant financier and entrepreneur who had been on the Polish negotiating team at the Paris Peace Conference of 1919. He had also been one of the first directors of the Bank of Poland, and in 1926 he had founded the Polish Radio and remained its managing director for ten years. Chouquette and her younger sister Wanda, who was known as Boule, had been brought up in a close and loving family and educated at a boarding school. They were well-groomed, with a keen fashion sense and a knack of charming people. But Zygmunt had fallen on hard times in the late 1930s, and since leaving school Chouquette had been working as a typist and secretary to help out her parents.

Stas visited her in Warsaw each time he travelled to or from Poznan University. They went ice skating at an open-air rink, or Chouquette would take him to her favourite church, St

Aleksander's in the centre of Three Crosses Square. That summer he asked Hieronim for permission to become betrothed, but Hieronim refused, saying he had not finished university, was not twenty-one and had not done his obligatory military service.

Zygmunt was equally unhappy with the relationship. He had worked for landowning aristocrats as a young man and disliked them, and Stas had a very unstable reputation. His wife Sophie disliked Stas on sight and considered the romance a disaster. But the story goes that Zygmunt reluctantly gave his permission to the engagement when Stas went to him that summer and told him that if he didn't allow Chouquette to get engaged he would kill him.

'So what could I say to that?' asked Zygmunt. 'I allowed it. What else could I say to such an argument? What could I do?'

CHAPTER SIX

Love at the Wolf Hunt

S ophie fell in love in January 1935 when wolves caused a scare at Dukla. A beggar's boots were discovered in the snow, and when no sign of the man was found people feared wolves had taken him.

Wolves were rare at Dukla, but the little town with its predominantly Jewish population lay in the foothills of the Carpathian Mountains, not far from wild regions and untamed forests where beasts of every breed roamed. The winter had been harsh, with freezing temperatures and heavy snowfalls, and the people of Dukla were terrified that wolves might have moved down into the surrounding countryside to search for food. A hunt had to be organised quickly. Wanda telephoned Count Zdzislaw at Dzikow, and asked him to send one of his sons with the gamekeeper Roman Sarnek to organise a hunt. As the oldest son Jas was travelling in China, and the second son Artur hunting in Lithuania, he sent his youngest son Andrew.

They drove up to the house in Andrew's tiny Fiat. Although he was Sophie's second cousin, they had not seen each other since she visited his home as a girl. Now she was a slender, auburn-haired beauty of seventeen, strong-willed, independent and full of escapades. She had lived in the country with her mother for nearly five years, and had grown fond of the big house. She was sociable and enjoyed meeting Wanda's many guests, but she was also a teenaged girl starved for the company of young men.

Andrew got out of the car and walked over with a smile, bowing to kiss Wanda's hand and then both cheeks. He turned to his young cousin with a laugh and greeted her too. He was a tall, good-looking fellow of twenty-six, dark-haired and full of laughter, affectionately known as Boubish. He was one of life's charmers: a great talker, a hard drinker and a man with many friends and admirers. While Sarnek spied out the land over the next few days, making the arrangements and gathering beaters, Sophie and Andrew were left alone. They were a perfect match for gaiety and adventure, and by the time the wolf hunt came round they had become close.

The day of the hunt was clear and crisp, the sky a perfect blue. Early in the morning the hunting party was driven on horse-drawn sleds to the forest and Andrew took his stand for the opening drive. With his gun on one arm and Sophie beside him in a tightly waisted fur jacket and matching hat, they waited for the hunt to begin. They stood close together, warm in each other's presence. As the first distant cries of the beaters and yelping of dogs cracked the air, Andrew bent down and wrote with his finger in the snow: '*Kocham Çie.*' 'I love you.'

Sophie said nothing. She clung to Andrew's arm. There are moments in life to be treasured without words, when the air seems to zing with intoxication. They stood breathless in the solemnity of the moment, two small figures under a broad sky in the bright midwinter landscape. Everything was still and silent, but she felt the warmth of his body against hers, and her body, mind and heart sang with happiness as she pressed against him and squeezed his arm. They did not kiss. For her it was too soon. She was seventeen and she had never kissed a man. For her, a kiss was a dedication for life. This soaring happiness was enough for now. Far away a horn sounded the start of the hunt.

They stood in the snow near a forest of pine trees, waiting for wolves to race out of the undergrowth. Over the past few days Sarnek had strung long lengths of rope around sections of forest at waist height. Strips of red or yellow cloth dangling from the ropes fluttered in the breeze, forming a barrier that wolves would not cross. The ropes cordoned off three sides of each section of forest, corralling the wolves. The dogs and beaters crashed through the trees driving them towards the open end where the hunters waited.

No wolves came loping out of the forest towards the hunters that day, nor the next. But by the time Andrew left Dukla he and Sophie had exchanged their first kiss. And that was the start of a commotion in the family.

Sophie's heart was full as she and Wanda stood at the door of the mansion waving goodbye to Andrew and Sarnek. She was dreaming happily of marrying Andrew when she heard her mother say: 'I'm glad he's gone. You were getting a bit too fond of each other, and you're too closely related.'

The words struck her with the force of a blow, but she said nothing. She and Andrew had plans to meet again. But they were indeed second cousins, grandchildren of two brothers from Dzikow, and as a result of generations of inter-marriage they had twelve great-grandparents in common. Marriage between such close relatives was discouraged, and it required a papal dispensation.

Neither Sophie nor Andrew knew it, but they were in fact far more closely related, as Hieronim and Wanda had been. Since Wanda was believed to be an illegitimate daughter of Andrew's father, Count Zdzislaw Tarnowski of Dzikow, her daughter Sophie was the old count's granddaughter, while his son Andrew was Wanda's half-brother and therefore Sophie's uncle. For a second generation in succession, Count

Zdzislaw's distant romantic adventure meant that a far too closely related couple were about to marry.

When Sophie and Andrew told their parents they wanted to marry, the family were alarmed. No one wanted a repetition of the disastrous marriage of Hieronim and Wanda. Hieronim knew by then of his blood relationship with Wanda, and he and Wanda led the opposition. Hieronim went to Count Zdzislaw and begged him to tell the young couple the truth. But the old patriarch would not do it. Hieronim and Wanda tried to dissuade Andrew and Sophie, but without Count Zdzislaw's backing they felt they could not tell them the truth and had no grounds for actually forbidding the marriage. Instead, they warned them that with so many ancestors in common they might not be able to have normal children.

When all the appeals and warnings failed to dissuade them, the family fell back on the church. A Jesuit priest went to see Sophie and Andrew at Dukla. He spoke at length about the family's distress and the church's belief that it would be better if they did not marry. On behalf of the family he asked them to sign pledges not to see each other for more than one week a year, nor to write to each other more than once every three weeks. They signed obediently. 'But the one thing they forgot was the telephone,' Sophie laughed.

They were so obviously in love and so determined to marry that the opposition crumbled after a year. Count Zdzislaw asked Bishop Wojciech Tomak of Przemysl, a family friend, to seek a dispensation for the marriage from Pope Pius XI. Wanda took Sophie to Dzikow on a visit that signalled the family's acceptance of the match, and Sophie remembered all her life how Count Zdzislaw welcomed her on the castle steps and folded her in his enormous embrace, like a bear hug.

'With all my heart I want to greet you, and yet I am so much against your marrying Andrew,' he told her.

It was only the second time she had met the old count, but she was inexplicably overwhelmed with adoration for him. Sophie and Stas loved and admired Count Zdzislaw, and when they learned later in life that they were probably his grandchildren they were untroubled. Sophie said she felt an extraordinary love for the old count that she believed could only be explained by the fact that he was her grandfather. 'Somehow, I can't explain it, but I loved him in a sort of way I've never loved anybody before or after,' she said. 'I just cannot explain that way of literally loving him, and that feeling of utter closeness, which he felt as well. I can't explain it, but I felt I couldn't have loved him in that sort of way had he been a more distant relation.'

Stas believed it too. 'I think I probably am Uncle Zdzis's grandson,' he agreed. 'He had a habit of saying "Hmm, Hmm, Hmm", and I catch myself doing the same. It's quite likely that I am.'

After the visit Sophie went to stay at Rudnik. She was sitting at breakfast with Hieronim when he handed her a letter from the old count, saying, 'Good God, it's amazing. I haven't seen a letter from Zdzis, he doesn't write to anybody. What has he written to you?'

He had written: 'Do come back as soon as you can. I miss you.'

Sophie and Andrew were betrothed at Dukla on 24 June 1936, before a small gathering of aunts and uncles, but it was not a happy occasion. Despite her beauty and maturity, Sophie retained a hint of the tomboy. She longed to go hunting with the men and kept a rifle in her bedroom and used to shoot crows in the trees from a small window at the back of the house to feed to her pet fox.

On the morning of their betrothal, she and Andrew were looking out of an upstairs window when she spotted a cat hunting in the walled, sunken fruit garden at the back of the house. She hated cats killing birds. 'Shoot it. Shoot it,' she told Andrew, handing him her rifle. He lent out of the window and shot the cat. The hunting dogs immediately took the carcass and fought as they tore it to pieces. When Wanda heard the din and learned what had happened she was furious. 'Go to your room and stay there,' she told Sophie. Then she turned to Andrew, who was twenty-seven, and ordered him to his room.

Wanda was still angry when they came down to dinner. They sat down with the small group of aunts and uncles, but something Sophie said irritated her mother. 'Take your food and go and eat in the pantry,' she snapped.

Sophie picked up her soup plate without a word and left. The occasion was ruined. Jan Szwab, the old Dukla butler, who adored Sophie, showed his disapproval of Wanda's action by serving Sophie first and presenting each dish to the guests with a generous portion missing.

Szwab was an institution at Dukla. He was already very old when Wanda and Sophie went to live there in 1930, and he considered the house his own. Every time Wanda found someone to help him, Szwab made life miserable for the newcomer until they left. He did not sleep much, and would go around the house very early each morning and wind up the many beautiful clocks. He was always ready to help Sophie, and she felt honoured that he took a liking to her. When the crows in the huge old linden trees behind the house grew too wily for her to shoot, he would discreetly shoot one of Wanda's chickens and feed it to her pet fox.

Not long after Sophie's betrothal, old Szwab died the perfect death of a faithful retainer. He knew his life was coming to an end and did not want to die in his own home, but in the grand old house to which he belonged, which he had served for fifty-two years. He had an armchair brought into his pantry and sat down without any fuss. He asked for each occupant of the house to come and see him, and said goodbye to them one by one. When Sophie was called to his side he was wonderfully affectionate, telling her he would always care for her and always be with her. It was only after he had died sitting in the armchair, surrounded by the things he had known and cared for in his long life of service, that Sophie realised he had been saying farewell to her. 'He never said the words "I am leaving you", and yet he was saying "I will be with you."'

Sophie left Dukla for good not long afterwards, after another disagreement with her mother. She had been angered by remarks Wanda made about Jas Tarnowski, Andrew's exceptionally handsome older brother, whom she dearly loved and admired. An intellectual and art connoisseur, Jas was unusual among the Polish landowning aristocracy, most of whom were mainly interested in managing their estates, hunting, riding and enjoying family gatherings. He had many friends among intellectuals and artists and was uninterested in life on a Polish country estate. He was also thought to be bisexual. The family once covered up a scandal in Warsaw when a young man in evening dress was found hanging by a silk scarf from a bridge over the River Vistula with a note pinned to his chest saying, 'Contact Count Jas Tarnowski'. The family bought up the entire edition of the newspaper that carried the story.

Count Zdzislaw passed Jas over and made his second son Artur heir to Dzikow. He bought Jas a farm in Kenya, where he made a name as a white hunter but frittered the farm away on extravagance and entertaining. But Sophie revered him as a man of great intelligence, knowledge and charm. When Wanda made derogatory remarks about his sexual tastes in front of the guests at her betrothal, she bit her tongue and kept quiet. But when Wanda repeated the comments a few months later when they were alone at Dukla Sophie lost her temper. 'You've told me all this already. I don't want to hear it again,' she said. 'You are saying it because you know that it hurts me. You must apologise or I will leave.'

Wanda never apologised for anything and did not apologise to Sophie now. But Sophie was equally strong-willed. A quick telephone call and the little Fiat bounced up to the house with Sarnek at the wheel and took her away. Sophie went to live with her father at Rudnik until her marriage. After waiting for two years, she and Andrew received a papal dispensation to marry and on the day they were married at Rudnik on 4 February 1937, a telegram of blessing arrived from the pope.

They went to live at Gora Ropczycka, a small estate previously owned by Andrew's mother where they settled down to plant orchards, breed horses for the military and start a family. Near the end of 1937 their first son was born.

CHAPTER SEVEN

Dzikow Country

For centuries, Andrew's family home at Dzikow had been the 'nest' of the Tarnowski family, as the Poles say, and his father Count Zdzislaw was its last great lord and patriarch. Big and powerful, with a broad brow and a dark beard, Count Zdzislaw had a commanding presence. When he entered a room people instinctively rose to their feet. Dressed in the silks and furs of the nobility, he resembled a Renaissance potentate who had stepped into the twentieth century. His prestige in the region was enormous and his status unique. 'In the whole neighbourhood for miles and miles around he was the man,' Stas remembered. 'He was the Lord Almighty. He was unrepeatable. I've never seen anyone, ever, who compared to him.'

Count Zdzislaw took his role at the head of an historic family very seriously. Before the Great War he was a hereditary member of the Austro-Hungarian House of Lords in Vienna. Although loyal to the emperor, he often held political gatherings at his Krakow town house to discuss prospects and proposals for achieving Polish independence. After 1918 he became a Senator of the Polish Republic and a leader of the Conservative Party. As a politician and public figure he did much to raise the family's prestige in the early twentieth century, just as Professor Stanislaw Tarnowski had in the late nineteenth century as a political thinker, historian and Rector of the Jagiellonian University.

Count Zdzislaw's passions were hunting and riding. He

was a fine shot and a great hunter who was said to be the last man in Poland to hunt wild boar on foot, kneeling to receive the charging beast on a spear. His sons Artur and Andrew were equally adept at hunting, and were thought to be the last men in Poland to hunt wild boar with knives. When the dogs brought the beast to bay they came up from behind, knelt beside it, seized its offside front leg and upended it with a swift heave, to plunge a hunting knife into its heart.

The count had a gruff manner, but he commanded unfailing loyalty and obedience in all who knew him. Something of a tyrant, his word was not questioned in the family. He was deeply traditionalist. Within his domain he would acknowledge only one greeting, the ancient '*Niech będzie pochwalony*' ('The Lord be praised'). If anyone greeted him on his estates with the secular '*Całuję rączki, Panu Hrabiemu*' ('I kiss your hands, Lord Count') he would wait without acknowledgement until the speaker realised his mistake and gave the correct salutation, to which he gave the traditional reply: '*Na wieki, wieków*' ('For ever and ever').

The house at Dzikow was neither ancient nor beautiful, for it had been destroyed and rebuilt many times during Poland's turbulent history. It had once been a fortified castle, but all that remained of its warlike past were parts of a ditch near the main gate where the defensive walls had stood. By the twentieth century it was a large neo-gothic country house with two wings set forward in a U-shape from the central block, the left-hand side housing the chapel, library and archives. To the right of the house was a separate kitchen block, built to prevent the smell of cooking from pervading the castle, but the unfortunate result was that meals at Dzikow were usually served cold. A large oval lawn in front of the house stretched down to the main gate beside the stables, the administration bloc and the covered riding school.

Carved on a stone tablet above the entrance of the house was the inscription: '*Pozwól nam Panie mieszkać w tym gnieździe Ojczystem, a racz obdarzyć zdrowiem i sumieniem czystem.*' ('Lord, allow us to live in this family nest, and give us health and a clear conscience.') They were modest sentiments for a family that had once enjoyed great power.

Those who lived at Dzikow before the war remembered it as a world apart. Stas, who visited as a young man, spoke of the castle and its surroundings as 'Dzikow country' and likened Count Zdzislaw to a king reigning over it. It was a self-contained world that was timeless, harmonious and reassuring. There were three or four generations of the family living in the castle at any one time. Long-term guests and distant relatives lived in apartments above the kitchens. The servants and retainers wore grey flannel livery with dark green piping and lapels, their buttons embossed with the six-pointed star and crescent moon of Leliwa, the ancient heraldic crest of all branches of the Tarnowski family. The surrounding estate was a hive of activity with forests and farms, huge fruit tree nurseries, a market garden, the stud farm and a host of small industries: vodka and liqueur distilleries, a brewery, a brick factory, flour mills, saw mills and commercial fishponds.

The twin pillars of life at Dzikow were a sense of family and respect for the older generation, and beneficence towards the people of the estate and the surrounding towns and villages. The family accepted their responsibilities towards their dependants as a natural part of life, nurturing lifelong relationships with governesses, servants, grooms, huntsmen, villagers, peasants and tradesmen. A sense of identity and belonging reached out from the castle to the people in the small town of Tarnobrzeg beside the castle gates and led to unusual loyalty. During a peasant revolt in 1846 in which hundreds of nobles were slaughtered across Galicia, Dzikow, alone of all the noble houses, was defended by its people.

The family had moved to Dzikow in the late sixteenth century after losing the southern city of Tarnow, its principal stronghold founded centuries earlier. The main branch failed to produce a male heir, and when the sole heiress married, Tarnow with its massive hilltop castle and Gothic cathedral containing the marble tombs of generations of Tarnowskis went with her. The family's greatness ended abruptly as its most powerful branch died out and most of its wealth and dominions were lost.

It was a junior branch of the family that moved to Dzikow. A royal decree granted it a stretch of the right bank of the River Vistula on which to found a new Tarnow that was named Tarnobrzeg or 'Tarnowski banks' but never grew to prominence. In the early twentieth century it was a small market town with an overwhelmingly Jewish population.

Count Zdzislaw sat on the town council and promoted local industries, public education and health services. He financed the building of schools and churches and built a hospital for the town. He also supported hospitals, high schools, orphanages and shelters for the homeless in other towns and villages, and after the Great War he created a foundation that looked after war veterans and the disabled.

During the Great War Count Zdzislaw risked his life more than once for his people. When the Russian army approached, he and his wife Countess Sophie set up a hospital for the wounded of both armies in the castle and flew the Red Cross flag. When the Russians first took the town on 15

September 1914, after winning a battle nearby, the count tried to save it from destruction. Michal Marczak, the Dzikow librarian and archivist, recorded in his diary that as the first Russian patrol trotted past the castle gates drunken men fired a few shots at them. The Russians rode up to the gates and angrily warned that the Red Cross flag would not be respected if they were fired on again. Count Zdzislaw walked over from the castle to reassure them. Then he walked alone into Tarnobrzeg, looking for Austrian troops in the hope of persuading them not to fight in the town.

'He met a large Austrian mounted patrol coming into town,' Marczak recorded. 'When he explained his intentions the major in command took the Count for a spy, put him in the middle of the patrol and ordered him to lead them to the Russian patrol.' The two sides met in the town square and unleashed volleys of gunfire. The Austrians fled and Count Zdzislaw escaped into the back streets, where a groom brought him a horse to ride back to the castle.

The war brought terrible sufferings to Tarnobrzeg and the surrounding villages, as it did to all of Poland, as foreign armies fought countless battles over the Polish lands and lived off the land, looting and requisitioning food, horses, carriages, farm carts and supplies.

Michal Marczak described what happened when the Russians took Tarnobrzeg in September 1914:

There was pillage and plunder on a large scale. They took or destroyed everything. There were terrible scenes of bestiality and licentiousness by night; all the shops were robbed and several Jews from Tarnobrzeg and nearby inns were hanged from trees.

Crowds of frightened people came to the castle seeking

protection, shelter and help . . . Every corridor and room in the kitchen building, the stable yard and the carriage building swarmed with crowds who had fled Dzikow village and Tarnobrzeg. It was difficult to move in the corridors packed with bundles and boxes, crying children and distressed women. Some took refuge in the castle offices and rooms, in the kitchens and in the servants' houses.

Count Zdzislaw organised relief, and Marczak wrote that no other Galician landowner made such efforts for his people. The count set up a soup kitchen in the estate office and ordered free distribution of firewood for the needy during the oncoming winter. But the Russians arrested him on 2 October 1914, after they had been occupying Tarnobrzeg for two weeks, because he was a prominent member of NKN, the Polish national independence committee in Krakow. He spent a month in a Tsarist jail before being released in poor health.

Early in October, after the count's arrest, Countess Sophie sent two wagons of supplies to the town, mostly for destitute Jews. She supplied shops with cheap produce and set up a shop in the stable yard. Crowds came to buy, even from across the border in Russian-ruled Poland. At the end of October she sent out two more badly needed wagonloads of flour and three wagons of salt.

After the Russians looted the town museum, their commander, Colonel Rachmanov, suggested to Count Zdzislaw that he take the Dzikow art collection under his protection. The count indignantly refused. The collection included priceless manuscripts, fine paintings and eighteenth-century miniatures, and historical mementoes that were Polish national heirlooms. Angered by the refusal, Rachmanov stole all the horses from the famous Dzikow stud at Wymyslow. There is a romantic tale about a stallion named Kondensz broke loose as the Russians drove the horses across the steppe and turned back to Dzikow, followed by a single filly foal. The two horses made their way to Wymyslow but nobody knew how Kondensz got the foal across the broad, fast-flowing Vistula. After the war Count Zdzislaw had a stone water trough with the stallion's name chiselled on it placed at the spot where the horses had emerged. It was set low so that horses drinking at the trough would bow to the name of the heroic stallion.

The Austrians drove out the Russians in October, but they retook the town at the start of November. 'At this time the region succumbed to almost complete ruin and destruction,' Marczak wrote. Heaps of bodies lay unburied, and dysentery and typhus were rife. People were so dispirited that most of the potato harvest that could have staved off hunger was left to rot in the earth.

When Count Zdzislaw returned from prison in November he ordered more distributions of firewood. Nearly a thousand wagonloads were sent out between November and March, and fifty people received free soup and bread at the estate office each day. With all schools in the district closed, he started a school for a hundred children in the estate office, recruiting the Prior of the Dominican priory in Tarnobrzeg and his own secretary to be among the teachers. He summoned the district clergy to a meeting and urged them to open temporary schools, giving them firewood and money for the teachers' wages.

By spring 1915 conditions were so bad that peasants around Dzikow were living in earth dugouts or makeshift shacks, but the Jews suffered most, huddling together in the small towns where they were often a majority of the population. 'Their fate was terrible,' Marczak wrote. 'Bullied and beaten by the oncoming soldiery, robbed of everything, they gathered in back streets and hiding places in hunger and sickness. After the second Russian invasion I saw Jews lying on the ground in the snow, or lying near a window in a building and not moving for two days. About four hundred Jews lived in Tarnobrzeg in these conditions.'

Countess Sophie opened a soup kitchen for the Jews early in March 1915. 'It is hard to forget the sight of the first meal given to these starving people in the presence of Countess Sophie, the founder of the kitchen, the fighting for a piece of bread and a bowl of hot soup,' Marczak continued. 'Four hundred and several dozens of Jews benefited from it.'

The front returned to Tarnobrzeg in May 1915 when the Russians were on their final retreat eastwards. They put artillery spotters in the tower of the Dominican church. The Austrians responded by shelling the church, holing the tower, destroying the vaulted roof of the nave, the baroque organ, the choir and the stained glass windows.

Count Zdzislaw, who was watching from the castle, risked his life by rushing to the burning church to rescue the miraculous icon of *Matka Boska Dzikowska*, Our Lady of Dzikow, which had hung above the altar for more than a hundred years. He removed the icon to the castle chapel, where it remained until October when the fighting was over and he ceremonially returned it to the church.

Count Zdzislaw suffered badly from asthma and emphysema, and by the 1930s he needed constant care. He was looked after by three servants named Walenty, Tadeusz and Pelc. Pelc, who had been his gun-bearer, took the night duty. He slept in a little loggia near Count Zdzislaw's bedroom on the ground floor, and if the count needed help he rang a bell.

But they had a cranky relationship and Pelc eventually started ignoring the bell. Count Zdzislaw then had a long string tied to a button on the old servant's livery and tugged it when he needed him. The system worked until one night he pulled on the string and Pelc's empty jacket came sliding into the bedroom.

During his gun-bearing days Pelc had been a drunken menace at the great hunts in the Dzikow forests to which Count Zdzislaw invited the cream of the Polish aristocracy. He was always sober when the hunt began, standing behind Count Zdzislaw and re-loading his shotguns. But by the third drive, when the count turned to hand him a gun for re-loading, Pelc was either staggering about drunkenly or stretched out unconscious on the ground. Count Zdzislaw was dumbfounded. Where did Pelc get the liquor? How did he do it? He had Pelc watched. No one could work it out, and it was a long time before the wily old man's trick was revealed. As the count's gun-bearer he was allowed to bring his own shotgun to hunts. Before he came he corked up both barrels and filled them with vodka, which he swigged surreptitiously while his lordship was shooting.

Count Zdzislaw was fond of his old gun-bearer in his gruff way. When Pelc lay dying, a servant came to his bedroom in the castle. 'Milord Count, things are very bad with Pelc. He is dying.'

'Hmm, hmm, I must go there,' Count Zdzislaw replied. 'Tell him to wait.' As usual, he took hours to get up, coughing and wheezing. By the time his carriage reached Pelc's cottage, the gun-bearer's body was laid out, candles were burning and women were weeping and praying. Count Zdzislaw stood in the doorway. 'Silly ass,' he muttered, 'couldn't you have waited for me?'

Count Zdzislaw died on 24 November 1937, aged seventy-five. His body lay in state in the castle chapel in a burial shroud made from a sheet, in accordance with family tradition. Twigs from every section of the Dzikow forests which he loved were placed in his coffin and numerous requiem masses were said in the tiny chapel.

Huge crowds came to the funeral. On a rainy, windy day Bishop Lorek of Sandomierz, a town just across the River Vistula, celebrated the solemn requiem mass in the chapel, and Count Zdzislaw's sons and closest friends carried his coffin to the family crypt under the Dominican church, escorted by soldiers with fixed bayonets. They were followed by a long procession of aristocrats, government officials, parliamentary deputies, politicians and academics from Warsaw, Krakow, Lwow and Poznan. 'Tens of thousands of peasants from miles and miles and miles away trooped to the funeral,' Stas recalled. 'It was amazing.'

Dzikow and Count Zdzislaw had represented more than anything else what the family stood for and what it treasured. The old count was succeeded by his son, Artur, who was a deputy in the Warsaw parliament, but less than two years remained before the Nazi onslaught on Poland that swept his world away.

CHAPTER EIGHT

Fool's Paradise

As war loomed in the summer of 1939, none of the family could have had any inkling of what was about to engulf them and their country, except perhaps Sophie who in the last days of August had a terrible premonition.

She and Andrew had just experienced the tragedy of losing their son. He was born on their estate at Gora Ropczycka in November 1937, and they named him after his father, but their joy grew to concern as he failed to develop normally, and in less than two years he was dead. By a cruel stroke of fate he died on 21 July 1939, the day Sophie gave birth to their second son. She was in a maternity clinic in Krakow when she received a telegram from Andrew at their home at Gora Ropczycka telling her of the child's death.

It was some time before she was well enough to travel home from Krakow, but on a beautiful August day she and Andrew began the journey with their new baby, whom they named Jan. Normally, they would have driven the 100 kilometres to Gora Ropczycka, but war with Germany was looming, the military were requisitioning private cars and the chauffeur had been called up, so they took a train.

As the train steamed into the station they saw through the shimmering heat that blood was streaming down one of the carriages. There were screams as the train halted and delivered up the first Polish victims of a war that had not yet begun. The train had been packed with military conscripts travelling to join their units, and seven peasant conscripts sitting on the roof of a carriage drinking home-made vodka had been decapitated by a bridge as it thundered towards Krakow.

Standing beside Andrew as the bodies were removed and the carriage was swabbed down, Sophie had a powerful foreboding that this blood and smoke and death were portents: a foul whiff of something that was about to engulf them. The horror of the scene never left her. More than fifty years later, as an elderly lady, she could still recall as if it were yesterday the blood, the screams and the dawning awareness that this was an omen of something monstrous.

Shaken, she and Andrew climbed aboard. Pushing along the packed corridor, with the nurse carrying the baby, she felt this train was a hearse carrying them towards God only knew what awful fate. As for Poland, well, dear God and Our Blessed Mother of Czestochowa, save Poland, she thought, with an absolute certainty that the future was atrocious and unavoidable.

The train pulled into the small country town of Debica east of Krakow where Stas met them with two young women. 'Zosia, darling,' he said, bursting with pride and smiling his beautiful smile, 'I want you to meet Chouquette, my fiancée. And this is Boule, her sister.'

Stas was about to turn twenty-one and was to enter the army's cavalry school at Grudziadz in north-western Poland in two weeks to do his military service. He had brought the two sisters to introduce them to Sophie and Andrew and spend a few days in the countryside at Gora Ropczycka. He wanted his family to meet Chouquette, and hoped that having guests in the house would help take Sophie's mind off the death of her son, who was buried in the churchyard on the hill behind the house.

Despite the threat of war looming over Poland the skies were blue, the sun was bright and the summer blazed on as they lived the last days of peace on the little estate at Gora Ropczycka with its manor house, stud farm and orchards amid the rolling hills and forests of southern Poland.

I can see them now, those five young people living the last long summer days of their beautiful, privileged world. I can hear the murmur of their conversations as they lunch near the house beside the pond in the shade of willow trees. They gallop across fields and along forest roads, their shouts and laughter rising above the gentle Carpathian foothills. It is a moment of utter clarity. There they are on the edge of the abyss. In a few days their country will be overwhelmed, their world will be destroyed and their caste will disappear into oblivion after many centuries at the pinnacle of power. That image of their energy, youth and innocence lives on in my mind's eye and colours for me the Poland in which they lived, which I never knew. I was not yet born then, but four of them were to be the people closest to me for much of my life: Chouquette and Stas, my mother and father, and Sophie and Boule, my aunts and loving friends. There they are, together for the first time in the bright August sunshine at the moment before the storm breaks.

They lived those days in a fool's paradise only slightly tinged with unease as Poland basked in British and French guarantees of protection against Hitler. The signing on 23 August of the Nazi-Soviet Non-Aggression Pact heightened their unease, but then Britain signed an Agreement of Mutual Assistance on 25 August, pledging to come to Poland's aid in the event of hostilities. And had not General Gamelin, the French Chief of Staff, formally undertaken to throw his divisions across the Maginot Line if Poland was attacked?

Had not General Edmund Ironside, soon to be Chief of the British Imperial General Staff, vowed that the Royal Air Force would match any German air raids on Poland with raids on Germany? So, confident in their own army which nineteen years earlier had seen off the Red Army, and with such allies in the West, what should they fear? It was all fraudulent, of course, Polish overconfidence and British and French bluff aimed at deterring Hitler without the intention or the means to help Poland in the event of attack.

Regardless of the growing threat, the household at Gora Ropczycka lived a carefree existence. Early in the mornings they went riding, and in the evenings Sophie drove Stas, Chouquette and Boule into the forest to hunt buck with Andrew. But Sophie's forebodings mounted as the days passed, until at lunch one day she blurted out that Chouquette and Boule should return to their parents in Warsaw.

'I know it seems awful to say such a thing, but the situation looks so ominous,' she argued. 'I feel war could break out at any moment and then it might be impossible for them to join their parents.'

Andrew and Stas brushed her fears aside: 'What sort of hostess are you, trying to get rid of your guests?'

Sophie believed all her life that Chouquette and Boule should have returned to Warsaw then. They were only nineteen and sixteen years old. The men's thoughtless reaction meant they would be caught far from their home and their parents when the war broke out, and would be swept into foreign exile with a group of people they barely knew.

But who can tell what might have become of them if they had been with their parents in Warsaw when the city was besieged by the Germans? Would they have survived the destruction, five years of Nazi occupation and the terrible

Uprising of 1944 in which 250,000 civilians died and the city was razed to the ground? Would they have lived, like their mother and father, to be marched out of the ruins by the Germans and into camps? Perhaps, who knows, they were fortunate to have been at Gora Ropczycka when the war began.

Both Sophie and Stas had clear memories of the day Hitler attacked Poland, on Friday, 1 September 1939. Sophie was woken very early by planes flying over the manor house.

> They were going so low that I saw the curtains moving and dust lifting off the road. I looked out of the window and I saw quite a lot of farm hands waving at the planes. Everybody thought that it was the British. They had promised us to fight if the Germans invaded, and so we were quite sure that they were making a show of strength. But then I put on the wireless and I heard a whole litany of towns that had already been bombed by the Germans and invaded by the Germans. And this is how we learned that the war had started.

Stas's recollection was that they were out riding that morning when they saw the first warplanes.

> We were going home, actually, it must have been about nine-thirty. And suddenly we saw a flight of planes overhead. Chouquette, who was working at the airport at Warsaw, said, 'Oh look, look, those are the new Polish bombers, the *Losy* [Elks].' Well, they weren't *Losy*, they were Germans on their way to bomb the nearby town of Debica or Rzeszow. And that's how we learned . . . But we didn't know that, we didn't hear the bombing, because it was too far away. And so we listened to the radio at twelve o'clock and then we learned that war had been declared. And I said, 'Hurrah, we'll show the

buggers. We'll be in Berlin in a couple of months.' Silly ass! I was certain we were going to win the war.

The blitzkrieg Hitler unleashed upon Poland from north, south and west was a new form of warfare more devastating than anything that had been seen before. The fighting began at 4.40 a.m. and 1,800,000 Germans poured into Poland with thousands of guns, tanks, planes. The Polish Air Force fought gallantly in its few outdated fighters, but could not prevent massive bombing of Polish cities and troops. The Polish army had only 150 tanks. They fought well, but by 6 September Krakow had fallen and the High Command was losing control of the situation. The next day the Germans were outside Warsaw. Most of the north and west of Poland was overrun by 10 September, and by 14 September Warsaw was encircled. Although the Polish forces inflicted a few reverses on the Germans, they were outnumbered and outgunned, inferior in troops, tanks, armoured vehicles, artillery and aircraft; they were overwhelmed by the most powerful military force in the world and they were smashed by the fast-moving *blitzkrieg* from land and air.

Polish military units retreated eastwards as best they could, hoping to form a line of defence in the south-eastern region of Lwow, with their backs to the Soviet and Romanian frontiers. But the German advance was too rapid, and on 17 September Stalin stabbed Poland in the back and sent the Soviet army pouring in from the east to link up with the Germans advancing from the west. The fourth partition of Poland that Hitler and Stalin had secretly agreed on 23 August was swiftly executed.

The Polish forces had lost 60,000 dead and 140,000 wounded when the fighting ended in early October. The civilian dead were uncounted. Warsaw, the capital, was devastated, and many cities and towns were badly damaged. The Poles had not been ready for the blitzkrieg, but they had just about accomplished what the British and French had asked of them during military discussions in the summer: to hold down the Germans for two weeks, the time France needed to launch an attack on Germany with up to ninety divisions. But French troops never crossed the Maginot Line. Neither France nor Britain fired a shot in Poland's support, and the RAF dropped leaflets, not bombs, on Germany.

Within hours of the start of the fighting refugees began arriving at Gora Ropczycka, bringing terrifying tales of bombing, burning towns and panic, chaos and slaughter on the roads crowded with slow-moving refugees and retreating troops. Day after day more refugees poured in, and soon they were sleeping all over the manor house and in the barns and stables. Many were relatives. They brought contradictory news and rumours that caused sudden mood changes from gloom to optimism, optimism to depression and then sudden hope once again. Disturbing news about German advances was contradicted by rumours of Polish victories and heavy losses of German tanks and planes. Few of the refugees remained long. They ate, slept and moved on to the east, fleeing before the advancing Germans.

September 3, the day Britain and France declared war on Germany, was a Sunday, and German planes machine-gunned worshippers leaving church in Sedziszów, a small town close to Sophie's and Andrew's estate, killing several people. But from then on each new wave of refugees arriving at the manor house brought rumours of Allied military successes against the Germans. Many people believed fervently that the British army was massing in Romania to the south to come to

Poland's aid. Even the sight of badly battered Polish military columns, defenceless against air bombardment, failed to shake the widespread belief among Poles in the early days of the war that Poland would be victorious in the battle with Germany.

As the young people waited at Gora Ropczycka during the first week of the war, not knowing what to do, German planes began circling ominously over the manor house at set times each morning and afternoon. Fearing they would attack, Sophie made everyone take shelter at those times in the ice house, which was hidden by trees under a bank near the pond.

Sophie had a narrow escape from death in the first days of the war. When a kitchen maid told her that her brother was very ill but the doctor would not visit him, Sophie sent someone to fetch the doctor, but he returned saying the doctor had suffered a nervous breakdown and would not come. She asked Stas and Andrew to drive to the nearby towns of Debica and Rzeszow for medicine. But all the pharmacies had been swept clean and they turned back when a German plane dived to machine-gun them on the road. So Sophie concocted a quack medicine for the maid's brother. She boiled apples, added salt and sugar and herbs to make the juice taste peculiar, poured the mixture into a medicine bottle and wrote a spurious Latin name on the label.

She took the medicine to the kitchen maid's home and found her brother with a high fever, dying of typhoid, his mother weeping beside him. She told her to give him the medicine every three hours. 'I felt that to give them even a false hope was something, rather than leaving them with no one coming to see him,' she said later.

Two days later she came down with a violent headache and a raging temperature. Andrew isolated her in the cellar of the manor house, and she lay there alone when everyone went to the ice house. But on the first day, the cellar door opened quietly and the kitchen maid came in.

'What on earth are you doing here?' Sophie asked weakly. 'Don't you know you should be in the ice house?'

'I would be in the ice house,' the girl replied, 'but you are here, Madame Countess, and so I'm going to be with you.'

Sophie somehow recovered quickly and on 7 September Andrew decided they should move to their hunting lodge in the forest, fearing the manor house would eventually be bombed. Andrew and Stas said they were only taking refuge temporarily, and confidently declared that the Germans would be defeated in a few months. But Sophie had another of her forebodings. She feared that leaving her home would be the beginning of a long flight that would take them away from Poland. Before they left that night she threw her passport into the fireplace and burned it.

'Are you mad?' Andrew demanded of her.

'No. I'm worried that panic is contagious and I don't want ever to leave my country and so I am making it impossible to leave.'

They piled into Andrew's new big blue Ford with the baby and his nurse and drove to the hunting lodge to settle for the night. But they had barely fallen asleep when someone knocked on a window and shouted that the Germans were only a few hours away. In the middle of the night they got up and got back into the car and drove north. They drove slowly without headlights, with Stas or Andrew sometimes having to get out to guide them round huge bomb craters in the road, and pushing slowly past crowds of refugees.

It was still dark when they reached the mansion at Rudnik, seventy kilometres away. Rudnik, too, was full of refugees.

They were sleeping all over the mansion, in the stables, the estate office and the farm buildings, and on haystacks on the grass in front of the house. Hieronim had slaughtered so many young cattle to feed them that his herd was depleted, and when Stas and Andrew arrived he sent them straight into the forest to hunt buck at dawn.

They returned with a buck and Stas drove to the nearby town of Nisko to volunteer for the army. 'No thank you, sir,' he was told. 'You have no military training and we will only take you if you have a car.'

That day, 8 September, was the last time Sophie and Stas attended Mass in the little wooden chapel in front of the mansion in which Sophie had been christened and married. The mass was celebrated by Prior Karol of Tyniec, an ancient Benedictine monastery overlooking the River Vistula above Krakow, who was fleeing eastwards with two of his monks.

'He celebrated holy Mass amid the roar of bombs falling on Rudnik (town),' Hieronim wrote beneath the prior's signature in the visitors' book. 'After the explosion of the first bombs he intoned the patriotic anthem *'Boże coś Polske.'* The anthem usually ends with the line 'Lord, bless our fatherland', but on that day they sang the nineteenth-century version from the times of Poland's partitions, which ended with the plea *'Ojczyznę wolną racz nam zwrócić' Panie* – 'Lord, give us back our free fatherland.'

Dozens of bombs exploded on the town, although not on Hieronim's estate. The Germans were aiming at the railway station, which was crowded with military transports and refugees. They destroyed the station and nearby buildings, killing eight people and wounding dozens.

Later that day Stas was showing Chouquette and Boule round the park and gardens of his childhood home when there was a shout and a stable boy ran up to him. 'Come quickly, Lord Count. An officer has shot himself.'

Stas ran round the lakes in front of the mansion, and beside the stables among the beehives in the cherry orchard lay the body of a Polish army colonel with a bullet in his head.

Hieronim recorded his death in the visitors' book: 'A colonel of a unit not known to me, who for several days looked for his regiment in vain, came here and committed suicide in the orchard. In that place is a cross.'

The colonel's name was Walerian Mlyniec. 'Colonel Walerian Mlyniec experienced a psychological breakdown,' wrote Rudnik residents Zofia and Zdzislaw Chmiel in their history of the town.

He had been a legionnaire under Marshal Pilsudski in the First World War, he had fought in the Bolshevik War of 1920 in defence of Warsaw and Lwow, and he could not come to terms with the collapse of 1939. He saw the bombardment of Rudnik, the military transports destroyed at the railway station, the dead soldiers who had not managed to reach the field of battle. He saw the defeated Polish army fleeing. Somewhere among this army was his regiment. On September 8 he committed suicide at the mansion where he was staying.

Amid the confusion, the young people discussed with Hieronim what they should do. He said they should flee to the east that night. He had heard on the radio that many bridges over the River San had been blown up to slow the German advance. But a nearby bridge was still standing, and he told Sophie and Stas they should leave before it was destroyed.

That evening Stas and Sophie said goodbye to their father for the last time. Although Stas's relationship with his father had long been difficult and distant, they took affectionate and emotional leave of one another. Stas knelt in Hieronim's study for the first time in his life to receive his father's blessing. Hieronim took a gold cross from his neck and hung it round his son's neck. It was a treasured heirloom taken from the body of Juliusz Tarnowski of Dzikow, the younger brother of Hieronim's father Professor Stanislaw Tarnowski, who was killed fighting the Russians in the Polish national uprising of 1863.

'I hope you will be brave,' he told Stas. 'Be a good soldier, and be sure you do not bring shame on the family name.' Stas kissed his hand and rose to leave.

Hieronim said goodbye to Sophie in the small salon with the beamed ceiling and hunting trophies on the walls. Walking over to the French windows that looked out towards the garden, he took an object down from the wall, removed it from its frame, rolled it up, wrapped it carefully and handed it to her. 'Take this with you. It is the first thing the Germans would take from here.'

It was a Polish national treasure: the personal standard of King Charles Gustavus of Sweden, captured at Rudnik during a seventeenth-century Swedish invasion. The incident, in which the king narrowly escaped with his life when he was surprised by Polish cavalrymen in the priest's house at Rudnik, is famous in Polish history. It was described by the Nobel laureate Henryk Sienkiewicz in his trilogy of historical novels beloved by all Poles.

Before the group got into Andrew's car and drove away from Rudnik, Hieronim asked Sophie and Stas to sign their names in the visitors' book. 'To dear Dad, may God bless you,' wrote Stas. 'We are now crossing the San, and may God grant us to return with the victorious army. (First time in Rudnik with my fiancée). Stas. 8/IX.39.' Chouquette signed her name below, and so did Boule and Andrew and Sophie.

Then they drove into the night, away from the rumble of guns. Sophie and Stas would never see their father again.

CHAPTER NINE

The Bridge over the River Dniester

With Andrew at the wheel, the big blue Ford nosed along in the darkness, headlights doused, sometimes pushing through crowds of refugees. There were seven of them in the car, including Chouquette and Stas, Boule, Sophie, her baby and his nurse. They were crammed so tight that Sophie, squashed against a door in the back seat, could barely move to feed her baby.

After they crossed the River San the sound of gunfire died away but there was no sign of Polish troops or any preparations for a line of defence, and Stas realised that Poland was being overwhelmed in a hopelessly unequal struggle. Their first instinct was to join forces with other family members, so they headed for Tarnawatka, a country estate about eighty-five kilometres east owned by Andrew's brother-in-law, Wladyslaw Tyszkiewicz.

They drove all night under a starlit sky along narrow, potholed roads through flat countryside dotted with a few villages and small towns and long stretches of forest. Day was breaking when they reached the low wooden manor house at Tarnawatka on the shore of Wladyslaw's vast commercial fishponds that stretched to horizons fringed with forests. Wladyslaw had gone off to the war, but his wife Roza and their five children were looking after sixty or seventy refugees who were sleeping all over the house, the stables and the farm buildings. The oldest of their children was Sophie's friend from convent school, Bisia, who was now eighteen. Some of the refugees were also relatives, and the morning air rang with greetings. But for Chouquette and Boule everyone they met on that feverish morning was a stranger. Accidentally caught up with a clannish group of aristocrats whom they barely knew, the two sisters felt insecure and frightened as each day took them further from their parents in Warsaw. Although Chouquette had known Stas since the start of the year she had only very recently met some of his family. Boule had disliked Stas from the start.

Over platefuls of eggs and sausages the new arrivals discussed with their hosts where to go next. That afternoon Andrew's elder brother, Artur, the young lord of Dzikow, drove up in a big chauffeur-driven Mercedes Benz. Artur had come from Dzikow, where he had learned that thirty people had been killed by bombing in and around Tarnobrzeg. The castle was not damaged, but his wife and children had gone and it was empty. He was in military uniform, heading for Lwow on military service, and he told them all to flee to the east as quickly as possible. In all Poland's many wars major battles had been fought in the nearby forests, and he expected the Polish army to regroup there and fight as planned, so it was not safe to stay at Tarnawatka.

Many of the assembled aunts, uncles and cousins took Artur's advice and decided to drive east together. The Tyszkiewicz children were given half an hour to get ready to leave with the smallest possible suitcases. They were told to think carefully about what to pack. It was difficult to choose, because they had no idea how long they would be away. Bisia crammed a suitcase with photographs and mementoes and all the jewellery her great-grandmother had given her for birthdays and Christmases. She did not take a change of clothes, reasoning that clothes could always be found, but not mementoes of her life. Then she wandered through her home for the last time, and coming to a pantry where her mother kept home-made preserves and crystallised fruit that were occasionally given to the children as a treat, she thought how sad it was to leave all this behind for the Germans.

Roza and her children said tearful farewells to the servants, the stable hands and estate workers they had known all their lives, and without waiting for nightfall or pausing to darken their headlights the seven cars, packed with forty-four aristocrats, servants, nannies and chauffeurs, drove off. The children thought it a great adventure and nicknamed the group The Gang of Forty-four, after Ali Baba and the Forty Thieves. But for each of them the journey they were beginning was to be the greatest turning point in their lives. At one moment they were comfortably established members of Poland's centuries-old elite, and in the next they had left everything they knew, loved and possessed, and joined tens of thousands of nameless refugees fleeing for their lives.

The children never dreamed they were leaving their home forever. The adults said they would drive to the Soviet frontier about 200 kilometres east and wait until things settled down. They believed they would be back in a month or two after the Germans were defeated. But Stas, Sophie and Andrew, and Chouquette and Boule were beginning to fear there would be no return home behind a victorious Polish army.

They drove north at first, heading for Klemensow, the main residence of the Zamoyski family just beyond the lovely Renaissance town of Zamosc. It was market day when they arrived, and as they reached the market square the horn of one of the cars stuck and caused near panic among the crowds of locals who thought it was an air-raid siren. Bearded Jews in long black coats and hats, with long sidelocks, rushed up to the cars, gesticulating wildly and shouting questions through the windows in heavily accented Polish. 'The Jews were frightened, terrified by the war, terrified of what was going to happen,' Bisia said. 'They didn't know, of course, what Hitler was going to do. Nobody knew. But they were frightened.'

At Klemensow they found their Zamoyski cousins had taken refuge in the nearby forests. The convoy turned round and headed east, hoping to reach Pomorzany, the estate of George Potocki, the brother of Wanda's lover Alfred, who was Poland's ambassador to the United States, near the Soviet border about 150 kilometres away.

It was September 10. Everywhere the German army was pushing deeper and deeper into Poland and cities were falling. The armoured divisions were pushing eastwards and the German airforce was bombarding everything in its path. Planes were swarming over eastern Poland, bombing and strafing military units, railways, cities and towns, and nowhere were the roads safe. It would not be long before the panzers arrived.

The seven cars drove through the night under dimmed headlights, past macabre scenes of war repeated many thousands of times across Poland during that nightmare September. The roads were again crowded with humanity. Families were fleeing on wooden farm carts piled high with possessions and pulled by horses. Trucks and cars bulged to overflowing. Many fled on bicycles or on foot, pushing handcarts laden with their belongings or carrying children. They passed burned-out houses, shattered tanks, wrecked gun-carriages and vehicles destroyed in dive-bombing attacks on columns of troops and crowds of refugees. They saw corpses in piles along the roadside – dead soldiers and civilians, horses and cows. Sometimes soldiers' graves lined the roadsides. They stood singly, or in rows of two, three or four, marked with makeshift crosses and the steel helmets of the fallen.

They drove until dawn, not daring to stop in the dark for fear of being separated. Sophie, who washed her baby's nappies during the day, sat squashed in the back of Andrew's Ford at night, breastfeeding the baby with a freshly washed nappy draped over her head to dry in the breeze from the car window. At dawn they pulled off the road, dispersed the cars and slept, thankful for the unusually fine weather that allowed them to sleep in ditches, woods and fields. They had little to eat or drink. Their jewellery and money was useless because it was impossible to buy supplies. No one along the road had much to offer, and no one would let refugees pay. Whatever they ate and drank came from the kindness of strangers. They experienced other acts of kindness. Sophie remembered stopping in a small town at dawn one misty morning, exhausted after a night on the road, and seeing an elderly Jew come out of a wooden house beside the road. When he saw her with her baby he beckoned, 'Come in, come in, my bed is still warm.' She accepted with relief.

Once or twice they made the mistake of starting to drive before darkness had fallen, or of staying on the road after daybreak, and each time German planes came screaming down with machineguns blazing and they jumped out and ran for their lives. Stas and Andrew threw themselves into ditches, lay on their backs and shot furiously at the planes with their hunting rifles. They had no hope of hitting aircraft flying at 500 kilometres an hour, but at least it made them feel they were fighting back.

Each night they saw more destruction: wrecked trains and railway lines, and towns blazing in the dark. Near the city of Lwow they saw the beautiful town of Zolkiew burning so furiously that the flames silhouetted the enormous medieval gate. Driving past Lwow, once the capital of the Austro-Hungarian province of Galicia, they saw the glow of flames from the burning city and heard sounds of war as General Kazimierz Sosnkowski, one of Poland's ablest generals and a good friend of Hieronim, rallied the Polish forces and gave the Germans a bloody nose in a ferocious battle.

The party was tired, shaken and hungry when they reached Pomorzany. The ancient castle seventy kilometres south-east of Lwow had once belonged to the seventeenth-century warrior King Jan III Sobieski. The present owner, George Potocki, was at his diplomatic post in Washington, but the estate manager welcomed them and put them up in the administration building. For two or three days the fugitives enjoyed comfortable beds, hot baths and good meals. Pomorzany was a beautiful haven, full of history and memories of Poland's wars against Tartars, Cossacks, Russians and Turks, a welcome respite after the frights and hardships of the journey. Their spirits rose.

But by 12 September the Germans were at the gates of Lwow, and it was clear they could not stay long. Across Poland the war was turning into a disaster. Warsaw was besieged and in flames. The government and ministries had begun evacuating the city on 5 September, and the General Staff started leaving the following day. Fierce fighting was continuing in many areas, but the backbone of the Polish army was broken, and despite wild rumours of British and French help no one saw any signs of preparations for a last stand near the Soviet and Romanian frontiers. Instead, people at Pomorzany told them there were signs of a Soviet build-up on the border, and they had to decide quickly what to do. Facing the nightmare that has always plagued the Poles, the impossible choice between falling into the hands of the Germans or of the Russians, the refugees decided with heavy and fearful hearts to leave Poland and cross into Romania.

It was a frightful decision for every one of them, and doubly agonising for those who were leaving behind a husband, parents or children as well as their home and country. They had never dreamed they would leave Poland. Chouquette and Boule must have been distraught, knowing their parents were in besieged and burning Warsaw. But they had no choice. How could two young girls like them have retraced their steps alone?

Roza Tyszkiewicz was terrified for her husband Wladyslaw, who had volunteered for emergency traffic-control duty somewhere near Lwow. He suffered from manic depression and she was tormented by the thought that he might return to Tarnawatka to find the manor house empty and her and the children gone. Her sister Zosia suffered similar agony: her husband was fighting with his regiment in eastern Poland. Should she stay behind in Poland to be with him, or take their children abroad to safety? All the wives and mothers hesitated terribly, and they were still full of doubts and fears as they left Pomorzany and headed for the Romanian border 120 kilometres south.

The crowds of refugees on the roads had swelled to huge proportions, all fleeing in the same direction in throngs so dense that they were almost propelled towards the border in a slow-moving mass. Sophie, who had been alarmed from the start by the prospect of leaving Poland, longed to turn back and return home. But the tide of humanity flowing southwards was so dense that it was physically impossible to resist.

They motored slowly through a vast and rolling countryside thickly covered with forest towards the very south-eastern tip of Poland where the broad and majestic River Dniester formed the frontier with Romania. It was Saturday 16 September, Stas's twenty-first birthday, when they reached the frontier. On that day, but for the war, Stas would have come into his inheritance at Dukla. He would have become independently wealthy as the owner of a small estate and a beautiful home surrounded by a park and gardens and packed with artistic treasures.

They reached the frontier town of Zaleszczyki, where the Dniester looped dramatically back on itself, so that the little resort town stood on a peninsula surrounded by water but for a narrow isthmus on the Polish side. Situated on a hill rising out of the water, it looked like a grand medieval fortress standing behind a fast-flowing moat, crossed by a single bridge leading to Romania.

Zaleszczyki was packed to bursting with refugees. Unable to find lodgings together, the travellers split up for the night and agreed to meet at the Catholic church for eleven o'clock Mass in the morning. They slept wherever they could. The fine weather still held and some of them spent their last night in Poland under the stars. Sophie and her baby found a space on the floor of a crowded room, her head resting on the bottom of a wardrobe that cut uncomfortably into her neck.

While they were at Mass next morning someone ran into the church and went up to the altar and whispered urgently to the priest. The priest turned to the congregation that filled every inch of the church and overflowed into the street. 'I've just heard that the Russians have crossed the frontier and

Professor Stanislaw Tarnowski, of the Jagiellonian University. The portrait, painted by Jan Matejko during his second term as rector in 1899–1900, hangs in the university's Collegium Novum at Krakow.

The lords in their finery. A 1930s wedding at Dzikow. Count Zdzislaw, lord of Dzikow, stands in the centre, hand on sword, close to Hieronim Tarnowski, with moustache. On far left, in uniform, is Artur Tarnowski, last lord of Dzikow. His brother Andrew is fourth from left, partly obscured.

Rudnik, Hieronim's mansion, after the battle between the Russian and Austro-Hungarian armies in 1914. There were ten shell holes in the house, the home farm was burned down and 4,000 acres of woods were destroyed. Some 3,600 bodies were dug up from graves in the park and gardens.

Rudnik after rebuilding was completed in 1926.

Stas and Sophie on the day of their First Holy Communion at Rudnik in 1929. Stas, who is ten, is already acquiring an aloof and arrogant look. Sophie, who is twelve, seems to have a mischievous twinkle in her eye.

Hieronim and Wanda in the forest at Rudnik in the early 1920s with Stas and Sophie, mounted on her first pony.

Stas at Dukla with a 14-point stag found dead in the forest.

Stas is 1934, aged sixteen, on a visit to Dzikow after leaving Downside, during which he shot his first stag. He is standing beside a tethered owl used as bait for shooting crows and birds of prey.

The wedding of Sophie Tarnowska of Rudnik and Andrew Tarnowski of Dzikow at Rudnik, 4 February 1937. Andrew wears the traditional finery of the Polish nobility. Behind, a cigarette in his mouth, is Stas, then aged eighteen.

Andrew Tarnowski of Dzikow as an Oxford undergraduate in the early 1930s, playing the minstrel at Pembroke College after a night out.

The wedding of Sophie (Chouquette) Jaxa-Chamiec and Stas Tarnowski at Belgrade on 24 October 1939. Chouquette is in front with two of Stas's young cousins from the family refugee convoy that fled Poland a month earlier. Stas walks behind with Boule, Chouquette's younger sister, partially obscured on his left.

Stas (left) and Andrew (second from left) as soldiers in the Polish army's Carpathian Rifle Brigade in Palestine with a group of friends during the Second World War.

Prince Youssef Kamal ed-Dine, uncle of Egypt's King Farouk, shows Andrew, Sophie (right) and Chouquette around the monuments of Upper Egypt in 1942. The prince, who hunted with family members in Poland before the war, lent Sophie and Chouquette a villa when they arrived in Cairo in mid-1941.

Russian tanks are advancing into Poland,' he said. 'Nobody knows what their intentions are, so if you want to leave now, the Mass is finished.' Shrieks of fear went up, and the church emptied as people began to rush to cross into Romania.

Soviet tanks had started rolling into Poland at six a.m. Stalin was planning to seize eastern Poland as secretly agreed in August by Molotov and Ribbentrop, the Soviet and Nazi foreign ministers. After only twenty-one years of independence, Poland was once again to be partitioned and wiped off the map. Zaleszczyki was only thirty-five kilometres from the Soviet border, and everyone feared Red Army tanks would arrive at any moment. Chouquette and Stas and their companions ran to the cars and drove straight for the Romanian frontier, any doubts about leaving Poland wiped away by their dread of the Soviets. They knew how the Bolsheviks had slaughtered Polish aristocrats and landowners in the Ukraine in 1917 and in eastern Poland during the war of 1920. They were terrified as the densely packed crowds of refugees inched towards the bridge over the River Dniester that marked the frontier. It was 17 September 1939, Chouquette's twentieth birthday and the most terrifying day of her life. It was also the day that the Polish president, the government and the commander-in-chief crossed the border into Romania to avoid being captured.

For Chouquette, the terror of leaving Poland was intensified by a furious row with Stas. They drove over the bridge in the back seat of the car of a dignified old aunt, arguing in whispers so that she could not hear them. But just after they had crossed, Stas lost his temper, grabbed Chouquette's hand and pulled off the betrothal ring he had given her, and threw it angrily out of the window. The ring was a nineteenth-century family heirloom. Stas and Chouquette were both dismayed by what he had done, and even fifty years later he expressed remorse. 'Bloody clever thing to do, wasn't it?' he admitted. 'We were both terribly sorry afterwards.'

Some of them had a foreboding that they would never return. Just before reaching the bridge, Aunt Maria Potocka, the youngest daughter of Count Zdzislaw who was known as Micia, stopped her car and got out. She knelt down and kissed the ground. When her niece Bisia asked what she was doing, she said she was kissing the soil of Poland because she knew she would never return.

Swamped by the flood of refugees, the Romanians had pulled their immigration and customs post well back from the river into a forest, allowing the Poles to queue safely on Romanian territory. The action probably saved many lives, because shortly after the family convoy had crossed they saw twenty-one planes fly over and bomb Zaleszcziki, setting the town on fire and destroying the bridge. They were cut off from Poland. There was no way home.

CHAPTER TEN

Into Exile

Sophie panicked when the planes bombed Zaleszcziki. She shook with terror when she heard the huge explosions across the river and saw the smoke rising above the trees. She had been frightened as they fled across Poland before the advancing Germans, but nothing like this sheer panic that made her want to hold her baby tightly and run blindly into the forest. It was not just fear. The bombing brought home to her that she was cut off from Poland. There was nothing she could do to help those left behind. Her determination not to leave her homeland had been futile. What she had most feared had happened. She had lost the home where she had settled into married life with Andrew; she had lost her father, her mother, her people and her country. Something in her snapped. Distraught beyond words, she wanted to scream and run and hide. She was twenty-two and it seemed that her life had lost all meaning.

Many in the queue wept with shock and anger at the bombing. Andrew tried to calm Sophie. Don't be silly, he said, taking her in his arms, there was nothing to fear. They were in Romania now. The Germans and Russians could not touch them. But this was unlike anything she had experienced before. Although she had modelled herself on her mother, never to show distress or weakness, she could not suppress her emotions. He held her for a long while before she recovered and they rejoined the queue for the customs post.

When they entered, an official asked for their papers. 'Excuse me, sir, I haven't got a passport,' Sophie said.

The official looked at her, a young woman who looked exhausted and tearful. He was an older man, with a kindly look.

'I burned it on purpose. I didn't want to leave Poland.' She fought back her tears.

Andrew handed over his passport. The official wrote down their details and gave them a document authorising them to enter Romania. He smiled and took Sophie's hands and folded them in his. 'You have left behind everything that you loved, and everyone that you loved, but wherever you go you will find love,' he told her.

What a strange thing, she thought. Like a blessing. His words touched her deeply and stayed with her. She would remember them all her life, and she believed they were true.

The seven cars drove away from the frontier, heading for Cernauty, the main town in the region. They passed Romanian military units moving in the opposite direction. The soldiers wore threadbare uniforms and straw sandals. Oxen pulled their field guns. If Poland had lasted only weeks against the blitzkrieg, they thought, the Romanian army looked as if it would only last days if war came.

Romanians had no ethnic ties with the Poles. The two peoples had often fought in the distant days of Poland's greatness, but their countries had friendly relations during the inter-war years and Romania had remained neutral when Hitler attacked Poland. It welcomed the tens of thousands of Polish soldiers and refugees who poured over the border. But Romania was in a precarious situation and was swinging towards the Nazi camp. The Soviet Union, Hungary and Bulgaria all coveted large chunks of the greater Romania created by the Treaty of Trianon in 1920, and Romania needed protection and security. The regime began gravitating towards Germany in 1938, when the western Allies backed down at Munich and let Hitler march into Czechoslovakia. Bucharest realised then that it could no longer entrust its security to France and the League of Nations. By 1939 German influence was predominant in the Romanian economy and a Romanian fascist party, the Iron Guard, was growing in strength. But it was not until June 1940, after the Soviet Union had seized the Romanian territories of Bessarabia and northern Bukovina, and Germany had conquered France, that King Karol joined the German camp.

As soon as Sophie and Stas and their companions entered Romania the large sums of Polish money they had were worthless. They were penniless except for the jewellery they had brought and a little money Stas and Andrew had got by selling their hunting rifles at the border. The once-wealthy aristocrats were gloomy and thoughtful as they stopped at a roadside Red Cross post and queued for glasses of milk and slices of bread. It was hot, and when they drove on they ignored signs indicating the direction for Polish refugees to take, suspecting they would lead to a camp. Instead, they drove into a small town. The peasants in the crowded market-place were alarmed by what was happening in Poland and showed them great sympathy. They gave them watermelons, maize, grapes, plums, pears and cherries and took them to an empty house on the square where they spent the night.

Next morning they used some of their Romanian currency to buy petrol and set off for Bucharest, the Romanian capital five hundred kilometres south. They drove past broad rivers, endless forests and dramatic mountains. They saw little strip farms with low, white-painted thatched cottages, horse-drawn carts and bullock carts, and backwardness and poverty along the road worse than what they knew in southern Poland. But in Bucharest they were surprised to find a city that was wealthier and more sophisticated than Polish cities. Thanks to Romania's oil wealth it was a bustling metropolis with fine avenues, magnificent nineteenth-century buildings, ancient churches and monasteries and delightful parks. Even shop-keepers spoke French, and Romanian high society was stylish, elegant and cosmopolitan, and buzzing with activity.

Roger Raczynski, the Polish ambassador, was a distant uncle of Stas and Sophie. He helped them settle down and gave them introductions that eased the shock of exile and poverty. Middle-class and aristocratic Romanian families did their best to make them at home, giving them clothes and toiletries. The children were lodged in an empty convent school, while the adults were showered with invitations to meals, entertainments and weekend stays in country homes.

But they stayed only a few weeks in Bucharest. It was becoming plain that Romania was moving closer to Germany. Gestapo agents were increasingly evident and the Iron Guard was growing more prominent. Fearing that Romania would soon go over to the Nazi camp, the convoy reassembled early in October and drove through the mountains of Transylvania to Belgrade. The Yugoslav capital, unlike Bucharest, was brimming with anti-Nazi feeling. Serbian nationalism was at a fever pitch, and the Serbs were determined to stand up to Hitler and fight if he attacked Yugoslavia. Wealthy Serbian families welcomed them eagerly and gave them comfortable lodgings. Chouquette and Boule were invited to stay by a wealthy lady who lived in a beautiful villa with her son and two daughters. She was warm and generous, and her dark-haired younger daughter Lilette became a lifelong friend of Chouquette.

Sophie and Andrew and their baby were put up by a French engineer called Pierre Fuziel whose wife had returned to France at the outbreak of war. He rummaged among her possessions to find Sophie scent, soap, a nightdress, slippers, clothes and shoes. The rest of the group took over the fourth floor of the Palace Hotel, a large, empty stone building in the centre of Belgrade that was owned by the French embassy. They believed the French secret service occupied the second floor as they settled into empty rooms off deserted corridors two storeys above. Andrew used his charm to scrounge odds and ends of furniture from Serbian friends and benefactors, and the ladies sold some jewellery to buy more. They also made cupboards and chests-of-drawers from tea crates and fruit boxes, nicknaming the makeshift furniture 'Le Style Sanduk XIII' from *sanduk*, the Serbo-Croat word for chest.

After they had all settled down, the ladies in the group began to consider the situation of Chouquette and Boule. They were not aristocrats and had no ties with the family apart from Chouquette's relationship with Stas. The aunts, including Andrew's three married sisters, considered them outsiders and decided that it would be best to regularise their situation. Coming from traditional families, and brought up according to conservative and somewhat autocratic principles, they decided that Chouquette and Stas should get married right away so that Chouquette and Boule could become a part of the group.

'We all felt that poor Boule and Chouquette, two young things who had arrived at our house more or less to spend the weekend, were in a rather horrible situation,' Sophie said. 'Chouquette was a complete stranger to most of us. Although you share your last bit of bread with your nearest and dearest, you're not prepared to do it for someone who is an outsider. So we wanted her to be in the family.'

Sixty years later Sophie's words ring with more *hauteur* than humanity. If those high-born ladies were good-hearted and well-meaning, why did they not just take care of two young and penniless girls without more ado? Why should Chouquette have to marry into their family to enjoy their solidarity? If the aunts had just accepted her and Boule as fellow refugees facing the same needs as them there would have been no pressure on Chouquette to marry Stas. But they pushed her into his arms, even though they knew of his violence, promiscuity and irresponsibility. It must have seemed to the aunts that he and Chouquette wanted to marry, but it was plain that they were unsuited. And no one made sure that Chouquette's real interests were considered.

Young people who saw her and Stas together in Belgrade remembered that they were as beautiful as two film stars. But under the surface they were as ill-matched as Stas's parents Hieronim and Wanda had been twenty-five years earlier. Everyone who knew them said two such incompatible people should never have married. Unlike Hieronim and Wanda they did not even come from similar backgrounds. Although Chouquette was tall and shapely, she was not physically or emotionally strong. She was a gentle, vulnerable woman who was always horrified by violent behaviour and unable to deal with it. Her upbringing had given her no experience of the kind of behaviour of which Stas was capable, and when he became violent she simply shrank from him.

It seems absurd that they married. Perhaps some families fall into a pattern of lovelessness that is repeated generation after generation. There had been no love in Stas's home, so how could he know what love was or how to give it? Although he had known Chouquette for about nine months, he may have just been infatuated with her beauty. He admitted on his eightieth birthday that they should not have married, saying, 'If it hadn't been for the war I should say that Chouquette and I would never have married. We were so completely different.'

The signs were clear enough before they married. They had fought in the back of the car as they crossed into Romania, and now Stas betrayed Chouquette on the eve of their wedding. On the afternoon of his last day as a bachelor he was lying naked on a bed in Belgrade's smartest hotel, the Serbski Kral, with the windows open to catch the breeze, when he heard someone calling: '*Schoen, schoen, kommen Sie hier.*' He saw a woman beckoning to him from a window on the floor above. No, he called back with a grin, you come over here. A few minutes later there was a knock on his door and an attractive young German woman came into the room laughing. 'I was unfaithful to my wife-to-be,' Stas said. 'I was married next day. Naughty boy, wasn't I?'

The wedding took place on 24 October 1939, at the Roman Catholic Church of Christ the King, a small mock Romanesque church on Krunska Street in the embassy district of Belgrade. The family put on the best show they could, and it was something of a social occasion, attended by diplomats and wealthy Serbs and White Russians who had befriended them. The French ambassador was there, an American diplomat and the Polish consul general.

Chouquette had no bridal gown and Stas wore a grey flannel suit, but they made a handsome couple. She was strikingly elegant as she walked with her sister Boule towards the church carrying an enormous bunch of white roses, a square-shouldered fur coat hanging open over a blouse and skirt, with her dark hair swept back and falling in thick waves to her shoulders. Father Matya Petlic, a Serbian priest, celebrated the wedding mass, and Andrew and the French engineer with whom he was staying were witnesses. A small black-and-white photograph shows the newly weds walking down the aisle smiling broadly. Chouquette is looking down shyly, carrying the roses and Stas is holding his head high.

Boule left Belgrade immediately after the wedding. Stas gave her money for a train ticket to Paris, where she stayed with relatives, and from there she travelled to the United States where she spent the entire war. Stas and Chouquette honeymooned disastrously at Makarska, a resort on the Dalmatian coast. They went with Sophie, Andrew and their baby to the villa of a Polish lady who grudgingly put them up in the off-season to repay loans Hieronim had made to her son in Krakow. But the Indian summer was well and truly over by the time they got there. It rained almost non-stop for two weeks and the villa was so damp that water was running down the walls of the rooms. There was no heating, the food was appalling – whoever heard of eating calves' hoof? Sophie asked indignantly – and the villa was so cold that Sophie struggled to dry Jan's nappies.

It was also a romantic disaster. 'All quiet on the Western front,' Stas announced each morning when he came down to breakfast. Relations were disappointing, he said. He and Chouquette returned to Belgrade before the two weeks were over, said goodbye to everyone and took a train to Paris. Stas was not a man to sit around hoping to avoid the war. He wanted adventure. He wanted to show his bravery. He wanted to fight Hitler. And so he set off with his young wife in November 1939 to travel across Europe and join the exiled Polish forces gathering in France.

CHAPTER ELEVEN

Under the German Boot

ack at Rudnik, the mansion emptied after the five young people drove off into the night. The last refugees soon fled eastwards and Hieronim was left alone with his aged mother, the housekeeper and the faithful old butler. Next day they heard more explosions as the Luftwaffe bombed the town again. A Polish cavalry squadron with rifles slung across their backs trotted wearily up to the house at nightfall and the officer, a young cousin, said they were the last unit before the advancing Germans. To Hieronim's anxious question he replied that the army planned to defend the River San, which was barely a kilometre from the house.

Alarmed that Rudnik would be engulfed in fighting as in 1914, Hieronim had a carriage harnessed and drove his mother several kilometres into the forest beyond the main road in front of the mansion, to get as far from the river as possible. They took refuge with one of his foresters who lived in a wooden house in a clearing among the larch, birch and pine trees. Sunflowers and hollyhocks taller than a man grew in the little garden around the house, and beyond the picket fence was a well, its bucket dangling from a ten-metre pole that pointed diagonally to the sky until it was released to let the bucket plunge downwards.

Hieronim recorded their departure for the forest in the visitors' book: 'Being unable to endanger my eighty-five-year-old mother, I went to the Lentownia forester's house, from where we returned home after a few days, having learned that there was no battle along the line of the San.' The words hint at his reluctance to leave the mansion even for a short time. He had not considered fleeing Rudnik with Sophie and Stas. After all the upheavals he had lived through he had no wish to face an uncertain future once again. It would have been the fourth time he had fled since 1914, and although he was still fit and active at fifty-five he no longer felt young enough for adventures into the unknown. How many times, he must have thought, must a man flee his home before he says, 'Enough, this is where I belong, and here I remain.'

A lifetime of memories bound him to Rudnik, from the day in August 1898 when as a boy of fourteen he had accompanied his mother and father from Krakow to take possession of the estate. He had spent idyllic summers swimming in the River San or roaming the tall, silent forests for mushrooms and wild strawberries. He had galloped across the broad forest meadows and driven along the dirt roads that meandered through the trees. He had shot roebuck grazing at dawn and dusk at the edge of the trees, and wild boar charging from the undergrowth with the dogs snapping at their heels. Here, too, he had begun to learn the arts of farming, forestry and estate management, which were to become his life.

Rudnik had witnessed his joys and woes since he brought his young wife there in 1914. He remembered the early years when he and Wanda had lived in *maly domek*, the wooden house where their children were born. No matter how painful his marriage had become, those years held memories of special sweetness. When Wanda and the children left, he had remained in the empty mansion, almost a recluse. But there were joyful memories, too: Sophie's christening in the wooden chapel among the trees, and her wedding twenty years later when they danced all night to gypsy violins.

But now there could be no doubt that the Germans would be at Rudnik in a few days. If he fled, there would be no one to protect his mansion and property, and should the gods of war ever allow him to return he would find them pillaged or destroyed as they were during the Great War. What would happen to the servants and estate workers? Too old to fight, and unwilling to start a new life abroad, Hieronim chose to stay and protect his home and people, or at least share their fate.

It did not seem a very risky decision. Although Germany was an ancient foe, German officers had generally behaved with decency during previous occupations, unlike the rapacious barbarism of the Tsarist Russian armies that bloodily put down Polish uprisings during the previous century and sent tens of thousands of Poles trekking into Siberia, and the savagery of the Bolshevik hordes who slaughtered all before them as they galloped into Poland in 1920. Hieronim had no inkling that the Nazi bestiality unleashed by the Germans this time would be far worse than anything Poland had suffered before. How could he know that Poland was marked for destruction, that six million Polish Christians and Jews were to be wiped out, and the rest of the Poles were to be reduced to serfdom before being murdered or deported to make way for colonists? He could not know that Poland was to become the Nazi killing field, turned into a land of concentration camps and death factories, with mass hangings and shootings in hundreds of villages, towns and cities for six long years. Ignorant of what was coming, he awaited the German army with trepidation but without undue fear.

The speed of the *panzers'* advance ensured that the Polish defence line along the River San never materialised, and on 13 September German troops swarmed unopposed into Rudnik. First came a phalanx of dust-covered motorcyclists wearing steel helmets and goggles, with sub-machine-guns slung across their stomachs, then files of foot soldiers, rifles in hand, moving along both sides of the road, followed by trucks carrying more soldiers. The streets of the little town emptied as they fired bursts of gunfire at houses and shot two civilian men caught in the open. Inhabitants hid in their homes or fled to the forest.

Having secured the town, the Germans searched the houses. They drove every man and every Jew they found to the square and made them lie face down on the ground under their rifles. In the evening the Jews were driven to the synagogue on Walowa Street, where they were shot and burned. Two synagogues, the Jewish bath house, the school and several houses on Walowa Street were burned down. A local priest noted what happened next:

> The church was surrounded for several days by so many German vehicles that it was difficult to get in or out . . . At the presbytery one could go crazy at night from the noise: the groans, the searches and all kinds of violence . . . The parish priest of Rudnik, Father Zagalak, was arrested with his housekeeper, Anna Kowalska. They were marched for an hour like laughing stocks through the whole town on their way to the court. In the end they were taken to the village of Kopki to be shot, but at the church in Kopki they were released and allowed to walk back. The priest's room in the presbytery was used from then on by the Germans as military headquarters.

German officers drove up to the mansion. Addressing Hieronim as Herr Graf – Count – they inspected the property and told him officers would be billeted in the house. They warned that he would be held responsible for any partisan attacks, acts of sabotage or hiding of Jews on his property, and the penalty was death. He, his mother and the housekeeper were restricted to two or three rooms off a ground-floor corridor while the Germans took the rest of the mansion.

The house now echoed to German voices and German laughter. Jackbooted conquerors strode beneath the pillared portico, sauntered through the hall past the curving wooden staircase and onto the polished parquet floor of the big salon with its immense, beautifully painted old porcelain stove, the ceiling spanned by massive larch beams. Officers lounged in the little salon where Hieronim and Wanda had taken their aperitifs and patted and kissed Stas and Sophie.

It is hard to imagine the humiliation Hieronim felt at having to move out of his bedroom and surrender his study, dining room and living rooms to the intruders. Although he spoke perfect German, he avoided contact with them as much as he could. He soon learned of the cruelties the Germans were inflicting on the town and nearby villages, and throughout Poland. He felt a bottomless distaste for these heel-clicking invaders who were invading his house and brutalising his people.

His mother Imcia was now a shrivelled old woman going blind from cataracts who tottered around looking like a witch and showed signs of dementia. She was so confused that she thought the Germans were guests arriving for a hunting party. Confined with her to a few rooms, Hieronim complained to his sister Etusia Esterhazy in Hungary that the eccentric old lady was driving him crazy with her constant demands. 'To keep Mama at peace will not be easy,' Etusia wrote back. 'I understand and share your feelings about the impossibility of doing anything in her presence.' She advised him to go to the estate manager's house to read and write. 'It will be quiet there and nobody will disturb you, even if she does come by the windows. And if you can't find peace there, go to the priest's house or somewhere – but do go and read and write . . . Do follow my advice, Imus dear, so that your nerves are not shattered. Many people depend on you.'

Hieronim had witnessed many tragedies in his life, but this, truly, was the hour when darkness covered the land. Poland's rebirth in 1918 had been the climactic event of Hieronim's generation, the fruition of more than 120 years of struggle and bloody national uprisings. For two decades he had watched the young republic grow in freedom and independence, and not a little chaos, while he rebuilt his property. Now, everything that had given his life meaning was being destroyed, and the seemingly invincible Nazi-Soviet alliance excluded all hope of Poland's restoration.

When the fighting Hitler began ended in early October Stalin annexed Poland's eastern territories and Hitler incorporated western Poland into the German Reich. All that remained of Poland was a central rump of thirty per cent of her territory under Hitler's control that the *Führer* designated the General-Gouvernement and placed under the rule of the Nazi Gauleiter Hans Frank. All laws and institutions were abolished in Frank's fiefdom, leaving the SS and Gestapo to reign unchecked in Warsaw, Krakow, Lublin and the Sandomierz region that included Rudnik. Poles are proud that their country produced no Nazi collaborators like Vidkun Quisling, the prime minister of German-occupied Norway, but the fact is that Hitler had no need of a Polish

Quisling since Poland did not exist. Frank's General-Gouvernement existed only to provide slave labour for Germany and sites for camps. All the Jews were to be exterminated, and eighty per cent of Poles were to be deported to the Soviet Far East to make way for German colonisation of their homeland. The five years of Nazi and Soviet occupation in Poland were far more ferocious than the regimes the Nazis later imposed on the conquered countries of western Europe, which were spared both the horrors of Soviet rule and the unrestrained brutality that the Nazis unleashed on the 'subhuman' races of the east.

The ferocity of the occupiers was matched by the exceptional harshness of the winter of 1939. From Christmas until April the forests bowed under abnormally heavy snowfalls, the meadows along the River San were deep under snow, and the drifts buried peasants' huts.

'This year's winter reminds me of the winter of 1928–29,' Hieronim noted in the visitors' book. 'The lowest temperature was –36 degrees celsius, and frost of more than twenty degrees was an almost normal phenomenon, so that I dare say the average temperature was –15 degrees celsius. The freeze lasted from December 26 to March 25.' When the Germans forced townspeople to clear the roads and railway lines, they suffered intensely from the cold, often wrapped in little more than rags. Many suffered from frostbite and many died from the cold.

While Hieronim settled into a frigid co-habitation with the Germans in his mansion, they imposed a ten p.m. to six a.m. curfew on the town. *Volksdeutsch* – Polish citizens of German descent, some of whom had been secretly pro-Nazi before the war – were installed in official positions. Forced labour was imposed. Radios were confiscated and possession of them was punishable by immediate execution. Secondary schools and higher learning institutes were closed and used as German barracks. Only technical colleges and primary schools remained open, the schools allowed to teach only singing, reading, writing, arithmetic, religion and gymnastics. Ration cards were issued, entitling Polish workers to 900 calories a day, Germans to 4,000 and Jews to less than 200 or nothing. There were shortages of petrol, salt, sugar and heating fuel, and people went cold and hungry. The bread queue formed at the bakery at dawn. Beef was reserved for Germans, and Poles caught with it could be executed. In October, the Germans rounded up the last of the 1,200 Jews they had gathered at Rudnik and marched them away. In December, trainloads of Poles expelled and deported from the western territories annexed by Germany arrived, hungry and frozen. Later, the trains would roll west carrying two million Poles to slave labour in Germany.

Like many Poles, Hieronim tried to protect Jews. The Gestapo repeatedly questioned him about Pan Glazer, a Czech of Jewish descent who was the bookkeeper at the wicker factory, which belonged to Hieronim's estate. He assured them time after time that Glazer was Aryan. But sometime in 1942 the Gestapo took Pan Glazer, his wife and thirteen-year-old son to the Jewish cemetery at Rudnik and shot them. Hieronim also hid Professor Erlich, a Jewish professor of international law whom Polish partisans spirited away from Lwow University to escape mass executions of academics by the Soviet NKVD secret police that followed Stalin's seizure of eastern Poland.[1] He gave Erlich a job as a bookkeeper in the forestry administration before he was moved on by the Polish underground.

The regime that Moscow imposed in the eastern territories

was even more brutal than the Nazi occupation. Skilled at massacre and deportations after Stalin's great purges of 1937 and 1938, the NKVD immediately set about liquidating all traces of the Polish nation in the areas they annexed. Stalin's aim was to wipe out not only class enemies but also Poland's political, professional and intellectual elite – anyone who was capable of playing a role in a future Polish state, whatever their racial origin. All representatives of Polish culture and education, whether Christian or Jewish, were to be exterminated or deported.

The NKVD arrested, imprisoned and deported up to 1.5 million Poles during the Soviet occupation of eastern Poland between October 1939 and June 1941. Many were sent to the Gulag, where the conditions were so terrible that nearly half were dead within a year. Among them were 100,000 Jews headed by Moses Shore, the Chief Rabbi of Warsaw who had escaped from German-occupied Poland. Many thousands more Poles and Jews were shot, including 25,000 reserve military officers captured by the Soviet army in September who were slaughtered at Katyn Forest and other NKVD killing grounds.

Despite the German occupation, Hieronim was able to travel occasionally. He went to Krakow to visit the Szlak and to Dukla to inspect Stas's estate, and he visited Wanda and Artur, who were living on an estate near the southern city of Rzeszow where they had moved in early 1939.

Like Hieronim, Wanda had not fled the advancing Germans at the start of the war, but waited for them to reach her new home at Zaleze, a small estate between Rzeszow and Lancut. They had been there a few months when the fighting began and the drone of aircraft, the scream of dive bombers and the roar of exploding bombs shattered the quiet of the countryside. 'Attention, attention. They are coming,' the radio announced in funereal tones as German bombers approached in the early days of the war. Zaleze was two or three kilometres from Rzeszow, and by day they saw smoke rising from the burning buildings and by night the sky glowed red.

There was no fighting around Wanda's estate, and they saw no German soldiers until the campaign ended. Calm had returned by the time a car drove up to the front of the large house and three or four German army officers got out and started looking around. Wanda, who spoke perfect Austrian German, could think of nothing better to do than to ask them in for a cup of tea. There was tension in the drawing room as they sat down. Artur, who was nine, remembered that when his mother poured the tea the Germans hesitated to drink and she realised that they feared poison. 'That's not the way we fight,' she told them, taking a sip from her own cup. The Germans laughed and drank.

Wanda was by now a woman of forty-seven, still tall and beautiful, and she was at last a lady of independent means thanks to Zaleze. She had left Dukla because she knew that when Stas came into his inheritance on his twenty-first birthday in September 1939 he would not want her there. Shortly before the war, he had learned that she had plundered his property by selling a house on the estate and selling the oil exploration rights to a French company. Hieronim had withdrawn her right to manage the estate and had taken over himself to protect Stas's interests. Although Artur always believed that his mother received Zaleze as a gift from Alfred Potocki, Stas believed she bought it for herself with money from Dukla.

Wanda still visited Alfred at Lancut, a few kilometres from

Zaleze, after the war began, but by then she had a new and very different companion. His name was Tadeusz Strugalski and he was a lieutenant in a frontier guards regiment. They had met when his regiment was stationed at Dukla in the late 1930s, and when it disbanded when the fighting ended Tadeusz had gone to Zaleze where Wanda made him estate manager. At thirty-four Tadeusz was thirteen years her junior, and he was as drab and inconspicuous as Alfred was exotic and flamboyant. He was short and stocky with thinning hair and the broad, flat face of a peasant. He had neither charm nor wit nor good looks, and he lacked wealth and position. But he was tough, brave and determined, and absolutely devoted, an ideal companion for Wanda in those dangerous times.

The arrival of the Germans did little to change the outward rhythm of life at Zaleze, although Jews on the estate were rounded up and herded into a walled ghetto in Rzeszow. The Germans told Wanda what crops to plant and took much of the produce. But no officers were billeted at the house. Wanda, her French companion Madame Leonie Rolland and Artur were still driven to church on Sundays in a carriage drawn by Idriss and Telwet, two beautiful Arabian greys.

Wanda sometimes drove into town in her carriage to plead with the Gestapo about the amount of produce they were seizing from the farm, or to try to prevent the deportation of farm workers for slave labour. She always spoke quietly but firmly, without any fear, no matter whom she was talking to. Artur said her pleas for the workers were successful, and none were taken from the estate or the surrounding villages during the occupation.

Little Artur enjoyed Hieronim's visits to Zaleze. He remembered him as a kindly man who was affectionate towards him. 'I always felt pretty close with Hieronim and vice versa,' he said. 'I remember when he visited us, not many times but several times, in Zaleze. He liked me and told me he felt close to me. He was a very nice man. Very gentlemanly. A gentleman in the sense of being gentle. But sad. There was a sort of aura of sadness about him.'

Early in October Hieronim went to Krakow for the first time since the fighting ended to take care of the Szlak, his town residence. Hitler had just taken a victory parade in Warsaw, and Nazi flags were flying everywhere in Krakow. Photographs of Hitler stared from shop windows, and huge red and black banners hailed the triumphant *Führer*. Armed patrols marched around the streets, and middle-aged German gendarmes directed traffic with metal half-moons hanging on their chests, steel helmets on their heads and rifles slung across their backs. The cafés around the great market square were crowded with German officers and weary-looking Poles with bronzed faces and stiff postures, whose ill-fitting suits and muttered conversations thinly veiled the fact that they were military officers embarking on new careers as underground agents.

Walking to the Szlak, Hieronim came across a shabby figure who seemed familiar. Looking closer, he recognised Tadeusz Komorowski, a Polish army colonel, whose sister Jadzia had been housekeeper at the Szlak for years. He was gaunt and bedraggled, almost unrecognisable as the dapper cavalry officer who had captained Poland's silver-medal equestrian team at the Berlin Olympics in 1936. He was on the run. He had been captured by the Germans during the September campaign but escaped from a prisoner transport. He was in Krakow to try to organise an underground resistance movement, and he needed somewhere to hide.

'Why don't you come to the Szlak?' Hieronim asked him, although the penalty for hiding escaped prisoners was death.

'We have German soldiers billeted with us, a general and some officers, but you look so different from usual that it should be all right. You can pretend to work as a gardener or in the kitchen.'

Komorowski accepted his offer. All went well for a few days, but then, very early one morning, the aide-de-camp of the Austrian general billeted at the Szlak woke Hieronim. 'I am sorry to wake you, Herr Graf,' he said, 'but the general is leaving in ten or fifteen minutes. He is not sure when he will return and he has something extremely important to tell you. He would like to see you as soon as possible.'

Hieronim and the general were sleeping in separate bedrooms in the first floor apartments of his sister Jadzia, who was trapped in Soviet-occupied Lwow with her husband. He put on his dressing gown and met the general in a small drawing room between the bedrooms. To his surprise, the general talked at length about the weather and other trivialities until he interrupted.

'General, I was told you have to leave very soon and you have something very important to tell me.'

'Well, Herr Graf, I don't know if it's so important or not, but it crossed my mind that your sister may come here,' the general replied. 'I don't know how long I shall be staying in your house and in her room, but perhaps there are some things she would like to take away if she comes.'

Hieronim was mystified. He had no word that Jadzia was about to return from Lwow. But as the general spoke he put a hand on his shoulder and guided him to an armchair. 'Please, Herr Graf, be seated.'

As he sat down, Hieronim got the shock of his life. On a table beside him, in plain view of both of them, was a framed photograph of Colonel Tadeusz Komorowski on horseback.

'I am sure there are things in this room that belong to your sister or perhaps even to you,' the general continued. 'Would you like to take some object away? I have absolutely nothing against it. Please, remove whatever you wish.'

Hieronim understood. The Austrian general was not talking about Jadzia. He was signalling that Komorowski had been spotted in the Szlak and was giving him a chance to get away. His capture there would have meant death for both of them at the hands of the Gestapo.

He replied as calmly as he could. 'I don't have the slightest idea what is happening to my sister. I don't know if I will ever see her again or if she will come here. But if you are so kind, General, let me get dressed and I will come back and perhaps find something I would like to take for her or for myself.'

The general left. Hieronim told Komorowski what had happened, and he left immediately. Komorowski would go on to become commander of the Polish underground Home Army under the *nom de guerre* 'General Bor' (Pineforest). It was he who gave the order on 1 August 1944, for the Home Army to begin the Warsaw Rising against the Nazis, which was one of the bloodiest and most tragic feats of arms of the war. While the Soviet army watched from across the River Vistula, 50,000 ill-armed Home Army soldiers fought for sixty-three days, longer even than the battle of Stalingrad, before surrendering. Up to 250,000 civilians were killed, and only 12,000 fighters marched out of Warsaw into captivity. Afterwards, the Germans razed Warsaw to the ground.

Before the winter was over Hieronim's nephew Wacek Bninski, who was staying at Rudnik, visited Krakow to see his family. Walking out of the Grand Hotel onto Slawkowska Street near the market square one morning he saw Pan Springer, the owner of the gunshop where Hieronim bought hunting ammunition, cleaning his shop windows. Wacek greeted him and they chatted. 'Do you have any news of Count Hieronim?' Pan Springer asked.

'Yes. He is in the country at Rudnik with his mother,' Wacek replied. 'Both his children managed to escape through Romania.'

'How is he doing? How is he feeling?'

'It is hard. There are Germans in the house.'

'You know,' said Pan Springer, 'we saw him in Krakow a few weeks ago and you could see on his face the tragedy of Poland. You could see how this man is suffering for everything that is happening to us.'

Throughout the first winter and spring under occupation Hieronim, like many other Poles, pinned his hopes for Poland's rescue on Britain and France. But the sudden fall of Norway, Denmark and France after Hitler turned on Western Europe in the spring and summer of 1940 smashed his illusions. By June 1940 Hitler was master of Europe and laying plans to cross the Channel and conquer Britain, the centre of resistance. As Polish hopes were crushed, Hieronim despaired. It seemed inevitable that England would fall and resistance to Hitler would end. In July he wrote to Stas in France, urging him to come home. There seemed no point in Stas and Sophie staying abroad if there was no more resistance to Hitler.

CHAPTER TWELVE

'For Your Freedom and Ours'

*S*tas joined the Polish army at a barracks in Paris soon
after he and Chouquette got off the train in November
1939. Joining the colours abroad to fight for their
country's freedom became almost second nature to Poles after
the eighteenth-century Partitions. From 1795 until 1918 Polish
legions had fought in many countries under the banner 'For
Your Freedom and Ours', offering their lives for the liberation
of their country and all subject peoples. Their campaigns had
sometimes been no more than acts of defiance with little hope
of restoring Poland's independence, but they had won them
renown abroad for bravery and helped to keep hope alive at
home. The spirit was enshrined in the opening line of the
national anthem: 'Poland has not yet perished, while we
still live', which was first sung by legionnaires fighting for
Napoleon in Italy. And so it was for Stas and tens of thousands of his countrymen who flocked to the colours wherever
they were to carry on the fight against Hitler: first in France,
and then as the war progressed, in Britain, Palestine, Syria,
Iraq, the Soviet Union and Iran.

Stas joined up at the Bessières barracks in the north of
Paris, which had been turned into a Polish army induction
centre and a camp for the reception of refugees. 'I'm
volunteering for the cavalry,' he told the recruiting sergeant.
Volunteers had the right under Polish army regulations to

enter the service of their choice and members of his family had always served in élite cavalry regiments.

'Oh no,' the sergeant replied. 'You've had no military training. We're only accepting men with military training into the cavalry. So you can have infantry or artillery.'

'Oh bloody hell,' Stas complained.

'Bloody hell, is it? And who asked your great lordship to come here?' the sergeant retorted, taking an instant dislike to the drawling young aristocrat.

Stas ignored him, but he had heard that infantrymen carried packs weighing twenty or thirty kilos. 'I'll take the artillery.'

To his relief he was drafted into a mounted artillery reconnaissance unit in the Polish Second Rifle Division. His first taste of army life was a training camp at Tenzy, near Poitiers in central France, from which he emerged early in 1940 as a corporal. Having always resisted discipline, he endured the training with distaste and developed a dislike for Polish professional officers, whom he considered martinets.

'The training was bloody awful,' he said. 'They loathed us. I was a bloody aristocrat and I treated all those people like . . . Well, I obeyed orders, but apart from that . . .' His arrogance caused him endless trouble during his military career.

He saw Chouquette only briefly that winter during rare visits to Paris on leave. She lived with Tante Eve, her mother's sister who was the wife of a Polish diplomat, and worked as a typist in a ministry of the Polish government-in-exile. But in February or March 1940 she realised she was pregnant and her doctor advised her to stop working. Tante Eve was not well off, and Chouquette soon grew short of money, so Stas decided to use family connections. He telephoned his great-aunt Anna Branicka, who lived at Montrésor, a chateau on the River Loire, and asked for help.

Great-Aunt Anna was the sister of his grandmother Imcia and she still enjoyed some of the immense wealth of her family. 'Ah yes, of course,' she said when Stas explained the situation. 'How much do you think Chouquette will need?'

'I haven't a clue,' he replied.

She sent Chouquette a monthly allowance. If Stas remembered rightly it was either three thousand or five thousand francs. In those days lunch for two at Maxim's, the best restaurant in Paris, cost thirty or forty francs and a good lunch for two in a normal restaurant cost ten francs, so Chouquette lived very comfortably during her pregnancy.

Paris lived in a state of suspended animation during the winter of 1939–40. Although France had declared war on Germany after the attack on Poland, it had done almost nothing to prosecute the war. Few Frenchmen wanted to fight for Poland. Amid reluctant preparations for war, life in the capital carried on normally while the French hoped fervently that it would just go away. There was a long lull that winter in the West, which was nicknamed the 'Phoney War', and there were rumours that France and Britain were putting out peace feelers to Hitler. Britain sent an expeditionary force of 400,000 men to help defend the Franco-Belgian border from German attack, but only half the men were in frontline units and they had little armour or air power and no offensive capability.

That winter Stalin attacked Finland, and in April Hitler struck in the north, invading Denmark and Norway. A month later he attacked the West. Holland was overrun in four days, Luxembourg in a day and Belgium in eighteen days. The French and British resisted for only forty-four days before France capitulated and the defeated British fled back across the Channel, leaving their equipment on the beaches of Dunkirk. French and British military commanders and politicians had expressed contempt for Poland's military effort in September 1939, but their combined armies did not resist much longer. Although Italy joined the attack on France on 10 June, the Western allies suffered nothing like the stab in the back that the Soviet Union inflicted on Poland.

When the Germans attacked France on 10 May 1940, the twelve thousand men of Stas's division were sent to help defend Belfort, a town at the southern end of the Maginot Line in the forests of the Vosges, near the German and Swiss borders. The main fighting was further north but Stas remembered two or three weeks of skirmishing around Belfort. He went on mounted patrols, spied out the land for the artillery and took pot shots at German soldiers with his rifle. He remembered waking one morning to find that the French had gone. They had pulled their guns out of the forts surrounding Belfort during the night and left.

'They just did a bunk,' Stas said disgustedly.

The French had been outflanked and were being attacked from the rear when they pulled out. Stas's division helped to cover the retreat of the French 45th Corps south to the Swiss border. When they reached the frontier at Saint Hippolyte on 19 June after two or three days of hard fighting, Stas was sickened to see French soldiers throw down their arms without a fight and cross to safety in neutral Switzerland. He made a quixotic attempt to rally a group of French soldiers. Sitting on his horse, the young Polish corporal harangued them in perfect French, trying to stir their patriotism by evoking the glory and pride of France and the memory of her great captains and kings, like Joan of Arc, Henri IV, Louis XIV and Napoleon. But it was no use. '*Que voulez-vous? Ils* *sont plus forts,*[*] the French soldiers replied, dropping their weapons and joining the queues of vehicles and men waiting to enter Switzerland.

As Stas and a friend from his unit, Zbyszek Morawski, sat on their horses watching helplessly, a few shells exploded not far away and French officers jumped out of their cars and ran to the border. Stas and Zbyszek looked at the long line of abandoned cars and then at each other: 'Oh my God, this is too good to be true.' They chose a nice-looking Peugeot saloon with its key in the ignition, unsaddled the horses and set them free, threw out the Frenchman's luggage, threw in their blankets and knapsacks and jumped in and drove across the border. As they passed a crowd of French soldiers an officer jumped into the road waving his arms.

'Hey, that's my car, my luggage,' he shouted.

'Go to hell,' Stas bellowed, accelerating past him. 'And damn the lot of you for cowards.'

Fifteen thousand French soldiers and the twelve thousand men of the Polish Second Rifle Division crossed into Switzerland on 19–20 June 1940. Switzerland was obliged to intern foreign combatants, and the Poles were disarmed and sent to camps, destined to remain there for the rest of the war. Zbyszek and Stas went to a camp near Lac de Bienne, west of Berne, the Swiss capital, but it was loosely guarded and after a couple of days they drove out in their French car and headed for Berne, hoping to ask the British Legation to help them get to Britain to join the Polish forces reassembling there. But Swiss police stopped them on the road, put them in jail for the night and drove them back to the camp next day. Two days later they drove out again, and

* 'What do you expect? They're stronger than us.'

made a wide circle round Berne to avoid police checks before entering the city from the east.

'I'm a nephew of Count Raczynski, the Polish ambassador in London,' Stas told the British military attaché. 'Could you let me have papers so I can get over to England?'

The attaché replied that Britain did not issue false papers. 'But I'm sure you both need civilian clothes and a little money.'

They got rid of their uniforms and left the Legation smartly dressed, Stas in a grey flannel suit with shoes, shirt and tie, and went to ask the Polish Legation to help them get out of Switzerland. But the charge d'affaires, whose name was Lados, brusquely ordered them back to the internment camp, and they walked out in a fury, slamming the door. Then they drove to Geneva and contacted Stas Radziwill at the Polish Red Cross, whom Stas knew. He put them up in his apartment for a few days and then smuggled them across the border into France in a Red Cross car and dropped them off in Annecy, a town in the Alps.

Stas and Zbyszek set out to reach Chouquette at Auch, a peaceful, charming medieval town at the other end of France near the Pyrenees where she had moved when the Germans attacked. Auch was in the unoccupied 'free' zone ruled by the collaborationist Vichy government of Marshal Philippe Pétain, but Vichy France was teeming with French police and German Gestapo. Stas and Zbyszek had no identity papers other than their Polish documents, but they managed to cross France by train and bus without being detected.

Chouquette was no longer able to receive money from Great-Aunt Anna. She was living in one of a network of hotels and villas subsidised as refugee hostels by the Polish Red Cross with money transferred through the American embassy in

France. One day she answered a knock on the door to find a dirty, bearded tramp whom she told to go to the back door where he would be given food.

'But Chouquette,' the man protested. 'It's me, Stas.' The story offended Stas's self-esteem and he later denied it indignantly. He said he had never grown a beard, never had a dirty face, and he was well dressed in the British attaché's suit after crossing France by train and bus.

Chouquette was six or seven months pregnant, and the three of them lived quietly at the villa, hoping to avoid the attentions of the authorities as they waited for the birth of the baby. It was one of the longest periods Stas and Chouquette spent together during their marriage. He learned to cook and sew and help about the house, but it was not a happy time. They had been married only a few months and had spent just a few weeks together, but the marriage was not working. Far from her country, her home, her parents and her sister, Chouquette was living in growing fear of what would happen to her and the baby she was awaiting. She had spent most of the winter and summer alone in Paris and Auch, and now that Stas had joined her she found him overbearing, impatient, irascible and violent. He was incapable of having a discussion without an argument, and unable to argue without losing his temper. Zbyszek saw him hit her one day, and was so outraged that he punched him and knocked him down the stairs. He was older and stronger than Stas, and he warned him that if he hit Chouquette again he would smash his face.

The situation in Europe looked hopeless after the fall of France, and they felt isolated and uncertain. Hitler seemed invincible as fleets of Luftwaffe planes attacked Britain daily during the late summer of 1940 in preparation for an invasion. They had no idea what would happen to them if they stayed in France, and their gloom deepened when Stas learned that Sophie's second son had died in Belgrade in July, less than a year old. Soon afterwards Hieronim's letter arrived, urging him to return to Poland and he decided there was nothing for it but to go home. They applied for visas to cross Europe and were awaiting them when a gendarme approached Stas.

'Tarnowski, are you mobilised or demobilised?' he asked.

Stas smelled a rat. 'Demobilised,' he answered. He wasn't.

'It doesn't matter,' the gendarme said. 'You're a Polish soldier. You'll have to go to the camp at Caylus.'

Stas thought Caylus was a concentration camp, but it was in fact a large French military camp where Polish soldiers were interned by the Vichy regime.

'What? Do I go right now?'

'No, no. That's not necessary. Come and report tomorrow morning.'

Stas had no intention of going to any camp. Although Chouquette was about to give birth, they said goodbye to Zbyszek and took a bus at six o'clock next morning, heading back across France, hoping to reach Switzerland.

It was a terrifying journey. They travelled without proper papers although French police and Gestapo agents were everywhere, and they feared that if they were caught they would be handed over to the Germans. They had a narrow escape when police stopped the bus before Toulouse, the nearest city, and checked the passengers' documents. For some reason they missed Stas and Chouquette.

France was in chaos after the German takeover. When they reached Lyon late at night the railway station was so crowded that there was not an inch of space for Chouquette to sleep. She was almost on the point of delivery, frightened, exhausted and hungry, but the whole of France seemed to be on the move. A taxi driver told them every hotel and boarding house was overflowing. 'The only place to sleep I can suggest is a brothel I know,' he laughed.

'Take us there,' said Stas. 'My wife has to sleep.'

They slept on a mattress under a table in a Lyon brothel. It was an exotic place to lay their heads, but they were far too tired to pay attention to the comings and goings around them as the ladies plied their trade. Next day they journeyed on, taking a train eastwards and up into the Alps to Annecy, the town from which Stas and Zbyszek had set out a couple of months before. From there they reached Annemasse on the Swiss border at the southern tip of Lake Geneva. They were in sight of their goal, but how could two Polish refugees without visas cross into Switzerland? There were armed patrols on both sides of the border With the Germans at their gates, the Swiss were fiercely guarding their neutrality and their frontiers. They would have to cross clandestinely, avoiding the patrols and finding a way through the barbed wire barriers. That afternoon Stas settled Chouquette in a restaurant and went to spy out the land.

I do not know to this day how they made that crossing. Stas said they did it at night, but how could Chouquette have managed it in darkness in the final stages of her pregnancy? She was only twenty and she had never been robust, and now she was worn out after the harrowing journey. It must have been a fearful ordeal. Stas said he carried her at times in his arms, but I still imagine her nearly fainting with exhaustion and fright as they moved slowly through the darkness. Somehow, they managed to avoid the patrols. Supported by Stas, Chouquette crept heavily past sleeping villas and scrambled awkwardly around barbed wire barricades. It seemed to take hours, but by dawn they were in Switzerland.

In Geneva they contacted a distant Polish aunt who sent Chouquette to La Pouponnière de Grange Canal, an exclusive maternity clinic in a smart residential suburb where soon afterwards, at seven o'clock in the morning on 18 September 1940, having beaten all the odds, I entered our warring world. Even today, when I am asked where I was born, I say it was very nearly in a Swiss ditch, but it might just as easily have been in a French internment camp or even a busy Lyon brothel.

Three days after I was born, Stas wrote a beautiful letter to Sophie and Andrew in Belgrade, apparently overjoyed at becoming a father but concerned about them both after the death of their second son.

First of all I want to tell you of our joy. You have surely received the telegram but I must write more extensively about it . . . His name is Andrew (after you, Andrew) Jan Zygmunt (Chouquette's father) Stanislaw (my grandfather) and Emeryk because father wanted it. Saint Emeryk is apparently our great, great uncle. . . . Zosinka darling, we both ask you very much to be his godmother. You know, darling, that we want to share him with you completely. Be a second mother to him and love him as your own as long as the Lord God does not give you yours.

He had heard that their house at Gora Ropczycka had been destroyed by the Germans and told them not to worry about where to live when they returned to Poland. 'Take Dukla as your own property, settle yourselves there and may it be the best for you,' he wrote. He told of his plans to join them in Belgrade, and enclosed Hieronim's letter advising them to go home via Hungary. 'God, how lovely it will be to see you again and maybe we shall all return home together,' he added. 'At any rate, we do not spend much money now and I know how to cook, so we will be able to manage very cheaply together, wherever we are, and that would be absolutely lovely for us.'

Like many self-centred people Stas had a deep streak of sentimentality that emerged in sudden enthusiasms and bouts of generosity. But they were fleeting gestures. He was too selfish to be capable of sustained affection. Even while he was writing generously to Sophie and Andrew, he was once again betraying Chouquette. Just as he had been unfaithful to her in Belgrade on the eve of their wedding, he now had a love affair in Geneva while she was giving birth to me. He even met his lover at the maternity clinic. Rumoured to be an illegitimate daughter of ex-king Alfonso XIII of Spain, she lived opposite and did volunteer work at the clinic.

After I was born they could not stay long with relatives or friends in Geneva because they were illegally in Switzerland and anyone caught putting them up might lose their residence permits and be expelled from the country. Chouquette and I were put up by a distant aunt, but Stas became a paying guest at a Roman Catholic monastery. Increasingly anxious to join Sophie and Andrew in Belgrade, he obtained Hungarian and Yugoslav visas with the help of his Hungarian cousin Bibi Esterhazy and then asked the Italian consul-general in Geneva for visas to cross Italy.

'But my dear fellow, how can I?' the consul replied. 'It's impossible. 'Italy and Poland are in a state of war. How can I send your request to the Palazzo Chigi?'

Stas was at his most charming: 'I have friends in Italy. Why don't you send it anyway? It makes no difference, so why not?'

'Well, you're a nice young fellow,' the Italian replied. 'I'll send it. But it's hopeless.'

Stas wrote for help to a first cousin of his grandmother Imcia in Rome, Princess Maria Radziwill, a famous figure among the aristocracy of Europe who was known as La Princesse Bichette. Before the Bolshevik revolution she had been one of the richest women in Europe. Although she no longer had her vast lands and immense wealth, she knew everyone, including the King and Queen of Italy.

Two weeks later Stas was summoned by the Italian consul-general. '*Voila*, your demand has been fulfilled,' the Italian told him, clearly astonished. 'How on earth did you manage that?'

'Oh, it's very simple. I've got an aunt in Italy.'

'Me too, I've got aunts. Who is this aunt?'

Stas had barely replied 'La Princesse Bichette . . .' when the consul interrupted. 'Ah, if you had told me Princess Radziwill is your aunt . . . Now I understand.'

Tante Bichette had obtained the visas by writing to King Vittorio Emmanuele himself.

When the couple eventually left Geneva they left a trail of debts and ingratitude. Hieronim received a letter from his sister Etusia in Hungary months later saying that people in Geneva had told her the clinic and the monastery where Stas had stayed were still seeking payment. 'From the letters, I see that these wild people did not say goodbyes or give thanks for all the cordial help they received,' Etusia wrote. 'Only Chouquette said something on the telephone.'

As they prepared to leave Stas met a Polish Jew named Monsieur Pam at a farewell party. When he told him his plans, Monsieur Pam, who owned a factory in Geneva, said he would like to help. 'Please don't be offended, but let's meet tomorrow,' he continued. 'I know what it is to be a refugee.' Next day he handed Stas two sleeping car tickets to Belgrade. Stas was taken aback.

'How can I accept that?' he said.

'Oh, but you must,' Monsieur Pam replied. 'I understand about being a refugee and I want to help you and your wife.'

When Stas began thanking him, Monsieur Pam interrupted: 'I've got something else for you,' and handed over a heavy envelope. Inside were 120 gold Swiss francs.

'I can't possibly accept this,' Stas protested.

'Take it,' insisted Monsieur Pam. 'If you get your estates back after the war you can return it. If not, it makes no difference to me.'

Stas and Chouquette took the train to Belgrade in January 1941, carrying me in a Moses basket. An Italian conductor took over at the frontier. 'Oh, Polish refugees!' he exclaimed. 'You can't travel like that.'

He gave them an extra sleeping compartment to show his sympathy for Poles. '*Barbari Tedeschi*,' they heard him mutter. 'German savages.'

CHAPTER THIRTEEN

The Road to Palestine

*W*hen Stas and Chouquette reached Belgrade in January 1941 the atmosphere in the Yugoslav capital was still fervently anti-Nazi, but their relatives had been kicked out of the Palace Hotel by Vichy supporters who had taken over the French embassy. They had scattered across Belgrade and Sophie and Andrew were living in a cramped apartment on the outskirts.

Stas and Chouquette moved in with them, but it was a tight squeeze. Since they brought me with them, aged four months, Sophie and Andrew gave them the only bedroom. Andrew, who had suffered tuberculosis as a young man and had the use of only one lung, slept on the sofa with Sophie on the floor beside him. The Polish nurse who had cared for their baby lay on a pallet in the hallway.

Sophie soon saw that Stas and Chouquette were not good parents. When I cried at night, as I often did, they passed me straight over her and Andrew to the nurse. No cuddling, no comforting, no patience. The nurse was still mourning Sophie's little Jan and resented having to look after another baby. She felt Stas and Chouquette were being inconsiderate as well as bad parents. Sophie shared her feelings but said nothing, because one did not question others in the family or say anything that might cause a disagreement.

She saw that Stas was treating Chouquette badly, but again she said nothing. Chouquette was being badly damaged by the experience of living with a hot-tempered, violent man and her unhappiness showed. She never washed a nappy. In a mute protest she let my soiled nappies pile up until there were no clean ones, a sign that she wanted nothing to do with Stas or the life he had led her into and the baby he had given her.

When there were no clean nappies, Sophie washed the dirty ones without a word. It must have aroused painful memories of her dead sons, and her hands felt like they were burning in the freezing water. It was a bitterly cold winter. The flat was unheated and they could only afford to light the boiler for a hot bath once or twice a week. It was a selfless act, and it probably prevented rows erupting in the claustrophobic flat. But she knew Chouquette was being mistreated and was miserable, and it would have been better to offer her sympathy and berate Stas for his behaviour.

An atmosphere of menace hung over Belgrade in early 1941. Hitler was rapidly extending his power over the Balkans and was threatening Yugoslavia more and more openly. There was no doubt about the Serbs' determination to defend their independence, but Stas and Chouquette, Sophie and Andrew decided after a few weeks it was best to move on.

Germany was being drawn into the Balkans by the military blunders of Hitler's Italian fascist ally Benito Mussolini. Italian forces had occupied Albania before the war and in October 1940 they invaded Greece, but the Greeks were fighting back and Hitler was preparing to come to Mussolini's aid. He had abandoned plans to invade Britain after the Luftwaffe's failure in the summer of 1940 to destroy the Royal Air Force in the Battle of Britain, and instead set about bringing the Balkans under his control before intervening in Greece. By early 1941 Hungary, Romania and Bulgaria were being absorbed into the Axis camp, and Yugoslavia was in danger of German invasion if it refused to follow.

It was dangerous to stay in Belgrade, but the road back to Poland had been blocked when Hungary joined the Axis camp. They abandoned the idea of going home but took heart from Britain's defiance of Hitler. They knew British and colonial forces were fighting the Italians in the North African desert. A Polish force was forming in Palestine to fight alongside them, and Stas and Andrew decided to join it.

The road to Palestine lay through a Balkan transportation network set up by the Polish government-in-exile to bring troops and refugees who had escaped from Poland first to France and then to Britain and the Middle East. They would be travelling along a prepared route with the help of the Polish diplomatic service and the military.

Sophie, again, did not want to leave. She put her foot down and told them quietly she would not be chased out of another country by the Germans. To leave Europe was just a step too far into the unknown. Stas and Andrew urged her frantically to come with them. The other relatives who had accompanied them from Poland had already left Belgrade to join a Polish refugee colony at the Dalmatian seaside resort of Crikvenica near the Italian frontier.

Sophie eventually gave way, but in a final act of defiance she gave the *proporzec*, the seventeenth-century Swedish royal standard, to a Serbian friend for safekeeping. It was strange to leave a Polish national treasure in Belgrade but it was Sophie's way of making a symbolic gesture, the next best thing to staying behind herself. 'I said to myself that if Belgrade was to be bombed to smithereens, let the *proporzec* perish there rather than run away with us,' she explained later.

They left none too soon. Hitler had given Belgrade what amounted to an ultimatum, demanding the incorporation of Yugoslavia into the Nazi new order. The Yugoslav Regent,

Prince Paul, delayed his response as long as he dared, hoping war would break out between Germany and the Soviet Union. But he gave way after a personal harangue from Hitler, and on 25 March his ministers signed the pact the Nazi leader demanded. Serbian nationalists were outraged. They seized power in Belgrade, abolished the regency and chased out Prince Paul. They proclaimed eighteen-year-old King Peter of age and renounced the pact with Germany.

Hitler reacted with equal fury, sending his bombers to pound Belgrade on 9 April and killing thousands of people. King Peter fled abroad and German troops marched into Belgrade and Zagreb, the Croatian capital, while Italian and Hungarian troops took over other parts of Yugoslavia they coveted.

We had left Belgrade by then, boarding a train to Greece in mid-March. As it crossed Greece the train chugged along slower and slower in stifling heat, stopping at every little station. Signs warned that the drinking water had been poisoned by the Italians. Having no food or water, they drank wine sold on the platforms. I have no idea how they washed me and fed me in my Moses basket. Sophie was so hot that she splashed red wine on her face and then felt horribly sticky. But she cheerfully volunteered to distribute patriotic Greek newspapers at stations and marched up and down the platforms shouting '*Zito Hellas!*', 'Long live Greece', and 'To hell with Hitler!'

They reached Thessaloniki in the middle of the night. The station had been bombed and a Polish diplomat led them with other refugees through the darkness to a room furnished with ancient wicker chairs. After a while they began to itch and scratch, but there was no sign of mosquitoes. Their arms were covered with bites before they realised the room had been a doss house to a long line of unwashed travellers and the chairs were infested with bed bugs. Unable to sleep, they brought out a pack of cards and played bridge until daybreak.

At Istanbul next day their luggage had disappeared, leaving them with only hand baggage and the clothes on their backs. After a few days, around 20 March they took another train packed with hundreds of Polish troops and refugees which puffed its way for three days across Turkey to the Mediterranean coast. It was so crowded that they took turns to stretch out and sleep for a couple of hours while the others sat or stood.

As the train crested the mountains before the final descent to the port of Mersin it slowed to walking pace amid meadows of spring flowers, and people hopped off to pick bunches of them and climb back on. Dropping towards the coast the scenery became almost tropical and they had their first sight of the Mediterranean glittering in the distance. Mersin was a squalid little town, but it was spring and the scent of orange blossom, roses and jasmine filled the warm air, and a few fine old houses surrounded by gardens and palm trees overlooked the sea.

There was not enough room in the accommodation assigned to the refugees, so Sophie and Andrew walked around town looking for a place to sleep. It was dusk and the muezzin's call to prayer sounded from the minarets. They passed beautiful houses with flagstoned courtyards filled with roses. As darkness fell they came to a house with a fountain playing in the courtyard and roses climbing the walls.

'I'm going to ask them if they can let us sleep here,' Sophie announced.

'But you don't know them, you can't.'

'Well, I'm going to.'

She rang the bell and a man came to the gate. Speaking French, she said they were Poles travelling to Palestine where her husband was going to join the army, but they had nowhere to sleep. 'I wonder if you know somewhere or other where we could spend the night?' she asked.

'Ah well, perhaps this would be convenient,' the man replied. He opened the gate and led them to a door on one side of the courtyard that opened into a long, windowless room with beautiful rugs piled on the floor and hanging from the walls. It was a carpet dealer's storeroom. 'If you don't mind, I'll be only too glad to let you stay here,' he said.

They slept there for three or four nights. Very early in the mornings, to make sure she was not observed, Sophie washed at the fountain. After a few days an old Polish tramp steamer named *Warszawa* sailed into the port to take them to Palestine. Hundreds of Poles assembled at the docks and the men climbed aboard on a rope gangway swaying precariously over the water. Sophie looked at it in horror. She was carrying an overnight case and Chouquette was carrying me in my Moses basket. They could not climb up without help, so Sophie called up in Polish: 'Captain, our husbands are up there, can they come down and help us up?'

'No, Madame,' came the shouted reply. 'They are enlisted men. They are under military orders and cannot mix with civilians.'

'But this is too dangerous. We need help. Send us sailors to help.'

A sailor came and helped them up. As Chouquette climbed aboard she handed me in the Moses basket to Stas, who had watched the scene angrily.

'Hey, you, get away,' an officer shouted. 'You women, don't mingle with the enlisted men.'

Stas was infuriated by his rudeness and wanted to punch him, but couldn't because he was holding me in my basket. But one of the men who had come on board stepped from behind him and punched the officer in the face.

'Bloody good. Well done. Thank you,' Stas said, delighted. 'And don't you dare be so bloody rude to my wife again,' he bellowed at the officer.

The battered old *Warszawa* sailed for Palestine on 26 March, with about six hundred passengers, most of them Polish men and their families going to Palestine to enlist. Sophie remembered that the boat was rusty and rickety and stank of sheep.

Dana Dushmaitich, the daughter of a Serbian diplomat and a Scottish mother, was on board with her family. They had also come by train from Belgrade, and they befriended my family during the voyage. 'The boat was disgusting,' Dana remembered. 'It was a filthy, dirty old boat. It was only fit to be torpedoed, which the Germans were trying their best to do.'

Sophie complained to the captain that Chouquette had been put in a cabin with eight people and the only space for my basket was on the floor. 'This is impossible,' she said. 'If anybody is seasick they will be sick on the baby. It is not acceptable.' She had seen an army officer alone in a cabin and demanded that Chouquette and I move there. After some grumbling, the captain agreed.

Sophie remembered that the stench below decks was so vile and the weather so fine that they spent most of the time on deck. Families were allotted small spaces on deck marked out in chalk, and my family found themselves next to Dana Dushmaitich and her family.

'The Tarnowskis all spoke beautiful English, and we

immediately made friends. So we all felt at home and made jokes and told each other stories,' Dana remembered. She was sixteen, and she and her sisters fell in love with me, the only baby on board, and took turns playing with me. I was six months old and so small that my parents had nicknamed me '*gnomek*', or little gnome. I must have been pretty smelly, because Dana and her sister Agnitsa decided to wash me. There was a shortage of water on board, so they went around collecting tea dregs in a bucket. Luckily, Poles drink tea without milk, and when the bucket was full they plunged me up and down in it as I screamed with delight at the first and only tea bath of my life.

There were anxious rumours of U-boat sightings among the passengers on the crowded deck as the *Warszawa* tramped eastwards out of sight of the Turkish coast, and turned southwards to sail past Syria and Lebanon. But there were no attacks, and we docked safely at Haifa on 28 March. Stas and Andrew were marched off the boat so fast that Sophie and Chouquette had no time to say goodbye before they disappeared in the direction of Latrun, between Tel Aviv and Jerusalem, and the depot of the Polish Independent Carpathian Rifle Brigade. They were there for three weeks before the brigade was transferred to Egypt for training at Mersa Matruh, a coastal fortress in the British defence line west of Alexandria. Soon, like the legionnaires of old, they would be fighting the Germans again in the North African desert thousands of miles from their homeland, 'For your freedom and ours.'

CHAPTER FOURTEEN

A Night of Betrayal

The troubles brewing between Stas and Chouquette in Belgrade burst into the open in Palestine, and it was Sophie who suffered most and found herself in a situation she had not imagined possible.

She had no money and only the dress she was wearing when they landed at Haifa. The Polish army lodged her and Chouquette for a few days at a hotel and gave them meal coupons and a monthly allowance of £11 each. It was not much to live on and they could not look for jobs because the British mandate authorities did not allow foreigners to work. When they had to leave the hotel Chouquette moved with me to Jerusalem, saying she wanted to have a sociable life. Sophie thought nothing of it, although she realised later that Chouquette had another reason for not living in the same city as her. She chose Tel Aviv, a modern Jewish city on the coast, thinking she could eke out her allowance by spending the days on the beach reading books from public libraries. She rented a room from an out-of-work architect from Vienna whose wife baked cakes for a café so that the apartment smelt delicious.

Sophie was glad of the sea, the sunshine and the warm Mediterranean springtime. She loved the beach, and was relieved to be free and in British-held territory after the long flight from Poland and living under the threat of German invasion in Belgrade. But she had few friends in Tel Aviv and she lived a solitary life, taking a bus to Jerusalem once a week to visit Chouquette, because Stas and Andrew had asked her to keep an eye on her sister-in-law.

She had not been long in Tel Aviv when she had an extraordinary encounter thanks to the daughter of the couple in whose apartment she was staying. The girl was an apprentice dressmaker, and Sophie asked her to make her a dress from the cheapest material. At the first fitting the girl asked if she was related to the Tarnowskis of Dzikow, and Sophie replied that she was not only closely related to them but was married to a son of Dzikow. At the second fitting the girl told her there was a very old lady living in Tel Aviv who came from Tarnobrzeg, the town next to Dzikow, who wanted to meet her. Sophie agreed, and a few days later she was taken to an apartment in the city.

She was let in by a very old lady wearing the wig of an orthodox Jewess who turned out to be the daughter of the lady she had come to see. As they sat together in the living room, the door opened and in came the most ancient woman Sophie had ever seen. She was very frail and blind, and shuffled towards her with her arms outstretched. Her daughter got up to help.

'No, no. Don't. I know exactly where to go,' the ancient woman croaked in Polish. 'I know where she is. I can feel her.' She tottered over and stopped in front of Sophie. Putting her hands over Sophie's head, she began to mutter blessings. Then, hands still outstretched, she uttered a long invocation in a sort of biblical Polish, while Sophie sat absolutely still. The ancient woman lowered her hands and spoke to her.

'When we were in Tarnobrzeg, your family watched over us when we were in difficulties,' she said. 'You are now in this town, which is our town, and I will look after you. Shops will give you whatever you want. Taxis will take you wherever you want. And we shall find you an apartment.'

Sophie was astonished and delighted. The old woman's words, expressing such gratitude and spoken so far from Poland, made her immensely proud of her family, particularly of Count Zdzislaw Tarnowski and Countess Sophie, whose good works during the Great War had won the gratitude of the Jews of Tarnobrzeg.

'Count Zdzislaw and his wife had a tremendous say in the country,' Sophie explained. 'It was because they never made any distinction between Jews and Poles, and gave their protection to all, that I was treated in this way in Tel Aviv. It showed what Dzikow meant and what Count Zdzislaw meant.'

The ancient woman kept her promise. Soon after their meeting Sophie was given a list of shops where she could obtain what she needed without paying, and a list of taxis she could use without charge. Then somebody came to invite her to view a rent-free apartment. She was deeply moved and grateful for the extraordinary generosity, but she did not stay long enough in Palestine to take it up.

She met another unique personality in Tel Aviv. Having coffee with a Polish officer at Cafe Noga, a favourite meeting place for Poles, she noticed a strikingly beautiful young woman sitting alone. After a while the woman got up to leave, but when she reached the little wicket gate that gave onto the pavement she turned back and walked up to Sophie's table. She introduced herself in Polish and they began talking. After a few minutes she said: 'I'm going to give a little party tonight. Will you please come?'

Sophie was immediately attracted to her. 'I'd love to come,' she replied.

The young woman's name was Irka Grabowska. She was legendary as a *femme fatale* among the Poles in Palestine. Fifty years later Sophie could not help giggling at her memory. 'She was indeed very naughty, and I loved her to bits. She did all the things that I would never dare to do, even if I felt like doing them. She was open and honest about it and she was amusing and had a heart of gold. And everyone fell for her, absolutely everyone. She could steal anybody's husband, or lover or anything. And the women loathed her. They were petrified of her, and I think I was the only female friend she ever had.'

They became close friends and often spent the day together on the beach. Although Sophie lived a quiet life, Irka sometimes took her to parties and introduced her to her men friends. Occasionally she heard vague hints and rumours that seemed to link Chouquette and Andrew. Irka mentioned them once or twice, but she shrugged them off. If they were true it would be an unthinkable betrayal and she dismissed them. She loved Andrew and trusted him completely.

But one day their peaceful existence was shattered. Returning in the afternoon to Sophie's room, they found a message from Stas saying he was back unexpectedly from Egypt on leave and had come to Tel Aviv looking for Chouquette, because he could not find her in Jerusalem. Sophie and Irka were wondering what had happened and how to find Stas when the telephone rang. It was Andrew. He said he was also back on leave but was staying in Jerusalem and he asked Sophie to join him that evening. She hung up and told Irka, who jumped to her feet and began pacing around the room.

'Do you know, it stinks,' she said.

'What are you talking about?' Sophie asked.

'Something is going on,' said Irka.

Something was indeed going on.

Sophie took a bus to Jerusalem and that night she and Andrew went out with Stas and Chouquette. As lowly corporals, the two men were not allowed in the better clubs reserved for officers, and they ended up in a club packed with boisterous Australian soldiers. Australians came to their table every few minutes and asked Sophie and Chouquette to dance. They explained patiently that they were with their husbands. After a while they moved on to a quiet little nightclub where a Jewish orchestra was playing Polish tunes from Krakow.

'You know, you shouldn't be seen with that Irka Grabowska,' Chouquette said to Sophie as they sat down.

'Oh! Why so?'

'Because she's so extremely good-looking, Zosia.'

'Is that a reason?'

'Yes, because you are not noticed beside her.'

Sophie laughed. 'Perhaps that's good advice. I don't know.'

The band played a tune that was special to her and Andrew and they got up to dance. She was spending so much time on the beach that she was very sunburned and her shoulder-length auburn hair was bleached light blonde.

'You look very lovely, you know,' Andrew murmured as they danced.

Sophie said nothing. She never knew what to say to compliments.

Then the blow came. 'You know, I think you will be even better looking later on, when you are about thirty,' he continued. 'What if we part now and get together again when you are thirty?'

Sophie knew at that moment that all the gossip about Chouquette and Andrew was true. Until then she had never thought for a moment to believe the rumours. She felt a sickening surge of fright, but outwardly she kept her emotions under control. Barely missing a step, she looked up at him in the dim light. 'You mean, you want us to separate now?' she asked.

'Yes, I'm in love with Chouquette. Please understand. Stas is not treating her well.' They carried on dancing.

'Well, I don't want it to happen in such a cowardly way,' she said. 'And I don't want Stas to learn about this in such a cowardly way.'

'Then talk to Stas,' he replied. 'Try to keep him occupied while I ask Chouquette if she wants me or him.'

Sophie returned to the table and Andrew took Chouquette onto the dance floor. Sophie was in turmoil but she made an enormous effort of will and chatted with Stas about anything she could think of – their childhood, their parents, life at Rudnik and Dukla. Most women would have dissolved in tears and told Stas what was going on, and he would probably have made a terrible scene. Sophie knew what he was capable of and wanted to avoid a scene at all costs. Her self-control was absolute. She chatted, watching Andrew and Chouquette from the corner of her eye.

Two British fighter pilots they knew joined them. Andrew and Chouquette danced on and on, moving slowly round the dance floor as they talked. It grew very late. They were the last guests in the club, and eventually they were politely asked to leave. They went outside and walked under the stars through the streets of Jerusalem to the house where they were staying. The British pilots came with them.

'Keep Stas busy again,' Andrew said when they got to the house. 'I want to carry on talking with Chouquette.' He climbed onto the flat roof and helped Chouquette up and they disappeared into the darkness while the others sat on a bank looking up at the stars and talking. Time passed, conversation flagged. They fell silent. One of the pilots, who could not understand a word of Polish, suddenly turned to Sophie and put a hand on her shoulder and gave her a sympathetic squeeze.

'You poor child,' he said.

Sophie felt tears of misery and anguish rising, but she was determined not to cry and resorted to anger as the best defence. 'Come down from there, you two,' she shouted. 'I want to go to bed.'

They came down after a while. The British pilots left and they went inside. Stas seemed to have no idea of what was going on. He and Chouquette went into the bedroom and closed the door. Andrew paced the living room, muttering and sighing heavily as Sophie prepared to bed down with cushions on the floor.

Suddenly, Andrew pulled out his service revolver, went to the bedroom door and knocked. Stas opened, in his underpants. 'What the devil do you want?' he demanded, looking at the revolver.

'Here, take this and shoot me,' Andrew answered. 'I am in love with your wife.'

Sophie let out a gasp of apprehension, knowing Stas's violent temper, but he took it in his stride. 'Oh, don't be a bloody idiot,' he said, kicking Andrew on the shin with his bare foot. They looked at each other, Andrew distraught, Stas unusually calm despite his cousin's words.

'Whatever happens,' Stas told him, 'there is a war on and it will make our decisions for us. But don't forget you're married to my sister.' He shut the door, leaving Andrew standing there with the revolver.

Sophie always thought of that moment as her brother's finest hour. For her, proper behaviour and absolute self-control in all circumstances were the paramount virtues, and for once in his life, she said, Stas had behaved perfectly, admirably. She was hugely relieved. But it was so unlike him to respond casually, even philosophically, to the news that his brother-in-law and closest friend was betraying him and his sister by having a love affair with his wife. Anyone who knew Stas would have expected the reaction Sophie had feared. Perhaps he stuck his head in the sand that night because the last things he wanted were a public airing of his treatment of Chouquette or a confrontation with Andrew.

His mistreatment of Chouquette was undeniable. Too many people witnessed his violence or reported her black eyes hidden by sunglasses for there to be any doubt of it. His temper was always explosive and his violence hair-triggered. He once erupted in fury at an imagined slight by a waiter in a Jerusalem restaurant by picking up his plate and throwing it at the wall, food and all. Perhaps the reason why he stayed calm that night after learning of Chouquette's unfaithfulness and Andrew's betrayal was that he really did not love her and did not care what she was up to. Whenever I asked him about his own adulteries during those times he would shrug and say it was to be expected, because he and Chouquette were almost continually apart from the moment they got married. Anyway, he added, she did not behave very differently. He even called her a social climber. I never heard him utter a word of love for her, nor regret for the way he treated her, nor indignation at her affair with Andrew.

If Chouquette was not important to him, Andrew was. Enormously important. He probably would have done almost anything to avoid a confrontation with Andrew, who represented Dzikow and everything he most admired and respected. The headship of the family was so important to him that his cousins from Dzikow were probably the only people in the world he was incapable of confronting with violence. They were more important than his wife, his marriage and his masculine pride. He did ask Chouquette next day, casually, if she was having an affair with Andrew. She had her answer ready. It was just a rumour, she said. They were just spreading the rumour as a joke to see how people would react. Stas said nothing. They were sitting in a field with Sophie and he pulled up a thistle and whacked Chouquette across the legs with it. That was all.

Sophie's reaction was different. Despite her self-control, she was a woman scorned, hurt and vengeful. When Andrew retreated, somewhat deflated, from the bedroom door and began settling down to sleep on the floor she was in no mood to lie beside him. Her stomach was churning and her mind racing. She sat up watching as he slept.

After a while she noticed his wallet on the windowsill and saw it was crammed with letters. She saw her handwriting, because she wrote to him almost every day when he was away in the army. So much had changed that night that she wondered what on earth she had written. She was beginning to understand that he must have betrayed her many times. As she pulled her letter out of the wallet, other letters fell out in Chouquette's handwriting. Deeply upset, she read her own letter, and thought what a fool she had been to write so lovingly. Then she read one of Chouquette's letters and had a wicked idea.

'Will you do something for me?' she asked Andrew next morning as he lay half awake.

'What?'

'I don't want to tell you, but are you ready to do something for me?'

'But what?' he asked.

'Either you say you will or I won't tell you.'

Finally, he gave up and agreed. Sophie reached for his wallet, took out a handful of letters, fanned them like cards and held them out to him. 'Pick one from me and one from Chouquette and read each of them aloud.'

He jumped up as if he had been stung and fell on his knees before her. 'I beg you, no. I can't. Please don't.'

She insisted. He refused, and then again. Then Sophie spoke. She looked at him and spoke quietly, carefully, without raising her voice. 'From this moment onwards, don't look upon me as your wife. If you are wounded or sick, or anything happens to you, I will not look after you. I no longer look on you as my husband.'

It was, apparently, the end of their marriage, but not quite the end of the drama. Irka came over from Tel Aviv that day, worried about Sophie, and saw from their faces that something dreadful was happening. When they were alone Sophie told her, and they plotted a small revenge. 'Should I try to seduce Andrew?' Irka suggested.

'I would be delighted if you managed to. Just to annoy Chouquette.'

Sophie laughed as she told the story because Irka got her man, apparently that very night, and Chouquette was not at all happy when she learned about it and realised what sort of man Andrew was. He had certainly wanted to protect her from Stas's bullying and was probably infatuated, but he was a serial womaniser and nothing would change him. He had a string of affairs in Jerusalem and Cairo during the war.

Sophie never really blamed Chouquette for what happened,

even though the affair continued for some time. She knew Chouquette was very young and vulnerable, and unprepared for the terrible uncertainties of the war, and she had known since Belgrade that Stas treated her badly. 'Stas has a very difficult character and I think that if he had been more under-standing, kinder, Chouquette would have been faithful to him,' Sophie said.

That was the closest she ever came to criticising her brother's behaviour or condemning his violence against my mother. But she expressed regret that she had not seen the trouble coming. She believed the affair began in the cramped Belgrade flat, although she was unaware of it at the time.

'I think it was a disaster that Stas and Chouquette came to stay with us, but we were living under one roof and if I like somebody I trust them,' Sophie explained. 'I never realised that any sort of feeling was being born between Chouquette and Andrew. Truthfully, I believe it happened because she had a difficult, hard life for which she was not prepared.'

Not long after that dreadful night Sophie and Chouquette moved to Cairo at the invitation of Prince Youssef Kamal ed-Dine, an uncle of King Farouk and third in line to the Egyptian throne. The prince was a friend of the family. He had been a pre-war hunting guest of close relatives in Poland. Andrew contacted him when they reached Palestine, saying he and Stas were in the army but their wives were living in straitened circumstances in Palestine. The prince spoke with King Farouk and arranged visas for Sophie, Chouquette and me, and invited us to accept his hospitality.

Once again, Sophie had no wish to move. The prospect of sharing a house in Cairo with Chouquette was not attractive. She refused, Andrew and Stas pleaded, and once again she succumbed. But she told Chouquette she had to behave respectfully towards her.

'I am prepared to live under the same roof with you, with the situation as it is, as long as we behave,' Sophie told her sister-in-law. 'The manners have to be Versailles manners.'

CHAPTER FIFTEEN

Cairo

The train to Cairo was crowded with British and colonial troops returning from leave in Palestine. Trundling southwards through the intense heat of the Egyptian summer, Sophie found it hard to sit in the compartment with Chouquette. They had nothing to say to each other, and she spent much of the journey standing in the corridor smoking and looking out at the empty spaces of the Sinai desert floating past.

The two women were hot, tired and rumpled, and feeling far from elegant, when they reached Cairo. As the train pulled into the station they were dismayed to see a crowd on the platform and a red carpet on which a distinguished gentleman in a Western suit and a maroon Ottoman fez waited.

Thinking he was Prince Youssef Kamal ed-Dine, they hurriedly touched up their make-up, smoothed their skirts and brushed their hair. But their hopes of making a dignified arrival collapsed when the porter collecting their baggage spotted my unemptied chamber pot under a seat and asked at the top of his voice who the smelly thing belonged to. Chouquette cringed. Her look of embarrassment and dismay made Sophie almost split her sides with laughter. The porter emptied the pot and slung it over his shoulder as he strode away with their luggage, but Chouquette ran after him and snatched it away and tried to hide it.

They got down from the train, and carrying me in my Moses basket and my potty, they approached the elegantly dressed gentleman, who turned out to be the prince's chamberlain. Completely unperturbed, he appeared unaware of what Chouquette was holding, and welcomed them graciously in perfect English before ushering them along the red carpet to a car with the registration plates of the Egyptian royal family. Only the chauffeur assumed an air of immense hauteur as he held the door open for a slightly crestfallen Chouquette, barely acknowledging her presence. Sophie laughed at the memory: 'Just think about it – the Prince, the royal car, we two titled ladies, and there we were with only a child and a dirty potty. How lucky that the Prince himself did not come to meet us at the station. It would have been a disaster.'

But Cairo welcomed them royally. Police saluted as they drove away from the station and more police saluted at every intersection as they crossed the crowded, noisy city and reached the outskirts where the car stopped outside a small, modern villa near Koubbeh Palace, one of King Farouk's residences. The villa, which the prince lent them for the next few months, was set in a small, well-tended garden and the interior was carefully decorated with flowers, with baskets of fruit set out on tables. A cook, a *suffraghi* or house servant and a night watchman lined up to greet them, and they found a bottle of champagne chilling in the refrigerator. After nearly two years of penury and uncertainty since escaping from Poland, it was like a dream come true and they sank into a life of luxury.

'We are living in a marvellous, delightful villa which is wholly at our disposal. We have a brilliant and simply extraordinarily well-mannered servant, and a cook who prepares us such tasty things that you can't even imagine,' Sophie wrote to Andrew on 7 July 1941, just after their arrival. 'Altogether it is a bit like a fairy tale.'

Prince Youssef dropped in to greet them after three days, a small, dapper, white-haired gentleman of about sixty, dressed in a tweed suit and tie despite the heat, with a silk-tasselled fez on his head. Slim and straight-backed, with a big, bony nose and a clipped moustache, he spoke fluent English and French. They talked about the journey from Jerusalem, their lives as refugees in the past two years, and about his hunting trips to Poland before the war, and he invited them to be his guests at the villa for as long as they wished. Before leaving he discreetly handed Sophie an envelope with money for them both and promised Chouquette to find a nanny for me. Sure enough, a Jewish nanny arrived soon afterwards. I was eleven months old and thanks to her my first words were Yiddish. They were calling me Boubi Pasha or Baby Lord, by then, and the names stuck, although they still often called me *gnomek* among themselves.

It was not easy for the rival sisters-in-law to share the villa, but they managed to live in peace by treating each other with the formality Sophie had demanded. Sophie thought the prince charming. She wrote to Andrew that he came for tea and brought a huge box of chocolates and two flasks of French perfumes for each of them, and a huge flask of English eau de cologne. He also provided them with American cigarettes and French wine that was brought to the villa each day. The prince called regularly, often leaving envelopes. He sent a car round most mornings with baskets of flowers and fruit and made it available to take them where they wished. Sophie grew very fond of their generous host. 'The prince is as good as a father to me and I haven't got the words to thank him,' she wrote after a year in Cairo. 'Heaven would want to bow to him. He has in him such marvellous delicacy – he simply has the gift of goodness.'

Cairo was bustling with the euphoria and intensity of war. Although Egypt played no part in the conflict and Cairo itself was never attacked, the country was under effective British control and the British had made the capital their headquarters for the campaign to drive the Italians and Germans out of North Africa. The fighting was hundreds of kilometres away, but in the teeming streets of Cairo Egyptians in long white robes mingled with a polyglot array of soldiers from Britain, Australia, South Africa, India and New Zealand, as well as Poles, Czechs, Greeks and Free French. Many were on leave from the front and they set a gay and festive tone for the city.

Sophie and Chouquette were soon moving in the most select circles. As guests of the royal family the homes of the Egyptian elite opened to them, and their beauty and charm and gaiety made them popular among British officers and diplomats. The British invited them to the Gezira Sporting Club on an island in the River Nile, with its racetrack and polo fields, golf course and cricket pitch, tennis courts and swimming pool. They had tea and chocolate cream cakes with cosmopolitan Coptic ladies at Groppi's, where Egyptian pashas could be seen in secluded corners of the garden, sipping coffee with their mistresses. They sat chatting with friends over gin and tonics on the raised veranda of Shepheard's Hotel, overlooking the crowds passing on Ibrahim Pasha street, as a piano trio played and elegant ladies in wicker armchairs sipped tea, hoping for an invitation for the evening. At the Continental-Savoy, run by a charming Swiss named Freddy Hoffman, they dined under the stars at the rooftop restaurant and danced in the nightclub. They went nightclubbing at the Turf, the Club Royale de Chasse et de Peche, the Muhammad Ali Club, and others like the Scarabee, the

Kit-Kat and the Deck Club that were on boats moored on the River Nile.

But life was not all party-going. Chouquette went to work for twenty-five pounds a month as a typist and secretary at Polish GHQ in a villa in Zamalek, a residential district. After a while she helped Ewa Thullie, a childhood friend from Warsaw and the daughter-in-law of a Polish general, to get a job with her. They had known each other since they were six and went skating together at an open-air ice-rink in Warsaw.

Ewa remembered Chouquette in Cairo well:

We had a lot of fun together, especially at work. We were two young, good-looking girls, and all the soldiers thought they could maybe catch us, gobble us up . . . My husband was in the army, so was Chouquette's . . .

Chouquette was a lovely person. She was extremely good looking, with fantastic manners. She was very elegant. She had a lovely figure. Everybody liked her because she had plenty of charm. She was very intelligent, and very helpful and friendly. If she could do something for somebody she was always willing.

She loved dancing. She loved her life. She was young, she was in a way freed in Cairo, because as a child she had a very strict life with her mother, and now she was free and she was trying to enjoy life.

One person who suffered from Chouquette's partying was me, little Gnomek. Sophie and Ewa often looked after me when Chouquette went out. Ewa remembered a time when I was sick with a fever of forty degrees Celsius and Chouquette pleaded with her to look after me and went off to a party in Alexandria, three hours away by car. 'You were a rather sad little boy, crying a lot. I was always very sorry for you,' Ewa recalled.

Sophie also found work. She volunteered for the International Red Cross, helping to trace missing Allied soldiers, and served at a military canteen outside Shepheards Hotel. She joined a group of British matrons who visited wounded soldiers in hospital, trying to cheer them up and handing out cigarettes and matches from little trays they carried like cinema usherettes. Sophie and some of the tougher ladies were asked to visit the burn unit, which was expected to be so harrowing that they were given a lecture on how to behave: show no emotion, look cheerful, mind what you say, never comment on the men's appearance and never use a mirror in case disfigured men saw their reflection.

The visits were beyond anything Sophie had imagined. 'You walked in there, and there were men, you couldn't really tell their age, with hands like claws and faces without lips, with part of the nose gone, with no ears, and with eyes covered with a kind of transparent skin.' She was moved by their courage and became a regular visitor.

One of the terribly wounded was Richard Wood, the youngest son of Lord Halifax, the former British foreign secretary who was ambassador in Washington. Sophie became friends with Sim Faversham, who was married to a daughter of Halifax, and he asked her to visit his brother-in-law. Wood had been hit by a shell that failed to explode but smashed his legs near the hips, and he was left more or less with a torso.

He made it hard for Sophie on her first visit, demanding, 'Why have you come to see me? Do you feel sorry for me?' It was some time before he accepted her, and she developed a great affection for him. 'I loved him with all my heart and admired him, his courage, and the wonderful way in which he would never pull any strings.' He showed her a letter from his mother Lady Halifax, offering to apply for permission to come to Cairo to be with him. A lady of her standing would certainly have been allowed, but he said that since other wounded men could not see their mothers he did not want her to come.

Sophie bought presents for the wounded to send home, and took convalescents on outings. A friend lent her a car at weekends, and she took a wheelchair case and two walking wounded each time. Sometimes they went to Shepheards Hotel and the nearby Ezbekieh Gardens where gazelles roamed, or they went to the zoo and took tea and fed the ducks.

When General Wladyslaw Sikorski, the Polish Prime Minister-in-Exile and Commander-in-Chief, visited Cairo in November 1941 Sophie and Chouquette were invited to meet him. Sikorski was a charismatic figure and Sophie revered him. He asked how they saw Poland's future. 'Do you think it should be as it was before the war?' he asked.

'No,' Sophie replied.

'What? Are you a Communist?' His blue eyes looked piercingly at her.

'Not at all, but I still think that no one should possess more than they can really care for and love and look after properly,' she answered, telling him that some estates had not been well looked after, but had been exploited by absentee landowners, and that was unacceptable.

'What a strange thing to hear, coming from you, countess,' said Sikorski. He asked what she was doing in Cairo and she said she was working with the International Red Cross.

'Why not with the Polish Red Cross?'

'Because there is no Polish Red Cross here.'

'Then you must start it,' he said.

'Shall we start it?'

'Yes, I expect you to.'

Sophie took up the challenge. There and then she asked Sikorski to authorise the Egyptian branch to wear khaki uniforms and short socks rather than the heavy navy blue uniforms and stockings worn in London that would be too hot in Cairo. He agreed.

'Then I want to ask you another thing,' she continued. 'Could we have a Red Cross with no ranks?'

'What? Now you are a Communist!'

'No, not Communist, but I realise that I'm fairly young and my husband is only a corporal, and later on Polish ladies much older than myself will arrive in Cairo. Their husbands will be colonels or majors or brigadiers, but having started the Red Cross I would be the boss with the highest rank, and I think that would be resented. Isn't it simpler to have no rank?'

Sikorski agreed again.

Chouquette presented me to Sikorski. I was fourteen months old, and he took me in his arms and put a small gold cross on a chain around my neck. 'I hope he will grow up to be a great patriot,' Sikorski said. I had the cross until I was a teenager, when it accidentally touched the bar of an electric fire and melted, but I still hold Sikorski's wish in my heart.

Starting the Polish Red Cross branch turned out to be tougher than Sophie expected. After Sikorski left, she went almost daily to the Polish diplomatic Legation to ask whether the authorisations and money she needed from the Red Cross in London had arrived. Nothing came for months until a Red Cross official named Modrzewski flew in from London on his way to Persia in the late spring of 1942 to make arrangements for Polish soldiers and civilians who were to be evacuated there from the Soviet Union.

Stalin had deported 1.6 million Poles to the Gulag between 1939 and 1941 after partitioning Poland with Hitler. But in the desperate days after Hitler attacked the Soviet Union and threatened Moscow, the Soviet leader began to deal with Britain and the London-based Polish government-in-exile as allies. He agreed with Sikorski on the formation of an army from among the Poles in the Gulag and eventually allowed the evacuation of 120,000 Poles to Persia to be formed into an army under British auspices.

The evacuees were starving, ragged and sick when they began to arrive in Persia, and Modrzewski was on his way to help the Polish army set up reception camps and medical services. He took Chouquette to Tehran to help him for a few weeks. She left me in Cairo, but when I was a boy I was told that she became friendly with the Shah and used to go riding with him. A love affair was implied, something Sophie also seemed to hint at when she wrote to Andrew about a letter she had received from Chouquette in Tehran: 'She is very busy in Tehran and especially with visits or rather audiences with the Shah of Persia. She devotes a huge part of her letter to describing his eyes, she is already greatly under his charm.'

But Modrzewski had forgotten to bring Sophie's Red Cross accreditation to Cairo and he could only leave her five pounds to get the Cairo branch started. He suggested she get financial help from the British.

'How do you expect me to ask for financial help here to start up the Polish Red Cross without any Red Cross documents or accreditation?' she snapped. Modrzewski said he would try to have accreditation sent from London, and asked what she would do with the money.

'You want to know?' she replied angrily. 'I am going to buy a large bouquet of flowers, and I will go to see the wife of the

British ambassador and ask her to take me under her wing, because I cannot start the Polish Red Cross without identification or authorisation, but maybe with the help of the British embassy it will be possible.'

'What? You're going to spend the money on flowers?'

'Yes. And it's your fault that I have to spend it that way.'

Sophie was friendly with Lady Lampson, the ambassador's Italian wife, and when she presented her with an enormous bouquet of flowers Lady Lampson telephoned Sir Duncan Mackenzie of the British Red Cross, who found Sophie a small apartment for an office and a big army truck. She got down to work, driving the truck herself to collect clothes for the evacuees reaching Persia. An unknown benefactor paid the office electricity bills; friends brought a typewriter and a sewing machine, and she persuaded others to put in a couple of hours' work a day.

She was up to her ears in work and by the time the Cairo branch of the Polish Red Cross committee held its first meeting the office was already partially equipped and the truck was standing outside half full of clothes waiting to be sent to the Polish refugees coming out of the Soviet Union. Sophie was enthusiastic and happy in her first real job and so busy, she said in a letter to Andrew, that she was unable to visit him in Palestine.

Despite having told him in Jerusalem that she no longer considered herself his wife, she was still writing to him almost every day with tenderness and nostalgia. 'My dearest Kaziu,' she wrote, using an intimate nickname, a few weeks after reaching Cairo. 'I don't know if you are already bored with my daily correspondence . . . but you are as silent as a secret and no tidings come to me from you. My Kaziu, be nice and write. OK?'

She wrote passionately on 17 January 1942, when he was still fighting in the desert. It was the seventh anniversary of the day they met, when Andrew went to Dukla for the wolf hunt, and she told him she was longing for him to come and visit her in Cairo. 'Kaziu, my own, I long so much to spend this day together, just the two of us, like the old days.'

But when Andrew visited Cairo he went out with Chouquette, not Sophie, and caused a rare confrontation between the two sisters-in-law. On the day he left, saying he was returning to his regiment, Chouquette asked Sophie to look after me for the evening. She said she was going out with someone else. I was unwell and restless and Sophie could not sleep, and late at night she heard a car drive quietly up to the villa gates and someone creep past her window to enter the house. Wondering why the car had not come up to the front door, she realised that Chouquette and Andrew must have lied to her, and next morning she confronted her, demanding that she observe their agreement to behave with perfect manners towards each other.

Prince Youssef Kamal ed-Dine took the three of them on a tour of Upper Egypt during Andrew's visit. They travelled in the prince's private train, which had a drawing room, a dining room and luxurious sleeping compartments. Red carpets were rolled out at stations whenever the train stopped, and staff lined up on the platforms to greet the prince. At Luxor, he took them personally round the ancient monuments, gesturing with his cane as he gave them explanations.

Sophie carried on writing to Andrew after he left Cairo, but it was no use. Another time when the three of them were together in Cairo early in 1942 he said a wealthy friend from his days at Oxford University named Angus McKinnon was coming as ADC to General Claude Auchinleck, the British Middle East commander-in-chief.

'He's bound to fall in love with one of you,' Andrew joked. Turning to Chouquette, he bowed and added: 'With you.'

'Well, I'm damned,' Sophie thought. 'I'll do my utmost so that this chap, whoever he is, falls in love with me.'

It was a turning point in Sophie's life, the moment when she decided to become fully independent. McKinnon did indeed fall in love with her and she indulged in her first brief love affair, making it plain for all to see. Although she carried on writing affectionately to Andrew her letters grew less frequent and she was sometimes sharp: 'I already know about your new flirt C. Badeni-Baworowska,' she wrote to him in Jerusalem in June 1942. 'I do not approve. But do what you like with your life.'

A month later she wrote that she had dined with McKinnon when he visited Cairo. 'He was more charming than ever . . . It seems to me that Angus is now truly under my charms, and probably because it does not matter to me any more.'

In fact, she was having the time of her life. Life was a whirl of parties: 'This is like being in heaven. I get to amuse myself perfectly every day,' she wrote. 'My life is seven hours of work (just like seven lean cows in the Bible) and then, whoopee. After that I sleep very little.'

Within weeks of her arrival Prince Ali Khan, the son and heir of the vastly wealthy Aga Khan, leader of the Ishmaelite sect of Islam, took her up for a spin in his light plane. It was her first flight and she enjoyed it hugely.

She made friends with General Stone, commander of British forces in Egypt, and his ADC Tiny Burton, and when Andrew was at Tobruk she wrote excitedly that they were sending him a crate of whisky.

Kaziu, remember, when the whisky reaches you, drink one to your wife's health, because, to praise myself, she was the one who arranged it. And I don't know that you shouldn't even send her a decoration, 'The Grand Cork of the Happy Water' . . . I am absolutely dreaming about a decoration that spins like a little windmill.

She even made an impromptu appearance at the Opera House, when the theatre manager unexpectedly pushed her onto the stage to announce the programme for the 1941 Christmas gala. 'I can't describe my stage fright when I found myself under the spotlights for the first time in my life,' she wrote to Andrew. 'Even now my heart is racing when I think about it . . . Can you imagine the Little Puppy on the stage? And the theatre was full . . . Even though it is after midnight, I have received telephone calls of congratulations.'

She met the Egyptian Queen Farida at a party given by Marie Riaz, one of Cairo's richest hostesses. King Farouk was there, but as a Muslim lady Queen Farida could not show herself in public. While Sophie was dancing a lady-in-waiting came and invited her upstairs to a room where the young Queen was alone. She liked to get out of her gilded cage and go secretly to society parties and watch unobserved. The two women peered down at the dance floor from between potted plants. They could only see the legs of the dancers but Sophie tried to identify them and tell the Queen who the King was dancing with.

Afterwards, she received an invitation to call on the Queen and drink sweet tea at the Abdin Palace, King Farouk's principal residence. Several times she was sent a numbered ticket for a public cinema and took her place beside several empty seats. After the film began Queen Farida came and sat beside her, wearing the yashmak or veil of a Muslim woman. 'I think I met her like that two or three times,' Sophie recalled. 'She was so lovely, and she had unbelievable charm. In her movements, as well, she had a gazelle-like quality about her.'

She also liked King Farouk enormously, although the British derided him as a fat despot. 'Oh, Farouk was terribly nice. Terribly nice. He was an amusing man,' she said. One evening when she was at a nightclub with friends, and the King was there with another party, he sent his aide de camp to invite her to his table. 'I moved from my table and went to his and saw that there wasn't an empty chair,' Sophie remembered, 'and I said: "Oh, there is no throne for me, so I'm going back."

'And the King immediately shouted: "A throne, a throne for Countess Tarnowska." Really, I found him very amusing and with a sense of humour, very human.'

She was embroiled at the time in a dispute with the Polish chargé d'affaires, Tadeusz Zazulinski. He was telling people around town he would have her sent to Kenya where the British were sending Polish refugee families evacuated from the Soviet Union. When she sat down beside King Farouk at the nightclub he leaned towards her and told her quietly that he had heard of the threat, and said: 'Look, you are my guest here in Egypt and no one will be able ever to send you away, anywhere, against your will. When you want to leave, you will leave, but no one will ever be able to make you go against your will. So don't worry about that.'

Sophie and Chouquette both had such a gay time in Cairo, making so many friends and going to so many parties, that some people thought they were a little too carefree. Stas said British officers nicknamed them *'Baksheesh'* and *'Maalesh'* – Arabic for a tip and something like 'Oh, all right, never mind'.

But Sophie was not always easy-going. 'She wouldn't accept invitations from just any Egyptian prince, you know,' Stas said.

Ewa Thullie, who knew them both very well, disagreed with the popular verdict. 'I don't believe Chouquette was doing as many bad things as people said. People love to exaggerate. Chouquette was doing well, she had friends, she was a very gay person and everybody wanted to be in her company. So of course people were jealous.'

As for Sophie, Ewa loved her dearly but thought that beneath the gaiety she was unhappy. 'There is not a thing that I didn't like about Sophie. You wouldn't believe how lovely she was, how pretty. She was really beautiful,' Ewa said. 'She was a very unhappy person but she never showed it. She was a very strong person. I mean her life with Andrew Tarnowski wasn't very pleasant, but she never complained.'

CHAPTER SIXTEEN

Fortress Tobruk

few weeks after Sophie and Chouquette reached Cairo, Stas was sent with the Carpathian Rifle Brigade to join the garrison at Tobruk, which had been holding off Rommel's Afrika Korps and several Italian divisions for four months.

The British-held Libyan port on the Mediterranean had held out since April 1941. Failing to take the fortress, Rommel had swept past it after driving the British out of Tunisia and had forced them out of the rest of Libya. In May he pushed the British back into Egypt. But the 38,000-strong garrison at Tobruk threatened his flank, and without the port of Tobruk his supplies had to be driven hundreds of miles across the desert under air attack to reach the front lines. General Sikorski offered to send the newly formed Polish brigade to reinforce the garrison in mid-1941. It was a way, he said with perhaps a hint of irony, for Poland to honour the Anglo-Polish mutual defence agreement.

Stas had been training with the brigade at Mersa Matruh in the Egyptian desert for three months when the order came to move. He marched out of camp with the Carpathian Artillery Regiment on the evening of 17 August 1941. The 682 officers and men boarded a train at nightfall and disembarked next morning three hundred kilometres east at El Amirya, near Alexandria. Stas was in the advance party of 192 officers and men driven in trucks to Alexandria the following morning.

'Alex bade us farewell with a beautiful morning and the hubbub of the streets of the Arab quarter as we drove through,' wrote Corporal Zbigniew Jakubski, who kept the regiment's official war diary. 'Arab boys watching the convoy go past soon realised who was in the trucks and shouted "*Dobra Bolonia*" ("Good Poland"), showing the sympathy of the Arabs for the Polish soldiers. From Sister Street, which we all knew well from recent visits, we turned into the port and stopped at the military harbour. It was 0640.'

They sailed at eight a.m. on three 1,600-ton British warships and only learned as they left port that they were heading for Tobruk, six hundred kilometres west. The sea was calm as the long, sleek vessels roared westwards, sending up huge bow waves. They ran close to the shore, British sailors manning the Bofors anti-aircraft guns, the Polish gunners relaxing under the blazing sun in cork lifejackets. The day passed to the throb of engines, sun sparkling on the sea. Mugs of hot, sweet tea were served at three p.m. An hour later they sailed past Mersa Matruh, their starting point, and suddenly at 5.30 p.m. two enemy planes dived out of the clear sky and dropped torpedoes that churned through the water towards them. One missed one of the boats by ten metres. The planes dived again, firing their guns, but missed and flew off under a hail of anti-aircraft fire. The flotilla roared on. Hot cocoa was served at seven p.m. and at nightfall they passed the Libyan frontier at Sollum. From there on they sailed along enemy-held coast under the threat of shore artillery.

'We increased speed and went at 50–60 km/h, as fast as a car, in complete darkness,' Jakubski wrote. 'There was a mood of excitement and expectation on the boats. We waited impatiently for our arrival at Tobruk, knowing that the worst part of the journey, landing at the port of Tobruk, was still ahead of us. At last a few weak lights loomed up before us; one of them proved, as it got closer, to be the light of a submarine moored in the port . . . it was 2345.'

Wooden barges came alongside and the men climbed down to them in pitch darkness, the top rungs of the ladders dimly lit by pocket torches held by sailors. By half-past midnight on 20 August 1941, the Polish advance party was ashore at Tobruk.

'The fortress of Tobruk received us in total darkness to the sound of artillery fire. Machine guns rattled often in the distance,' Jakubski wrote. 'Our arrival was accompanied by bright flashes of gunfire from the fort artillery and by the distant light of enemy flares that illuminated the lines of soldiers coming in to reinforce the fortress.' Amid the flickering sights and distant sounds of night-time battle the Polish soldiers in khaki shirts, shorts and knee-length stockings with British helmets, kitbags and rifles, assembled in a square near the port.

After a half-hour march along bomb-cratered roads past wrecked Italian colonial houses they climbed into trucks. The Australian drivers chatted, telling them drinking water in the fortress was heavily chlorinated and salty and all the food except for bread came out of tins. Cigarettes and beer were rare, sometimes handed out only once a month, and then maybe one bottle of beer between several men and a handful of cigarettes each.

They drove for an hour past piles of wrecked trucks and Italian bombers. Reaching a range of hills, they got out and scrambled through the darkness along a ravine-like riverbed to the headquarters of the British 51st Royal Horse Artillery, the regiment they were relieving. As dawn lightened the sky they took cover because enemy planes often bombed and machine-gunned early in the morning. They sheltered among the rocks all day. The next day they took over the British regiment's twelve 25-pounder and nine 18-pounder guns and went into action, firing their first 270 shells. The rest of the regiment arrived in a couple of days and the armoured and infantry regiments followed within a week under General Stanislaw Kopanski, the brigade commander.

Tobruk was besieged by 33,000 Italian and German troops. The Poles helped to defend the western sector, the most vulnerable and dangerous part of the perimeter. German troops were 500 metres away on Ras el Medauar, a heavily fortified hill that bulged inwards over the defences. Further north towards the sea, Italian troops manned the Twin Pimples, another heavily fortified hill.

The Polish positions were only five kilometres from the coast, but they might have been deep in the desert. 'Clouds of heavy clay dust billow up from the valley and there is no way of hiding from it. It gets into everything,' Jakubski wrote. 'We are covered with dust which sticks thickly to the skin. We find it in our food, in the tea, sometimes in our teeth, it is a plague . . . We suck small green lemons which give the illusion of satisfying our thirst.'

On their first evening they had a grandstand view as twenty-three Stuka dive-bombers dropped like stones through puffs of anti-aircraft fire to attack the port. Four days later forty planes attacked with 1,000-pound bombs, setting a ship on fire, damaging a barge and destroying houses. An anti-aircraft gun was hit, killing four British soldiers, but three planes were shot down. Hundreds of bombs and shells hit the fortress every day, and the simplest activities required great caution. For Sunday Mass the Polish gunners built an altar of empty petrol cans and scattered under shelters and among the rocks during the service so as not to provide a target for enemy planes.

On 1 September, the second anniversary of the invasion of Poland, a hundred German planes dropped hundreds of bombs and a hurricane of shellfire hit the fortress. 'For half an hour we witnessed real hell,' Jakubski wrote. Fifty-five shells hit the regiment's sector and four enemy planes bombed and strafed it. A gunner who was slightly wounded became the regiment's first casualty. Two days later towering clouds of sand cut visibility to a few metres. Blinded and deafened, with sand in their eyes, ears and mouths and driving like needles into their skin, the men crouched behind any shelter they could find.

For most of Stas's comrades, Tobruk was their first chance to fight the Germans since the fall of Poland. They had scores to settle and they patrolled aggressively. 'Our patrols go out daily, sometimes penetrating two or three kilometres into enemy lines,' Jakubski wrote. 'There are daily poundings, shooting from near and far, throwing grenades and often fighting with bayonets. Often, too, not all return from patrols, so the defenders of Tobruk offer up victims every day as a result of patrolling and also from air bombardments and shelling.'

The patrols went out on moonless or overcast nights. Reconnaissance patrols of up to eight men mapped out enemy positions. They cleared paths through minefields, set booby traps and crept up to detect work on enemy fortifications; they listened for the language of the enemy troops and for any indication of a change in the strength of the besiegers. They stayed out for hours, and sometimes a single camouflaged soldier remained all day, observing a German or Italian position.

Fighting patrols of up to ten men probed the enemy positions and snatched prisoners for interrogation. Sometimes the Poles mounted attacks with seventy or a hundred men, testing enemy readiness or diverting attention from major operations by the garrison forces elsewhere on the perimeter. On 30 August a patrol from Stas's regiment attacked the Italians with bayonets and grenades, causing many casualties. Another ten-man patrol assaulted an enemy position of forty or fifty men, killing about fifteen for the loss of one dead, two missing and three wounded.

Stas went out several times with Adolf Bochenski, a sergeant-major in the Carpathian Lancers Regiment, the brigade's armoured unit, who was renowned as the bravest man in the Polish army. They met at the training camp at Mersa Matruh in Egypt in April 1941. 'When I arrived at the brigade Adzio Bochenski came to inspect me. "Who's this Tarnowski?" he said, and we became friends. He used to go on patrol all the time in Tobruk and he used to take me on patrol occasionally. It was great fun.'

Bochenski went out fifty times in nearly four months. He was awarded the *Virtuti Militari*, Poland's highest medal for bravery, and twice won the *Krzyz Walecznych* or Cross of Valour. He had a narrow escape in the desert when a bullet went through his helmet without injuring him, and from then on he wore the same helmet until he was killed at Ancona in Italy in 1944. 'He took that helmet as a lucky charm,' Stas recalled, 'and when he lost it he said: "Well, I'm sure I'll get killed tomorrow." And he left his letters and possessions to Andrew, because they were living in the same digs, and he was killed on patrol by a mine next day.'

Stas was in a fighting patrol that got badly knocked about by the Italians on the Twin Pimples, and in another attack he fought hand-to-hand in the Italian trenches. 'It was the only time in my life I stuck a bayonet into somebody,' he said. 'Most unpleasant thing, and I didn't do it properly because you should twist your rifle when you stick the bayonet in, and I stuck it in just like that and it was rather hard to pull it out again. The poor Italians! They didn't want to fight, anyway. They were delighted when they were taken prisoner. *"Polacchi, amici,"* "Polish friends," they said.'

Stas loved the fighting. He was in his element. Trying to be as brave and dashing as possible and look unconcerned in battle, he did his best to bring honour to the family name. He volunteered for the most dangerous night-time patrols and attacks on enemy lines, and stayed out all day in exposed positions in no man's land as a forward artillery observer directing the regiment's fire.

'The war was a hell of an adventure. I enjoyed it enormously,' he said. 'Obviously, excuse the expression, I shat in my pants every now and then. But I always tried to be in the very thick of it. I often got myself into a situation that was quite unpleasant, when I would have preferred to dig myself underground instead of going on in the attack. But one doesn't remember things like that afterwards. One remembers that one was scared stiff but didn't show it, and that's one thing I never did.'

He soon won a reputation for bravery but once again his arrogance led to bad relations with his officers. 'I was always very polite to everyone, but I would not stand any high-handedness from the officers,' he said. 'On duty I was absolutely disciplined, but off duty I was myself and couldn't care less about them. I didn't keep saluting and saying, "Yes, sir." When I was off duty I was off duty. I was myself, a *grand seigneur*.'

When General Sikorski visited the brigade in November 1941 after his visit to Cairo he inspected Stas's battery. 'I was a corporal then, and when Sikorski came they told him I had escaped from internment in Switzerland and I was the first soldier to arrive from Switzerland to join the Carpathian Brigade. Sikorski looked at me and said: "I forgive the corporal his desertion." Silly ass.'

The implication that he should have sat out the war in an internment camp, and needed to be pardoned for having escaped and travelled across Europe and the Middle East to join the brigade, infuriated Stas. He lost his respect for Sikorski. He was not aware that Sikorski considered the interned Second Rifle Division as a strategic reserve to be reactivated when the situation in Europe changed, and that he had issued orders forbidding escape from internment in Switzerland under pain of court martial.

By November the desert nights were bitterly cold. German air raids hit the naval convoys from Alexandria, interrupting the garrison's supplies of cigarettes, beer, toiletries, mail and even their pay. When supplies eventually arrived during a huge sandstorm the men got eight cigarettes each instead of the usual fifty, and there was no beer. They were choked by sandstorms and lashed by cold winds and rain as they awaited the start of Crusader, a British offensive from Egypt intended to smash the Afrika Korps and chase the Germans back across Libya. An all-night downpour on 18 November flooded the trenches and bunkers so badly that a soldier of the newly arrived Czech battalion next to the Poles drowned in a bunker and the besiegers and besieged agreed to a truce while everyone cleaned up and dried out.

On November 21 the Poles made a diversionary attack as garrison forces broke out to link up with the British Eighth

Army offensive. The Polish gunners began rapid fire before three a.m. and by the time the guns fell silent they had fired 11,046 shells. At dawn two hundred armoured vehicles sallied forth to the sound of bagpipes and a hundred Carpathian Lancers and a Polish-Czech fighting patrol launched a diversionary attack to the west, killing thirty Italians in hand-to-hand fighting.

The break-out stalled in the face of stubborn German resistance. Not until the night of 26–27 November did it link up with New Zealand troops advancing from Egypt. The battle continued until early December when Rommel was forced to withdraw and the siege was lifted after seven and a half months.

The garrison joined the Eighth Army chasing the Germans and Italians westwards. 'We leave Tobruk without regret, glad to be undertaking mobile warfare and to take part in the great British offensive in the Libyan desert,' Jakubski wrote. 'We are proud that it was given to Polish soldiers to take part in the defence of heroic Tobruk, the fortress now famous in the whole world.'

The Polish troops went into action in the desert on 15 December at Gazala, forty kilometres west of Tobruk, where the Germans and Italians had turned and inflicted heavy losses on the British and Australians. They attacked up a slope against Italians dug into an escarpment and overran a series of strongpoints. 'Our men go into the attack splendidly, giving a very good example against very heavy machine-gun fire. They go as if to a dance,' Jakubski wrote. By evening the Poles had seized most of the enemy positions, capturing twenty officers and 391 men of the Pavia Division for the loss of twenty dead and a hundred wounded. Resistance stiffened at dusk and fighting continued into the night. Next morning the

Carpathian Lancers regiment attacked in armoured personnel carriers and captured eight officers and 330 men of the Seventh Bersaglieri Regiment. The Italians fled, leaving the Poles victorious after a two-day battle that cost them twenty-nine dead.

The next day, 17 December 1941, was one Stas remembered all his life. 'I'm the one who took the most senior Italian officer prisoner,' he told me. 'At Gazala I asked to be sent on patrol and got an old tank which had no gun, couldn't shoot. So I just had an ordinary tommy gun. There was a chap driving the tank and a third chap with me, maybe a fourth. And we came to a sort of wadi (river bed) and I saw several Italian cars and Italians messing around. So I fired my tommy gun and said, "*Mane alto!*" ("Hands up!") And of course the Italians "*mane alto*", and I took prisoner the headquarters of an Italian Bersaglieri regiment. The colonel's name was Ugo Barbatti. If I remember rightly he was the officer commanding the Seventh Bersaglieri.'

Nearly sixty years later at the Sikorski Institute in London, which holds the archives of Polish military units that fought in the West, I found the exploit in the war diary of the 7th Battery of the Carpathian Artillery Regiment. In cramped handwriting it recorded that on 17 December 1941, the Artillery Regiment and the 2nd Battalion Carpathian Lancers joined up at Gazala to form an assault group and advance westwards on Derna. They passed a mass of weapons abandoned by the fleeing Italians and reached the coastal escarpment from which they could see the Mediterranean. The diary continued:

The observation tank with the Cadet 2nd Lieutenant Tadeusz Sawicki, Corporal Tarnowski, Corporal Jozef Safianyk and

Corporal Zacharewicz went to investigate the terrain ahead. When they went ahead the tank took prisoner Colonel Filippo Barbatti, commander of the Seventh Bersaglieri Battalion, Captain Sangiorgio and 34 prisoners.

Stas's name leapt from the page. I felt a surge of exhilaration when I saw it. In Warsaw I asked him if he received a medal. 'What, for popping off my tommy gun?' he laughed.

He had a contretemps with an officer when he returned with the captured Italians that might explain why his leading role in the exploit was not even recorded. 'When the colonel of Bersaglieri reported to me I treated him rather nicely because I left him his field glasses and revolver and I sat him on the tank and all the rest of us walked back,' he said. 'When we got back, the commander of the Polish troop saw the field glasses on the colonel's chest and grabbed at them, wanted to take them for himself. And I said: "Sorry, this is my prisoner." I wasn't very popular for that. That's probably why nothing was said about it.'

But he received the *Krzyz Walecznych* for the Gazala action. The citation read:

On December 16 and 17, 1941, . . . he volunteered to go as an observer under heavy enemy artillery fire, endangering his life to link up with the infantry, and as an observer under heavy fire he constantly informed the battery commander of the movements of our infantry and the enemy's movements. On December 17, 1941, during the attack by the 4th Company he went at his own request with the forward observer 2nd Lieutenant Liszka, giving another outstanding example under enemy fire.

By 21 December the Eighth Army had driven Rommel deep into Libya and the Polish brigade hoped that after four months of fighting they would be withdrawn from the front. But General Kopanski was ordered to halt and send the artillery regiment back to support a South African assault on the coastal fortress of Bardia, east of Tobruk, where 5,000 Germans and Italians were holding out. So on Christmas Day 1941 the regiment turned round. They drove all day and spent a cold, windy night in the desert without tents. Starting again in darkness at six a.m., they drove without headlights through battlefields littered with destroyed tanks and carried on all day and into the night. By ten p.m. they heard the boom of artillery and saw British planes swarming over Bardia.

The assault began at dawn on 31 December after a bombardment by the Polish gunners. Stas volunteered as a forward observer and was paired with a South African spotter in a perilously advanced position. They had to keep cool heads and report accurately as the South African troops rapidly overran the enemy, because the gunners had to know the exact positions of both sides at all times.

General Kopanski watched the battle and mentioned Stas in his war memoirs: 'The forward observers: Lieutenant Ledochowski, Second Lieutenants Nowakowski (in the tank), Stojowski, Michel and Palka, Corporals Budzich and Tarnowski, worked with great self-sacrifice and a considerable proportion of them were wounded.'[1]

Stas thought he should have received another medal at Bardia. 'I did something there. I don't quite remember what,' he said. 'I took a few prisoners and whatnot. I was going to be proposed for the *Virtuti Militari* but the regimental commander said, "No, he's undisciplined," which was not true.'

After the capture of Bardia the regiment returned through the desert to rejoin the brigade. They were overjoyed to learn that they were to be withdrawn to Egypt for a rest. But before they could leave Rommel launched a counter-offensive after receiving new tanks in Tunisia and drove the Eighth Army back towards Tobruk. The fighting kept the weary Poles in the desert for another two months.

Stas's regiment retreated through sandstorms so dense that the truck drivers were blinded. Even driving nose-to-tail, trucks sometimes strayed into the column alongside them. They drove in cold, wind and rain and slept without tents with their boots on, ready to drive off at first light, their rear patrols often exchanging fire with the Germans coming up behind.

Morale slumped and exhausted Polish soldiers fell ill in droves. Stas fell ill with pneumonia and was evacuated to Alexandria on 29 January 1942, and that was the end of his desert war. From his hospital bed he telephoned Chouquette who took a train from Cairo for their first meeting since the dramatic events in Jerusalem seven or eight months earlier. That was when she gave Stas the rose whose petals I would find in a leather wallet fifty years later.

The Carpathian Brigade soldiered wearily on for a few weeks, its guns and vehicles deteriorating and health and morale declining. Casualties mounted and the artillery regiment's strength dropped to 599 men from a peak of 866. At last on 18 March the Poles were withdrawn to Egypt. In May they returned to Palestine and moved to Iraq, where the brigade was reinforced with men evacuated from the Soviet Union and expanded into a division that fought throughout the 1944–45 Italian campaign in the Second Polish Corps commanded by General Wladyslaw Anders.

Three months after the brigade's withdrawal Rommel broke through the British defences at Gazala and reached Tobruk. On 21–22 June 1942, he captured the fortress and its new garrison of 19,000 British troops, 9,000 white South Africans and 5,000 Indians and native South Africans. Winston Churchill, the British Prime Minister, called it 'one of the worst blows of the war' and two days later Rommel's panzers crossed the border into Egypt.

CHAPTER SEVENTEEN

Defiance

*R*ommel drove the British before him like chaff after capturing Tobruk. He pushed deep into Egypt and reached the desert railway halt at El Alamein in late July. He was within a day's march of Alexandria and was threatening to drive the British out of Egypt and seize the Suez Canal. Everyone in Cairo knew the exhausted troops facing the *Panzers* at El Alamein were making their last stand after retreating for five months. The Germans were only 95 kilometres from Alexandria and 240 kilometres from Cairo. Only a miracle could stop Rommel capturing them. There were fears that Alexandria could fall in twenty-four hours and Cairo in three days, and that Rommel would seize Egypt and the Suez Canal and push on into Palestine.

The British panicked. They called it 'The Flap'.[1] Cairo was in turmoil. Huge crowds besieged the banks and blocked the streets. Smoke rose from administrative, diplomatic and military buildings as the British burned files. Military headquarters and the embassy on the banks of the Nile were in such a hurry that half-burned papers rained down on Cairo on what became known as Ash Wednesday. Crowds thronged the railway stations and trainloads of evacuees left for the relative safety of Palestine, hundreds of kilometres away. Cars loaded with possessions headed for the Suez Canal and the Sinai Desert, and shiploads of evacuees sailed from Suez to South Africa. Outside the city, beyond the Pyramids, truckloads of exhausted soldiers, and guns, armoured cars and supply wagons were pouring down the road from the desert in full retreat towards Cairo.

Many Egyptians were happy at the prospect of being rid of the British, who had been their colonial masters since the 1880s. When the Afrika Korps' radio, operated by Rommel's troops from El Alamein, broadcast its famous invitation to the women of Alexandria – 'Get out your party frocks, we're on our way' – shopkeepers in the ancient port city began hanging out welcome signs in German, and ladies got ready for a Victory Ball. Even Cicurel's, a Jewish-owned Cairo department store, secretly prepared to welcome Rommel, as Peter Tunnard, an officer in the Scots Guards, found out. Looking round the store for a present to send home, he went behind the counters and found a Nazi flag hidden in the shelves at the back. He pulled, and a long string of swastikas fell out.

As Cairo emptied of the British and their allies, Sophie put her foot down. She had already been chased out of Poland and Yugoslavia; she had left Jerusalem. Nothing would make her flee again. She and Chouquette were living at the National Hotel, a staid establishment mainly inhabited by retired British people in the centre of Cairo where Prince Youssef Kamal ed-Dine had moved them in November 1941 for safety.

Chouquette, who was just back from Tehran, packed her bags to leave for Palestine. She pleaded with Sophie to come with her, but Sophie refused. She carried on going to work every day at the Polish Red Cross until everyone else had left and there was nothing she could do alone. As the end of June approached, the Polish Legation and military headquarters told her to leave with growing sharpness, but she ignored them. At the end of the month she was summoned to military headquarters and told the times of the last transports for Palestine. Then she was summoned to the Legation, where the chargé d'affaires Tadeusz Zazulinski ordered her to leave. 'I said I didn't have to go because although I was working in the Polish Red Cross I was not a soldier and I didn't have to listen.'

She and Zazulinski had a row. 'Let me know when you are in some concentration camp and I'll try to send you a parcel,' he sneered.

'Let me know when you're coming back to Cairo, and I'll meet you at the station,' Sophie shot back.

Andrew wrote from Palestine, begging her to come, but on 1 July, the day Chouquette left, she wrote him an extraordinary letter and sent it with her sister-in-law, saying she was convinced the Germans would not take Cairo. If she left Cairo now she feared there would be no return, just as there had been no return to Poland or Belgrade. She would only leave if the British and their allies won a victory, and then she would follow them to Tobruk and Gazala. She felt deep inside her that a great victory was coming.

But she knew how grave the danger was, and ended with an emotional farewell as if she might never see Andrew again.

> I am keeping all your photographs and your childhood prayer book. I say goodbye to you and I thank you for what you were for me in life, for having been the best, best friend . . . someone who is still to this day my dearest, most beloved . . .

Chouquette left that night with me, and next day Sophie drove alone to an intersection on the main road out of the city and watched the evacuation rolling past. 'You could see cars with bundles on top heading in one direction for Palestine, and you could see lorries full of soldiers taking the other road towards Alexandria and the desert. And I decided, "I'll be damned, I'll take the train and go to Alexandria, to be closer to the front.'" She wanted to be near the troops at the decisive hour.

Alexandria was a three-hour train journey from Cairo. The train was almost empty, and it was stopped on the way by an air-raid alarm. When it arrived the streets were blacked out and deserted after German bombing two days before. Sophie had little money, but she decided to splash out and stay in the luxury Beau-Rivage hotel on the seafront Corniche for two or three days. She was the only guest. 'When I went down from my room to have a meal I had all the waiters around me, and with the compliments of the management I got the best bottle of wine in the cellars,' she remembered. 'And I could hear the guns of Alamein.'

They were the guns of the first battle of Alamein from 1 to 4 July 1942, when six divisions of British and colonial troops stopped Rommel breaking through their lines and at last halted the long German advance from Tunisia. The sound that reached Sophie 95 kilometres away was very faint, barely a sound at all. Olivia Manning, author of *The Levant Trilogy*, who was in Alexandria during the second battle of Alamein in October, described the sound of the guns then as no more than a shudder in the night air, a vibration in the ground beneath her feet.

It was one of those moments in Sophie's life when the projector seems to slow down and everything grows still, like a frozen frame of film, and the image is preserved forever. Such moments speak of the essence of people and places and of the times they live in. Chouquette and Stas, Boule, Sophie and Andrew had experienced such a moment in August 1939 in their last carefree days before their world changed. The picture of Sophie sitting alone in the empty dining room of an

Alexandria hotel, as close to the fighting as she could get at the most critical moment of the desert war, speaks of her quixotic and indomitable spirit. She was just a slender woman of twenty-five, but she was unbreakable. Her presence there was an inspired, stubborn act of faith, a solitary gesture of defiance against the Germans and whatever else life might bring.

She described her visit to Alexandria in her usual matter-of-fact way: 'I am at Alex, it is wonderful,' she wrote to Andrew. She was staying in a marvellous hotel on the sea shore, eating grapes and peaches during long days on the warm sand, and she had forgotten about the chaotic days when everyone was fleeing Cairo.

Rommel's failure to break through in July brought 'The Flap' to an end. He made a second attempt in September and failed again, and in October General Bernard Montgomery sprung his carefully prepared trap and routed the heavily outnumbered and outgunned Germans in the second Battle of El Alamein and chased them hundreds of kilometres back to Tunisia, where they eventually surrendered. Before the end of July 1942 evacuees were returning to Cairo. Sophie was there to greet them as she had promised.

Zazulinski, the Polish chargé d'affaires, apologised for his angry outburst. 'He excused himself madly,' she wrote on 22 July. 'I tried to believe him. I agreed with him without a pause . . . I hid my enmity in my pocket and was just very inaccessible, and he twisted and turned like an eel.'

Chouquette returned, bringing me with her, and rejoined Sophie at the National Hotel. I was lucky to be alive. I had caught typhoid fever in Jerusalem and nearly died at the age of twenty-two months. I had such a high fever that Stas, who was on an officer's training course in Palestine, expected to be told I was dead whenever he went to the hospital to visit me.

Back in Cairo Sophie learned of my illness. 'After my return from Alexandria I learned that the Gnomek is very sick and since then I have been writing to Chou. I am very alarmed about him,' she wrote. She had often cared for me in Cairo, and must have feared that I would die like her two sons.

CHAPTER EIGHTEEN

Little Gnomek

Stas, Chouquette and I left Egypt not long after El Alamein. Stas wanted to train as a parachute commando with the Polish Special Forces in England, and Chouquette's affair with Andrew had ended by then.

Stas may have thought that moving to Britain would get him back into action quicker than staying with the Carpathian Brigade, which remained in Palestine and Iraq for many months being reorganised and expanded. Or perhaps he wanted to switch units because of bad relations with his officers. He may even have been encouraged to leave the regiment. Whatever the reason, General Kopanski backed his request for the transfer and gave him a glowing citation: 'Corporal Cadet Officer Tarnowski was one of the bravest soldiers of the Carpathian Artillery Regiment. He twice distinguished himself in battle – at Tobruk in a sally of the Lancers Regiment and at the battle for Bardia – and he was decorated with the Cross of Valour.'

Stas moved from Palestine to Cairo in September 1942 in readiness for our departure and was attached to Polish military headquarters. He was laid low by a bout of jaundice, but when he recovered he was ordered to escort a Polish journalist to observe the battle of El Alamein in late October. They drove off in a jeep with a pistol and a tommy gun and on 4 November watched the British break the German lines and start chasing Rommel. After following the advance 400 kilometres west to Bardia, where Stas had fought nearly a year earlier, they drove on before the advancing British and headed for Tobruk, which was held by the Germans.

'We were the first jeep fired on from Tobruk by the Germans,' Stas said. 'We turned back, and about half way back we met the front of the advancing British troops, armoured cars and tanks, and lots of them were blown up by mines. We had travelled that road, it was mined all the way, and nothing had happened to us.'

Back in Cairo Stas joined in the social whirl. He met Irka Grabowska, the *femme fatale* from Tel Aviv whom Sophie had brought to Egypt. Irka was driving a Red Cross truck by day and a sports car by night, and had a succession of wealthy lovers. But she also had time for Stas. 'I had her,' he admitted. 'Most people did. She was very attractive.'

Then he fell in love with Samicha, a beautiful Coptic woman who led him into the desert one night. Stas was usually only too happy to take his pleasure with a woman, but he had fallen heavily for Samicha's Levantine charms. When she stripped under the moonlight he was shocked, because he loved and respected her, and refused to make love. 'She took three months to forgive me,' he laughed. By then it was too late, because we left for England.

We sailed from the port of Suez on New Year's Day 1943. Two years and three months old, I toddled up the gang-plank with Stas and Chouquette onto the transatlantic liner *New Amsterdam*, which had been converted into a troopship. We sailed for South Africa, taking the long way round to England, because the Mediterranean was swarming with German and Italian ships, planes and submarines. Sophie came to see us off, waving goodbye as the great ship, bursting with troops, pulled away from the quayside and steamed out to sea. She was happy in Cairo and had decided to stay.

General Kopanski had arranged for Stas to have officer status for the voyage, so we had a cabin to ourselves while thousands of men of the First South African Division who were returning home after serving in the desert slept in the corridors and on stairways. Instead of cruising down the coast of Africa in a heavily protected convoy, the *New Amsterdam* steamed alone straight out into the Indian Ocean for several days and then turned and made a top-speed dash for South Africa, a tactic used by troop-carrying liners fast enough to outrun the U-boats. The voyage took about ten days, and crowds of white South Africans were at the docks to cheer the returning troops at Durban.

We were due to take another ship to England, but instead of leaving right away we stayed in South Africa for nearly four months. Stas had made friends on the *New Amsterdam* with the general commanding the South African division, who gave him letters of introduction to friends and an invitation to go lion hunting. Since no Polish forces were fighting in the West at the time, he obtained permission to take a later ship to England. The delay probably saved our lives because the ship on which we were supposed to sail, the transatlantic liner *Empress of Canada*, was sunk off the coast of Sierra Leone on the way to England in March 1943 with the loss of nearly 400 lives.

Stas left Chouquette with me in Durban and went to stay for several weeks on a farm beside the Kruger National Park game reserve, where he became friends with the park manager, Mrs Leo Lyons. 'Once I got there they all invited me and I had the time of my life,' he said nostalgically. 'Oh, it was great fun, lovely country . . . It was the best time of my life. It was wonderful.'

He shot a black-maned lion but found it was too easy. 'A wonderful animal like that, it doesn't stand a chance,' he said. After that he stopped hunting and never shot another animal or bird in his life.

He also had a brush with death while tracking a lion through the bush. Looking up as he followed the trail, he saw a snake on a branch above him poised to strike. At that instant his tracker threw an *assegai* from behind him and speared the snake, a deadly yellow bush mamba. If it had struck, he would have been dead in twenty minutes.

It must have been late April 1943 when we embarked at Cape Town. Stas and Chouquette spent little time together during the voyage. Both made new friends and were too busy for each other and probably for me. I have a picture of myself on board, a real *gnomek*, a dark-haired toddler of two and a half in shorts, a short-sleeved shirt and sandals standing alone on deck, grimacing in the sunshine with a rope quoit in each hand.

Chouquette spent her time getting to know a tall and handsome Scottish major in the Black Watch regiment named Malcolm Wolfe Murray. He was returning home to his two small sons in Scotland after losing his wife, who had died when her ship was torpedoed on the way home from visiting him in Palestine.

Stas was on the prowl, as usual, having a romantic adventure with a young girl named Paddy Gordon, whom he met on board. 'She was only sixteen, very attractive,' he remembered. 'I didn't actually, you know, but . . . Good Lord, those were the days.'

I have no memory of our arrival in England, but I suppose it was a cold, grey day in early May. England was a pinched and dismal place in those days and for years after. I was not yet three, and I don't remember being with my parents after we arrived because Stas went away to Special Parachute Units for training and Chouquette enrolled at an Oxford secretarial college. Or was it London first as a secretary at one of the ministries of the Polish government-in-exile, and then Oxford? I'm not sure, but she made lots of friends and led a pretty successful social life.

All I remember of the next three or four years are jumbled snippets and faded images of people and things: the wail of an air-raid siren; the growl of a V1 or V2 rocket before the engine cut out, and the long, menacing silence before it exploded; sunshine and long grass and buttercups in a beautiful field somewhere in England. Did my mother send me for a while, for the holidays, perhaps, to a foster family in the countryside? I remember a nursery school at Oxford with children playing on a lawn, and not knowing how to mingle with them. How could I, having lived abroad in a hotel and in a villa with a nanny? I had probably never played with another child in my life. I probably didn't speak English. I must have been a boarder at the school, because after a while there was a school play and when I had to perform alone on the stage I saw my mother sitting in the front row of the audience. I hadn't seen her for weeks, or was it months? I was sitting beside a cardboard tree with a paper spider dangling beside me, petrified as I began to recite 'Little Jack Horner, sat in a corner, eating his curds and whey . . .' Right there, rigid with fright, I forgot my lines and got up and fled from the stage, rushing straight to my Mummy and burying my face in her lap. There was sympathetic oohing and aahing from the motherly audience. But so much for Tarnowski bravery! Stas would have been furious. I knew I had been a coward.

Was it at that school that I did something awful, because the headmaster locked me in a dark cupboard under the stairs and afterwards left me alone in a room for hours? Was I developing Stas's temper already? It was certainly at Oxford, because Uncle Philip, Boule's husband, came haring up from London to rescue me. Boule, my darling aunt, was with him, and I think he shouted at the headmaster before they took me away. I remember he was very angry. But that must have been after the war, because Boule spent the whole war in the United States and only married my beloved Uncle Philip, Philippe Boulasse, a Frenchman who was the epitome of Gallic wit and charm and urbanity and kindness, after the war was over.

I stayed for a while with an English family in a rather dark and gloomy house in London. I wonder why. They were a dry and distant couple with a son who didn't want to know me, and I felt out of place and crept about like a mouse. I remember walking in the streets of London, my big, tall, handsome father holding my hand. I hero-worshipped him with his neat military moustache and swept-back hair, and his crisp khaki uniform with the parachutist's beret, and felt wonderful beside him, and wondered why the women walking by kept looking at him. The streets were full of bomb sites where whole buildings had been destroyed, leaving gaping cavities as though giant teeth had been pulled by an evil German dentist.

I remember my mother and father together three times, once among the huge marble columns and floors of Blenheim Palace near Oxford, the home of the Duke of Marlborough. Chouquette made lots of friends in English high society. She was brilliant at it. She was beautiful, and graceful. She spoke perfect English and French. She had a shy smile and a quick, gay laugh, and everybody loved her. We spent one or two weekends at Blenheim. Stas played bridge with Bertie, the duke, and won seventeen pounds one evening, which gave him a shock because he thought he was playing for pennies. It was more than his monthly pay as a second lieutenant in the Polish army. If he had lost, he wouldn't have been able to pay up. That was probably during the war, because he was in uniform. He never went to Blenheim after he was de-mobbed because he couldn't have afforded to tip the servants.

I remember Stas in his army uniform, hanging by his hands from the landing above the main stairs at Houghton Hall in Yorkshire, the home of my mother's dear friend Joyce Lady Fitzalan-Howard. Chouquette and Joyce, and her sister, Alathea Lady Manton, shrieked, 'No, Stas, no!', hands to their mouths in fright, as he swung forward and jumped to the floor of the hall, landing with an expert parachutist's roll. After he finished the parachuting course and won his para-chutist's wing he loved to show off his jump and roll whenever he got the chance, and to strut the streets of London in his immaculately creased officer's uniform with the red-and-white Poland flash and the paratrooper's half-wing, with the grey beret sitting proudly on his head.

I loved Houghton. The grown-ups wanted me to be friends with Auntie Joyce's daughter Lizzie-Ann. Lizzie-Ann was nice, and pretty, but she was a few years older and much taller than me, and I must have spent a lot of time instead behind the green baize door with the servants Ming-Ming and Eileen because just the memory of their names brings back a wonderful feeling of warmth and intimacy that I can't remember from anywhere else in my childhood.

Joyce and Alathea, who was known as 'The Rabbit' –

Chouquette was 'The Mouse' – were my mother's best friends in England. She used to stay at Alathea's flat in Fountain's House in Mayfair, which must have been the most feminine place on this earth: all silks, satins, soft carpets and cushion upon cushion, pink everywhere, and heavy curtains with deep pelmets, dressing tables crowded with make-ups and scents and hand mirrors and hair brushes, and the whole flat filled with a lingering perfume heavy on the air, the scent of a woman. Auntie Rabbit was lovely: gaunt and twitchy, hoarse, chain-smoking and affectionate. Charm and concern poured from her long, lined face and from every aristocratic word she spoke. 'Dahling Chou', she would say before every anxious sentence. Or 'dahling Boubi'. Dahling. Dahling. Dahling. It was the most important word in her vocabulary. She and Joyce were so homely. They cocooned Chouquette with love and luxury and comforted her as she adapted to her somewhat spartan new country while Stas was away training for the battles ahead, and for all I know they protected her from him when he came to London on leave.

The last time I saw my parents together, or rather heard them together, was in London just after the war. I had had an operation by a South Audley Street eye surgeon to correct a terrible squint, and I woke up in darkness with my eyes bandaged to hear them having a row beside me as I lay in bed. I think they were arguing about me. What best to do for me, or with me, I suppose. Stas kept raising his voice and it got deeper as he grew more and more impatient and came close to bellowing. 'Oh Stas,' I think I remember my mother saying. 'Oh Stas.' That was all. I was six. I can't remember if I cried.

CHAPTER NINETEEN

The Villa Tara

S ophie stayed in Cairo after we left for England and remained there until the end of the war, thriving on a heady mix of high society, hard work and exotic adventures. She was almost twenty-six when we left, a woman in her prime, and the next few years were the best of her life. She formed many close friendships with unusual and exceptional personalities, and she was so much at home in the boisterous *milieu* of wartime Cairo that she said it was there that she really grew up.

Of all the relationships she formed during the war years, the strangest began on a Sunday afternoon as she was going home by taxi from a lunch party. She saw a crowd of Egyptian men gathered in a street and told the driver to slow down. 'What do you think it is?' she asked him.

The taxi stopped. She got out and saw that the crowd was being entertained by a man worrying two mongooses in a cage. Sophie immediately decided to rescue them. Assuming an air of self-assurance, she called out loudly: 'I am buying them for ten shillings' and pushed through the crowd to thrust the money into the man's hand and carry the cage to the taxi. Only when she walked into the hotel, and venerable British residents uttered indignant exclamations as a bellboy carried the mongooses through the lounge, did she notice that they were playing with a very large reusable condom. She giggled at the memory.

Her new pets were so alike that she gave them a single

name: Kurka. She kept them in her room and they became completely tame, but when hotel staff came in they hid under the bed and growled like a dog. At night she shut them in the bathroom but they always managed to get into her bed. In the heat of Cairo she slept with only a sheet and tucked it tightly round her so that the mongooses could not get under it, but they always did, and cuddled up to her and slept along her back.

'If I moved they would give me a warning bite so that I wouldn't squash them. So I had these bites at the top of my back, and the evening dress I had was décolleté at the back and people used to say, "Oh Sophie, what is that?" So I said, "Oh, it's nothing, it's mongooses."' She laughed.

Her only bad experience that year occurred after General Sirkorski was killed in July 1943. His plane crashed while taking off from Gibraltar on the way to London after a second visit to the Middle East. It was a terrible blow to the Polish cause because he was Prime Minister and Commander-in-Chief and the only Pole whom the Allies respected as a national leader.

Polish officials in Cairo, who were unhappy that Sikorski had put an independent-minded woman in charge of the Polish Red Cross there, got rid of Sophie after his death. Orders were issued allocating ranks in the Red Cross branch, overruling Sikorski's agreement with Sophie. When she refused to accept a rank, Polish military police stopped her in the street and stripped the Polish eagle from her cap. For a while she stopped working for the Red Cross.

But that summer, she had fallen in love with William Stanley Moss, a captain in the Coldstream Guards back from the final defeat of the Afrika Korps in Tunisia. As someone described him, Billy Moss was very tall, good-looking and devilishly languid. He was an adventurer with a literary bent and an attractive air of unaffected self-deprecation. 'He was extremely good looking, he danced well, he was amusing. He was a very good companion,' Sophie said.

Billy had just joined SOE or Special Operations Executive, whose agents were dropped into Nazi-occupied countries to help partisans organise resistance, and was waiting for his first assignment. He had been staying at Shepheards Hotel but left when extra beds were put in his room and strangers moved in. One of them made a pass at him, and Billy had to knock him out. Now he was sleeping at an SOE safe house, a barrack-like flat that the inmates dubbed Hangover Hall.

It was Billy who introduced Sophie to the glamorous young men of the SOE who became her companions and friends. The first was Patrick Leigh Fermor, another officer with a literary talent just back from the mountains of German-occupied Crete. He and Billy had found a splendid villa in Zamalek, an exclusive, tree-lined residential district on Gezira Island in the River Nile, and wanted Sophie and two young English ladies to share it with them and a group of friends. They described the villa with its gardens front and back, a driveway up to the balustraded front steps, a ballroom with a parquet floor, a large dining room, a drawing room with a fireplace, and six or seven bedrooms. The roof was ideal for sunbathing, and the Gezira Sporting Club was nearby.

Sophie was considering the idea when one of the young ladies fell in love and pulled out. The other soon followed suit. 'I know that the next thing is you'll call it off, too,' Billy lamented. 'You must come.'

'No, I can't possibly come,' she replied. 'I can't be the only girl with all these boys. I mean, what do you think my reputation would be like?'

'Please come or we'll be bankrupt,' Billy and Paddy Leigh Fermor pleaded. 'We've paid the deposit and we have to pool our resources. Come and see how lovely the place is. Your mongooses will be so happy.'

They thought up an imaginative ruse to satisfy her concerns for her honour, inventing a fictitious chaperone, Mrs Khayyat, who was to move into the villa with her. So Sophie left the National Hotel and for several months she was the only woman in a household of British secret agents, several of whom became her lifelong friends. At the beginning, the men would apologise to visitors for Mrs Khayyat's absence. 'Mrs Khayyat is so sorry that she can't join us but she has a terrible headache.'

They called the villa Tara, after the legendary strongtown of High Kings in Ireland and Scarlett O'Hara's plantation home in the American South in *Gone with the Wind*. For a few months in 1943 and 1944 it was home to half a dozen young SOE officers between assignments, whose riotous parties and eccentric goings-on made it a centre of Cairo social life. Besides Billy Moss and Paddy Leigh Fermor, the inhabitants included the jovial Arnold Breeme, who had been on a mission in Yugoslavia, and Billy McLean and David Smiley, who had been in Greece and Albania, and before that in Abyssinia. Then came the quixotic Rowland Winn who later dropped into Albania, and finally Xan Fielding, back from some derring-do among the partisans on Crete.

Colonel David Smiley remembered it as the happiest time of the war. 'I loved it. I really loved it,' he remembered at his home in London. 'We were all such good friends. I don't ever remember an angry or cross word. We all got on frightfully well.'

Sophie was hostess, housekeeper and presiding spirit in their Bohemian world. She collected the money for the rent, food and drink; she supervised the excellent Egyptian cook and the *suffraghis* who skimmed about in scarlet *tarbooshes* and long white *galabias*; and she organised the dinners and parties. She loved it, and when she was invited out she was the belle of the ball escorted by dashing young British officers, and she knew how to make an entrance. David Smiley thought most of the occupants of Tara were a little in love with her. 'She was great fun. She had this sort of Polish accent which was rather attractive and she was a very good-looking girl. She was a lot of fun to have around.'

The boisterous band acquired nicknames that they inscribed on a bronze plaque on the front door of the villa. It announced the occupants of Tara as:

Princess Dnieper-Petrovsk	(Countess Sophie Tarnowska)
Sir Eustace Rapier	(Lt-Col. Neil 'Billy' McLean, DSO)
Marquis of Whipstock	(Col. David Smiley, OBE, MC)
Hon. Rupert Sabretache	(Major the Hon. Rowland Winn, MC, later Lord St Oswald)
Lord Hugh Devildrive	(Major Xan Fielding, DSO)
Lord Pintpot	(Arnold Breeme)
Lord Rakehell	(Major Patrick Leigh Fermor, DSO)
Mr Jack Jargon	(Capt. William Stanley Moss, MC)

They launched Tara with an outrageous party that ended in the small hours with a delighted orgy of smashed glasses and broken window.

One night, at the Club Royal de Chasse et de Peche, Billy Moss and Patrick Leigh Fermor dreamed up a plan to kidnap the commander of the German forces occupying Crete. David

Smiley remembered that everyone helped to work out the details:

> We all planned that particular operation in the bathroom at Tara. We were all pretty well stark naked and on the wall was steam, the walls were tiled. I remember we were drawing with our fingers on the wall, a sort of road was here; we'd be able to stop the German general's car there, we'd have a covering party there – all that sort of stuff. But it was all in the bathroom.

Billy and Paddy left for Crete in April 1944 and with Cretan partisans kidnapped General Karl Kreipe, the German commander on the island, and spirited him back to Cairo in one of the fabled commando exploits of the war, which Billy Moss described in his book *Ill Met by Moonlight.*[2] His account included a moving reminiscence of the farewell party at Tara on the night he and Paddy left, which he wrote in a cave in the mountains of Crete.

> How often I think of that night . . . the faces grouped round the lacquer-red table in the corner of the drawing room, intimate by the light of four tall candles . . . four o'clock in the morning, waiting to leave for the aerodrome . . . drinking and singing . . . Sophie in a huge Hebron coat, the sleeves flopping over her fingertips; David, shivering in his extraordinary dressing-gown which is embroidered with Lumpers on guard before Whitehall; Pixie, all four paws in the air, fast asleep on a couch in the corner; and the people who had come to see us off . . . Gertie (Wissa), like the quinquireme of Nineveh rolling at anchor in a British port; Denise (Menasce), on her back upon the chaise-longue; Alexis (Ladas), with appendix just

removed, singing Phillidem; Inez Burrows, enormously decolléré, happy in the role of Hungarian peasant. . .and then Billy (McLean) had come in, a towel round his waist, smiling shyly and giving us these two volumes (the Oxford Book of English Verse and the collected Shakespeare), one to Paddy, one to me, saying that they had been with him in Albania and would surely bring us luck. I have them before me now.

The non-stop partying told on the liquor supplies, and Sophie suggested they should make vodka. As a child in Poland she had seen flavoured vodkas and liqueurs made by pricking fruit with a needle and pickling it in alcohol. 'Oh yes, how do you make it?' the men asked.

'Well, it's based on pure alcohol and there is a garage where you can buy good, clean alcohol in great big gallon containers.'

They bought gallons of spirits and poured them into a bath. They used prunes for flavour because they could not find fresh cherries or plums, and Sophie gave the men pins to prick the holes. 'We pushed the prunes into bottles and poured alcohol in,' she said. 'The boys were getting sticky and they were being very bolshy. They were awfully curious about how long it would take before the vodka was ready. So I said, "One should leave it at least six weeks."

' "Ha, that's much too long," they said.

'They were trying it to see if it was terribly raw, and in the end there was none left. And I must say, that vodka never waited its six weeks and we didn't go on with it but we decided to do something quite different with the alcohol, to buy tomato juice and make Bloody Marys.' But David Smiley said they once served the raw spirits at a party and one of the guests went blind for a day or two.

They lived lavishly on back pay accumulated during

months in the field. They gave lunches on racing days at the Cairo racetrack, and whenever one of the group was going on a mission they threw a party. 'There would be a big party and a car would call, and those who were going to be dropped into enemy territory left just like that. Without a goodbye, without anything,' Sophie remembered. 'We never allowed ourselves to be anxious about them. We believed that to be anxious was to accept the possibility of something dreadful happening to them.'

Their guests included King Farouk, Egyptian princes, foreign diplomats and Coptic and Levantine socialites, Allied generals, military officers and diplomats and journalists, writers and SOE secretaries. 'The Poles, of course, were the worst,' David Smiley said. 'They used to come and let their pistols off and shoot the bottles and things like that. They were a bit wild.'

Even the servants contributed to the exotic lifestyle. 'We were having a very pleasant life there, giving these parties,' Sophie said. 'We were giving Abdul the *suffraghi* a certain amount of money for them, but apparently he was not able to manage. So, without us knowing at all, he would stand at the little gate onto the street holding out his *tarboosh* to collect money from people who were leaving.'

She found out what Abdul was up to when David Smiley asked if he could join them at Tara, saying with a laugh that it would be cheaper for him than living elsewhere. 'What do you mean?' asked Sophie. When he told her about Abdul she was horrified. She called him and demanded: 'Abdul, what are you doing?'

'Oh, but Madame, you wouldn't have parties if Abdul didn't do that,' he replied.

Sophie laughed. 'He was buying more shrimps or rice or

whatever it was with the money he collected so that we could have our parties.'

The gardener found a more gruesome way to make money. He came to Sophie during a lunch party carrying a headless chicken in a flowerpot, its wings still flapping feebly. 'Mongoose, mongoose,' he said, thrusting the flowerpot at her. Kurka had bitten off the chicken's head.

The sight was so revolting that every man at the party put his hand in his pocket and thrust money at the gardener. 'Go away, go away,' they told him. He went, clutching the money. But that was not the end of the story.

'The next time we had a lunch party the gardener bit off the head of a chicken and again brought it in a flower pot. Quite mad!' Sophie said. 'It was just as revolting as before. He thought it was a good way of getting money for the house.'

Kurka came to a sticky end in the spring of 1944 after attacking a parrot in the next villa. The bird was unhurt, but the neighbour was an important Englishman. The local head of SOE summoned David Smiley and Billy McLean and ordered them to chain, muzzle or shoot Kurka. They ignored him, but a week later Kurka killed the parrot. They were summoned again, given formal reprimands, and ordered to shoot the mongooses. 'It so happened that I had rather a good .22 silencer so I was nominated the executioner. I got behind the poor brutes and blew their brains out,' David Smiley said.

The only other Tara resident I came to know years later was Rowland Winn, who became Boule's second husband after the war and inherited the title Lord St Oswald and a stately home in Yorkshire. Uncle Rowland was a colourful, quixotic figure. He was chivalrous, generous and gregarious and a true eccentric, though perhaps not quite as eccentric as his father who when invited for the weekend arrived with his jazz drums, pulling a stuffed bulldog on wheels. David Smiley remembered that the bulldog's mouth opened and shut as it rolled along.

Rowland had reported on the Spanish civil war for Reuters news agency and the *Daily Telegraph* and spent his twenty-first birthday under sentence of death in a Republican jail in Barcelona, from which he was extricated by the British consul. From Cairo he was parachuted into Albania and later dropped into Siam. When the Korean War broke out in 1950 he volunteered and won a Military Cross. Later he tried his hand as a bullfighter, novelist, government minister and Member of the European Parliament and was an energetic spokesman in the House of Lords for noble causes, including the cause of a free Poland. But at Tara he was a bit of a figure of fun thanks to his explosive personality and his clumsy gait, caused by a congenital disease.

He sported large moustaches at the time, which were waxed daily by his barber, like the enormous moustaches of King Fouad, the father of King Farouk whose picture was on every wall in Cairo. Aunt Sophie thought they were ridiculous and did a terrible thing. 'One day I walked in and he was fast asleep on the sofa in the drawing room. And I went straight up to my room, got a pair of scissors and cut off one moustache. It was a horrific thing to do, and the moustache was hiding a scar on his lip.'

She also hid Rowland's Eighth Hussars' kepi, which he wore wherever he went. 'When he was asleep I would take his kepi and put it behind a picture on the wall,' she told me. 'When he woke up Rowland would say, "By God," and you know how he thumped the table. "My God," he said, "It's amazing. Where could it have gone?" He would sort of trot around the whole place, buzz off to town, come back with another one, and then boom, the original would reappear. We were doing silly things like this because we were all living together and teasing one another.'

According to David Smiley, Rowland broke an ankle practising suicide after the actress Louine McGrath jilted him. 'I remember him jumping off the dining room table, and I said, "What are you doing, Rowley?" He said, "I'm practising committing suicide." In fact I believe he did jump off the roof and broke his leg.'

Sophie remembered the incident differently. Rowland had been ordered to guard Italian prisoners building roads instead of being selected for the SOE. He considered it a complete disgrace to his name and dignity. 'He came back home extremely depressed and rather bolshy, and all the boys got to drinking far more than usual,' Sophie said. 'They got very tipsy and there was a mantelpiece in the drawing room and they started jumping off that mantelpiece and doing the parachute roll, and showing me how to do it. In the end I got bored with this and I decided to go to bed. I went to bed and after a time someone knocked on my door and said, did I have an aspirin? So I just gave an aspirin, didn't ask any questions. And ten minutes or maybe fifteen minutes later, again there was a knock at the door and they asked for another aspirin. And I immediately said, "What's all this? What does it mean? Is anybody trying to commit suicide? I'm not going to give them all the aspirins." So then they said, "Ah, but Rowland has jumped."

'And Rolando, after having tried several jumps from the mantelpiece, decided to jump from the balustrade outside, forgetting, because it was pitch dark, that there were flower pots underneath. And he jumped into them and broke his ankle. So the boys came up to my bedroom door and said, "Look, Rowland is in great pain. God knows what he's done. You must give another aspirin. So I decided to go and find out. Pixie the Alsatian dog followed me and the first thing he did was jump on Rowland's bed and Rowland almost screamed with pain." '

Uncle Rowland was invited to join SOE shortly afterwards and parachuted into Albania, but he broke his ankle again as he landed in the mountains. His leg was set in a splint by a horse doctor and he rode through mountains on a mule until he took part in something like a cavalry charge with the partisans and the mule fell on him and broke his leg a third time.

The fun at Tara ended early in 1944. The war in the Balkans was beginning to wind down and SOE was moving to the Far East. The villa's owner was probably reluctant to renew the lease after all the damage they had done, so at the end of April Billy Moss, Sophie and a few others took a large flat in Zamalek which they again christened Tara.

She wrote to Andrew in May, making her final break with him, telling him in the most affectionate way that she was in love with Billy. 'Darling, forget me, do not call me with the memories of what has been – something so marvellous, like velvet, that came to me and you from nowhere,' she wrote. She was no longer the little girl filled with dreams whom he had met at Dukla, she continued. The war had brought difficult times and she had grown up far from him. Although she still feared to lose the last bit of his affections, she told him her feelings had changed and he must now build a new life without her. She would never be able to return to the empty home at Gora Ropczycka 'which once was my whole world, to everything that no longer exists, to the land that would remind me every day of my childless motherhood'.

She married Billy in Cairo in April 1945, just before the war in Europe ended. He was about to be dropped in Siam, and fearing that he might not return, they decided to marry before he left. She asked a Catholic bishop to annul her marriage to Andrew, explaining that they had been very closely related and she feared that this was the reason for the death of their two sons. The bishop was unsympathetic, particularly after learning that they had received a papal dispensation to marry. He lectured her about an Egyptian woman who had seven abnormal children but then had a normal child, and told her she lacked patience and Christian humility. Sophie thought him cruel. She stormed out and joined the Greek Orthodox church, then she divorced Andrew and married Billy in an Orthodox ceremony. Prince Peter and Princess Irene of Greece attended the wedding, and her friend Princess Emine Toussoun of the Egyptian royal family gave them a magnificent reception.

CHAPTER TWENTY

Tides of Misfortune

ack in Poland, with German officers billeted in his home, Hieronim suffered one disaster after another as the war continued. His mother died early in 1942, at about the time Stas was in hospital in Alexandria. Imcia was eighty-eight and had survived her husband the professor by twenty-five years when she died at Rudnik on 23 February 1942.

'Today at half past one in the morning after a week's illness, without suffering, Mama ended her life in death,' Hieronim wrote in the visitors' book. He asked the Germans for permission to take her body to Dzikow to lay her beside the professor in the family crypt beneath the Dominican church, but they refused and so she was buried under a plain concrete slab in the town cemetery at Rudnik. Perhaps it was fitting that she should lie barely a kilometre from the estate she had bought for the family.

She was buried on a bleak winter's day. A black and white photograph shows a bareheaded crowd kneeling or standing around the open grave, framed by leafless trees silhouetted against a dull sky. The coffin is on the ground beside the grave and the black-robed parish priest Father Stefan Zagalak kneels at its foot reading prayers. Hieronim is kneeling in the mud beside the coffin, his head bent over it in prayer. His nephew Wacek Bninski and the housekeeper Pani Sarnecka kneel beside him. His sister Jadzia Bninska and two dozen friends, relatives and neighbours crowd around them. The balding head of the faithful butler Wojciech Hass peers from the crowd behind the priest, his thin, pale features pinched and lined.

Twenty-five mourners signed the visitors' book, and beneath their signatures Jadzia added her own farewell to her mother: 'I arrived on February 23 after receiving news of Mama's worsening condition. After receiving the Blessed Sacrament she ended her life at 1.30 a.m. on February 23. May her memory be blessed by all of us to the end of our lives, and by our descendants, and may her spirit rise from her to God.'

Her death brought Hieronim no respite, and tragedies continued to rain down upon his head. The very next entry in the visitors' book is in the form of two small flowers that he taped onto the page, beside which he wrote in his tall, clear hand: 'Primroses from the Szlak – the last, for how long? Picked 16.IV.1942.' What he meant was that within two or three months of losing his mother he also lost the Szlak, the historic Krakow mansion in which he was born, which had played a large part in the family's life for nearly seventy years. The Germans had looted many of its finest contents in 1939: Flemish tapestries and medieval armour and weapons that adorned the walls, paintings including a triptych by the romantic Polish painter Jan Matejko and the great store of old Persian carpets collected by previous owners. Now the Germans told Hieronim they were going to take over the house and turn it into the headquarters of the Hitler Youth in the *General-Gouvernement.*

He tried for months to fend off the blow, turning to friends and connections in Austria and Hungary, and representatives of the German government in Poland. His efforts may have delayed the seizure of the Szlak for a while, but in May 1942 the Germans gave him forty-eight hours to clear out his possessions and leave.

Hieronim and his nephew Wacek went to Krakow and hurriedly packed books, archives, correspondence and papers from the professor's study into crates and sent them to the nearby Benedictine monastery at Tyniec for storage. He sent the great dark Gdansk cupboards, oriental chairs and tables and the ancient porcelain tiles from two magnificent stoves to the estates of relatives outside Krakow.

Hieronim must have felt a remorseless fate was stripping him of everything he loved, and his distress seems to have made him increasingly gloomy and nervous. When his cousin Franciszek Mycielski invited him over to his estate at Wengierka for the wedding of his administrator to a much-loved governess named Karolcia, he made a complete fool of himself. Vodka was served after the wedding ceremony and the toasts and speeches, and after the dinner dancing began. Unfortunately, Hieronim could not take his liquor, a trait he had passed on with a vengeance to his son. Like Stas, drink made him bad-tempered and rude, though unlike his son he did not often drink too much and it never made him violent. After a while, he found the party too much for him, and he suddenly became truculent and declared at the top of his voice, 'I won't drink vodka with riff-raff.' Silence fell and everyone watched as he went weaving towards the French window and out into the garden where it was raining heavily.

After he had been gone a while his cousin sent Michal the butler with an umbrella and a raincoat to see if he was all right and bring him in. A few minutes later Michal returned still carrying the umbrella and raincoat and looking disturbed. 'The count is going to hang himself from an apple tree,' he said. There was consternation among the guests and the butler was hurriedly sent back to try to persuade Hieronim not to hang himself and come inside. A few minutes later

Michal returned once again and reported: 'The count has not killed himself. But he won't come inside and has decided to leave. He is walking to Jaroslaw.'

Jaroslaw was a town several kilometres away and it was still raining heavily. So Franciszek ordered a horse to be harnessed to a trap and went after him himself. Half an hour later he returned with poor Hieronim soaking wet and shivering, and took him upstairs to dry out and sleep it off.

While Hieronim's misfortunes threatened to overwhelm him at Rudnik, Wanda found that she needed Tadeusz's support more and more at Zaleze. In late 1941 she detected a painful lump in one of her breasts and realised that she probably had cancer. Courageous as ever, she mentioned it to no one except Tadeusz, and did not seek medical treatment because she did not want to leave little Artur. The only hint she gave that all was not well was in a letter she wrote to Sophie in December 1941. Without mentioning herself or her health, she wrote that she was giving Artur into Sophie and Andrew's care. Sophie, who was in Cairo, was alarmed. 'Perhaps this means nothing, but to me it is extremely disturbing,' she wrote to Andrew, who was fighting with the Carpathian Rifle Brigade in the North African desert.

Despite her illness, Wanda and Tadeusz had turned the estate at Zaleze into a centre of anti-Nazi resistance. As a former regular officer, Tadeusz had begun underground work in the clandestine Home Army, and he used his role as estate manager as cover. He operated under the *nom de guerre* Kos, or Blackbird, and sometimes spent long periods away on missions. Home Army fighters often took refuge in the house or the farm, and their commanders sometimes gathered in the house to plan guerrilla attacks on the Germans.

Partisan activities in the area increased after Hitler attacked the Soviet Union in June 1941. The resistance began attacking German supply trains heading east for the front in the Soviet Union. The railway that crossed southern Poland from Krakow to Rzeszów and on to Lwow in the east was a supply line for the German offensive and it followed the boundary of the estate as it passed Zaleze. Home Army fighters would jump onto a train, kill some German guards, and toss out supplies, weapons and ammunition to be picked up by their own people before jumping off. The fighters, who were often from the estate, once found several wagons full of miserable Italian soldiers sent by Mussolini to the eastern front, who begged for their lives. They also found Red Cross food parcels addressed to Allied prisoners-of-war that the Germans had stolen, and threw out as many as they could. Tadeusz gave a couple of the packages to young Artur, who enjoyed a feast of tinned bully beef, spam and chocolate.

The trains were well guarded and German reprisals for the partisans' attacks were merciless. After one successful raid, troops rounded up hostages in Rzeszow and posted notices in the streets that if there were more attacks they would execute ten Poles for every casualty they suffered. The attacks continued and they carried out their threat.

The Germans must have suspected that something was going on at Zaleze because in 1941 they billeted a man in the house to keep an eye on things. He was a fat middle-aged civilian from the Rhineland who turned out to be slow-witted and affable. He took a liking to little Artur and tried to make friends, and once brought him a .22 rifle from Germany as a present. His name was Lorer, and the clandestine activities carried on under his nose. Home Army fighters sometimes stayed in a hiding hole above the bathroom, and a wounded fighter once spent two weeks there without him noticing anything. He saw nothing unusual in Tadeusz's long absences, and his presence in the house turned out to be the best possible screen for the underground activities, since his failure to report anything unusual must have allayed any suspicions the Gestapo had.

While Tadeusz was away on underground missions, Wanda helped to channel funds for the Home Army. Allied planes dropped loads of cash by parachute from the London government-in-exile that had to be passed on by the resistance from one underground cell to another before usually ending up in Warsaw. The gullible Lorer sometimes came in useful. Wanda once recruited him to help her take 2.5 million zloties to her cousin Jan Zamoyski at his estate at Klemensow about 100 kilometres north of Zaleze. She packed the notes into a bulging moneybelt, tied it around her waist under her dress, and invited Lorer to accompany her to Klemensow, saying she had to make an urgent visit to discuss important administrative matters and offered him the chance to look around one of Poland's stately homes. Lorer eagerly agreed, the Home Army provided a car for the journey, and thanks to Lorer's presence they were waved through several German checkpoints along the road without being searched. When they were finally stopped, Lorer got out to remonstrate with the soldiers, and while he was busy talking to them Wanda wound down the car window and without a word pointed to her stomach, which was bulging with the moneybelt, as though she was pregnant. At the same time, Lorer told the officer in charge he was a Nazi party member, and they were waved through.

As soon as they reached Klemensow Wanda gave the money to Jan Zamoyski, but he whispered that the Gestapo were about to arrive and she had to leave immediately. She invented an excuse to leave in a hurry and bundled the bemused Lorer back into the car without the expected tour of Klemensow. According to Artur, the Polish government-in-exile decorated Wanda in London in 1947 with the *Krzyz Walecznych* for her wartime service.

As the fighting in the Soviet Union continued and partisan activities intensified around Zaleze, the Gestapo grew increasingly suspicious that something was going on at the house. Artur, who like many Polish children worked as a local messenger for the underground, remembered running into the drawing room one day to find his mother pale and drawn, sitting stiffly erect with a uniformed Gestapo officer beside her. He had come in from the farm, and Wanda scolded him in Polish for having dirty fingernails. The German, who understood Polish, beckoned to him and took his hands and examined them while making a comment in German to Wanda. She told Artur later he had threatened to make her watch him pull out Artur's fingernails one by one if he got the slightest suspicion that she was working for the Home Army.

All over Poland terrible things were taking place. As soon as the German army invaded Poland, *Einsatzgruppen* killing squads began operating behind the advancing troops. In September and October 1939 they murdered 10,000 unarmed Polish civilians in the streets, and mass shootings and hangings took place in countless towns and villages throughout the country. After a few weeks the Germans began herding Jews from all the villages and towns into selected urban areas, and by April 1941 they had imprisoned all Poland's 3.5 million Jews in walled ghettos where they were left to starve slowly. In the Warsaw ghetto, where half a million Jews were confined, 2,000 were dying of sickness and starvation every day by June 1941 when Hitler invaded the Soviet Union. Even so, he ordered the pace of the killing to be stepped up. As the German army sliced into the Soviet Union, *Einsatzgruppen* totalling three thousand men were sent in behind the army. They shot entire Jewish communities in town after town from the Baltic Sea to the Ukraine, and within six months they had slaughtered up to a million people. Later in 1941 Hitler launched his 'Final Solution'. Death camps for killing Jews on an industrial scale were built on Polish soil at Chelmno, Sobibor, Belzec, Treblinka, Majdanek and Auschwitz-Birkenau. By mid-1944, when the tide of war had turned against the Nazis and the Soviet Army fought its way into Poland, the camps had exterminated six million Jews, or one-third of the world's 1939 Jewish population.

The killings continued for year after year and it was sometimes impossible for people in the *General-Gouvernement* to be unaware of what was happening. Artur witnessed a terrible scene in Rzeszow one hot summer day. As he sat in the carriage outside the Gestapo offices on May 3 Street, waiting for his mother, he heard furious shouting and cursing, and saw a column of emaciated people being driven along the street towards him by SS guards.

They were a ghastly, pitiable group of about a hundred Jewish men, women and children, ragged and pitifully thin after months of starvation in the ghetto, and they were being marched out of town to be shot. Whenever one fell, screaming SS men clubbed them with rifle butts, while all along the street, which had been turned into a Germans-only area, windows and doors of houses opened and Germans came out onto their doorsteps and balconies with their wives and children and jeered at the Jews and cheered on the SS.

Artur remembered the scene all his life, and he also remembered the attitude of some of the Poles around him to what was happening. Jews had made up about one-third of the town's pre-war population of 40,000 people, and some locals expressed deep dislike for them. Artur heard people on the estate at Zaleze and round about say through clenched teeth: 'Oh, those Germans, awful as they are, they are doing one good thing, getting rid of this Jewish pestilence.'

Wanda twice tried to save Jews from the Nazis. The Germans sometimes brought men from the ghetto to work on the estate, and one of them slipped her a note from the former estate accountant. It begged her to plead with the SS for his life, and said he would watch from a house by the ghetto wall that overlooked the town square for her to drive by in her carriage and signal with a handkerchief if she succeeded. Artur remembered her setting out to drive into town to try to save him, and returning home hours later, shaken and miserable. 'I couldn't, I couldn't,' was all she would say. Wanda did not drive past the ghetto in her carriage and she did not give a signal to tell the accountant she had failed.

Artur believed the SS had demanded a price she found too high to pay. 'My mother was a remarkable beauty and I wouldn't be at all surprised if the Germans made all manner of insinuations and demands,' he said. 'I'm sure she wouldn't have any of it. Rather die than that.'

But on another occasion she risked her life to stop an SS officer shooting a Jewish boy. The officer's name was Kruge. He sometimes came to stay at Zaleze to watch the household, and brought his wife and small son with him. He was so vicious that he taught the child to stamp on chicks in the farmyard, and applauded him, to the despair of his wife, who was a pious and gentle Catholic who disliked everything that the Nazis were doing in Poland.

Wanda and Artur were walking on the estate with Kruge, who was inspecting the harvest, when an urchin came up and begged for food. Kruge grabbed him. 'You're a Jew, aren't you?' he hissed, reaching for his pistol. As he drew the weapon from its holster, Wanda grabbed his arm to stop him shooting, and he let go of the child in astonishment. The boy ran away and Kruge turned on Wanda in a cold fury and without saying a word raised his pistol and aimed it at her.

Artur watched, petrified. 'I was frozen to the ground as she stood there without flinching, looking him straight in the eye. Slowly, Kruge replaced the pistol in the holster.'

It would not be Wanda's last brush with death before the war was over.

CHAPTER TWENTY-ONE

Back to War

*A*fter parachute training in England Stas joined a Polish airborne commandos training course at Court in East Sussex, and when it ended six months later General Kazimierz Sosnkowski, the new Commander-in-Chief, came from London to take the passing-out parade. It was early 1944. Sophie was still in Cairo, living in the Villa Tara surrounded by her glamorous entourage of secret agents. Andrew was in Italy as aide de camp to the regimental commander of the Carpathian Lancers, who were part of the Polish Second Corps that captured Monte Cassino and a string of Italian towns from the Germans.

Sosnkowski was a good friend of Hieronim and a fine soldier who had played a big part in Poland's defeat of the Red Army at Warsaw in August 1920 and had fought well in the September 1939 campaign. Since Stas was leader of one of the half-dozen commando patrols on parade, and the only man who had been decorated for bravery in action, he was first in line for inspection. He saluted the general and gave his name.

'Oh, you're the son of Imus?' Sosnkowski asked, using Hieronim's nickname.

'Yes sir.'

Sosnkowski turned to his entourage. 'Of course, this is one of the five men to be commissioned as officers after the parade?' he asked the commanding officer.

'No sir,' interrupted Stas, who was still only a corporal after four and a half years of war, despite having completed an officer cadet training course. 'You need too much Vaseline here for that.' Stas's attitude to authority certainly lacked the requisite obsequiousness.

Sosnkowski said nothing but saluted and moved on. Stas's comrades expected him to be disciplined, but the school commandant came to him half an hour later with an ingratiating smile and said, 'Don't worry, I've fixed it. You're going to be commissioned, too.'

Stas was promoted to the rank of second lieutenant on 1 March 1944, ready and eager to go into action as an airborne commando. But months passed and nothing happened, and he grew frustrated. His old comrades of the Carpathian Brigade, now the Carpathian Division, had been fighting in Italy since early 1944. The Normandy landings took place in June and the Polish First Armoured Division that had trained for years in Scotland went into action in France under General Stanislaw Maczek, but the Polish commandos remained idle.

Finally, after a six-month wait, they were taken in September to an airport near Peterborough to be dropped behind enemy lines in north-east France. They were to destroy railways, bridges and telephone lines and recruit some of the many Polish coalminers in the region for sabotage operations.

They paraded, fully armed and equipped for battle, before General Marian Kukiel, the minister for national defence in the government-in-exile, who made a speech and wished them luck. But then shortly afterwards, Kukiel summoned the patrol leaders and told them the drop was cancelled because Allied forces had advanced across France much faster than expected and were already approaching the drop area. When he heard that, Stas lost his temper. 'If that's the case I've had enough of this bloody mess,' he shouted. 'I want to join Maczek's armoured division.'

'How dare you speak like that!' a colonel exploded.

'I bloody well dare because it's a disgrace to be in this uniform and not be sent into battle,' he shouted back. He was right. All the Polish forces in the West except the airborne troops were fighting in France and Italy. In Warsaw, the Home Army had risen against the Nazis on 1 August and was fighting a terrible battle in desperate need of support, while the Soviet army stood by on the other side of the River Vistula and Britain and the United States sent few supplies and no reinforcements. The Polish Airborne Brigade trained in Britain had been earmarked to help the uprising, but without Soviet co-operation the Allied air forces were unable to drop them on Warsaw. Stas and his fellow commandos felt frustration and rage at their impotence.

Since his demand for a transfer to the armoured division had been refused, Stas slipped away to London next day and went to Polish military headquarters where he asked General Kopanski, his former commander at Tobruk who was now the Chief of General Staff, to transfer him to General Maczek's armoured division. Kopanski, who was always helpful to Stas, gave him a written movement order on the spot, and a few days later he flew to France to join the Polish 10th Dragoons Regiment, a motorised infantry unit at the forefront of the fighting.

On his first evening in France he met his cousin Jas Tarnowski, Andrew's oldest brother, who was Maczek's aide de camp. They had not met since fleeing Poland five years earlier. Jas invited him to Maczek's headquarters, and at dinner somebody asked him if he knew the life expectancy of a dragoon in action. 'I said I didn't have a clue, how could I? And they said, "Just over 20 minutes."'

The First Polish Armoured Division had been fighting in

France for nearly two months and was already covered in battle honours. It was Stas's new regiment that on 19 August had linked up at the town of Chambois with American troops to close the Falaise Gap, trapping up to 50,000 German soldiers in a pocket and bringing the battle of Normandy to a close. The fighting was so fierce, SS troops climbing on top of Polish tanks to drop grenades inside, that the dragoons had lost 254 dead, missing and wounded – twenty-seven per cent of their strength – in their first two weeks of action.

The regiment was in the vanguard of the division when Stas took command of a thirty-man platoon on 1 October 1944, as they were about to cross into Holland after fighting across much of France and Belgium. He and his men went into battle sitting on top of tanks or in open armoured personnel carriers and jumped off to press home their attacks on foot. 'Of course, the tanks were under fire from anti-tank guns,' he said. 'But they were also fired on by machine-guns, which of course the tanks ignored, but we on top of them did not. It was quite a lot of stiff fighting, and the Germans were bloody good soldiers.'

In his first action his platoon took prisoners and Stas was furious to see his men robbing them of their possessions. 'I had my officer's swagger cane, so I sloshed them in the face with it,' he said. Another officer had to persuade him that since his men had risked their lives it was better for them to rob the prisoners than leave them to be robbed by non-combatants at the rear.

As he had at Tobruk and in the Western Desert, Stas did his best to be in the thick of the fighting and make a show of unconcern in the face of danger. Despite his bravado and deliberate risk-taking he survived seven months of hard fighting with barely a scratch, while his thirty-man platoon

The wallet Chouquette sent Stas at Christmas 1941 when he was fighting in the North African desert with the Carpathian Rifle Brigade. Stas kept the wallet, the photograph of Chouquette and me as a baby, and the remains of a rose she gave him, for fifty-seven years.

Stas (centre) in the North African desert with his friend Adam Gorayski (right) and another Polish soldier.

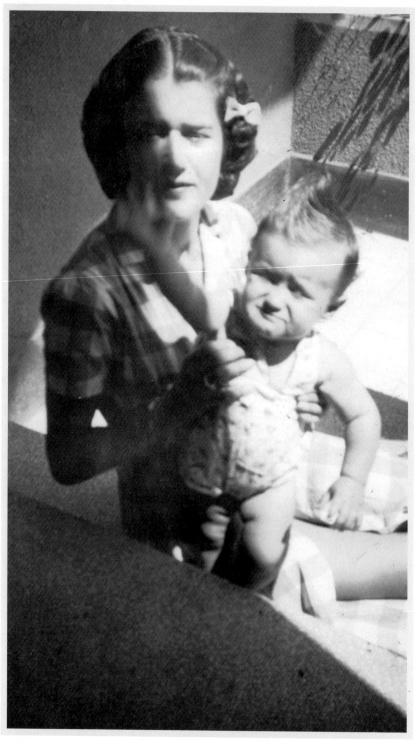

Chouquette with me in Cairo in 1941; I was known as the *gnomek* or little gnome.

Sophie dressed as Scarlett O'Hara for a 'Gone With the Wind' ball in Cairo during the war, a cigarette, as always, in her hand.

After the war. Chouquette with her second husband Malcolm Wolfe Murray at their home at Glenternie, near Peebles, in the Scottish Borders.

Me (centre) on a 1950s skiing trip at Murren, Switzerland, with step-brothers James (right) and Angus Wolfe Murray.

Grouse shooting in Peeblesshire in the 1950s. Chouquette is third from right, back row, beside Angus, who towers above her. I am seated in front, third from right, with my half-sister Tessa first on the right. Our host Alistair Balfour kneels in front, his wife Elizabeth standing beside him.

Stas is London in the 1950s with William (Billy) Stanley Moss, second husband of his sister Sophie, who as a Second World War SOE commando captured a German general on Nazi-occupied Crete; he told the story in his best-selling book *Ill Met by Moonlight*.

Stas with his second wife Ada Lubomirska in the garden of their Ealing home with four of their children, (left to right) Adam, Michal, Iza and Sandra. Soon afterwards, in 1957, Stas left on his fateful return trip to Poland.

Back at Rudnik in 1957, eighteen years after fleeing Poland, Sophie and Stas are warmly welcomed by former employees of Hieronim's estate and their families. They have just finished an open-air banquet offered in defiance of the Communist authorities.

Stas (right) and cousin Jas Tarnowski present the *proporzec* (banner) of seventeenth-century Swedish King Karolus Gustavus to the Polish ambassador in London. The banner was captured at Rudnik during a Swedish invasion of Poland. Stas and his sister Sophie gave it to the Wawel Museum in Krakow in 1957.

The terrible triangle. Ila Straszewska and her lovers, Stas (right) and Jurek, on a hike through the Bieszczady hills of south-eastern Poland in 1972.

Stas looks pensive during a visit to one of the former family castles on my second visit to Poland in 1972.

Stas types away during the 1970s at his freelance translation work in the back garden of his little house in Warsaw.

Rudnik, derelict in 1991, with me (left) and my half-brother Adam. During our visit an old retainer described the scene in 1944 when the Communists expelled Hieronim from Rudnik.

Me with my wife Wafa', sitting on my favourite old love seat at Drwecck 21, the little farmhouse we bought in 2000 in the Mazurian lake district of northern Poland.

lost forty-six dead and wounded, and despite constant reinforcements only four or six men were still on their feet after he led the platoon into its final action of the war. 'Still, my men liked me because I took the same risks as they did. I didn't lead them from behind,' he said.

He was dynamic and imaginative in battle, and an inspirational frontline officer, and within a month of joining the dragoons he had won his second *Krzyz Walecznych* or Cross of Valour during an attack on the Dutch towns of Gilze, Oisterwijk and Rijen. The citation reads:

> At the town of Rijen during a night battle his platoon was surprised by enemy fire from fixed positions. Second Lieutenant Tarnowski quickly overcame the confusion, and thanks to his personal leadership and the fact that he first rushed the enemy with grenades he saved the platoon's position and turned the situation to its advantage and even took prisoners.

He was also a fine shot with a rifle. When it came to shooting Germans he led by example, and he was proud of his prowess. 'I know I killed for certain forty-seven Germans, which is quite a record,' he boasted. 'After the Special Forces training I was an excellent shot. I really was a brilliant shot.'

He remembered a time when his platoon was holding an island on the River Meuse. German troops were on the opposite bank 250 or 300 metres away. His first cousin Stefan Zamoyski came on a visit from division headquarters and said he wanted to do some shooting. Stas gave him a rifle and Stefan took a pot shot at a German soldier hanging out washing. 'The German looked up and shook his fist,' Stas explained. 'So I took the rifle and took a shot, and hit him, like that.'

But Stas was soon in trouble with his superiors. Once again his courage was matched by his arrogance and contempt, and the consequences were disastrous. In the regimental commander Colonel Wladyslaw Zgorzelski, Stas came up against a man as tough and bloody-minded as himself, and the result was a series of rows and a battle of wills that as a junior officer he could not win. Zgorzelski was a courageous soldier decorated with an honorary British DSO and a Polish *Virtuti Militari* for the action at Chambois, where he had been badly wounded. But he was a rigid disciplinarian and a tyrant to his officers. 'He either favoured somebody or he didn't,' one of Stas's ex-comrades said. And he came to hate Stas.

The trouble began soon after the colonel recovered from his wounds and resumed command of the 10th Dragoons in early 1945 when the regiment had reached north-west Germany. Stas was leading a seventy-man armoured reconnaissance patrol along a side road, and the leading troop carriers ran into fire from deadly German 88mm anti-tank guns and what looked like a battalion of troops. He halted the column and reported to regimental headquarters that he could not advance further. After a while he saw the German infantry begin withdrawing, but the anti-tank guns remained, and he reported back to headquarters.

'Send your carriers ahead,' Zgorzelski ordered.

'That's impossible, I know the guns are still there,' Stas retorted.

'It's an order.'

Within minutes of resuming the advance the leading Polish armoured personnel carrier was destroyed by an 88mm shell and Stas was nearly decapitated by another. Luckily, he had got into the last carrier to be able to see what was happening. When he gave the order the carriers advanced as fast as possible, but the Germans opened fire and the first was hit and the three others turned back.

'And that's when I got my helmet blown off my head,' Stas said. 'I felt a shell go just over my head, and the slipstream blew my helmet off. It wasn't the explosion of the shell, just the shell passing over my head.' He immediately ran to the stricken carrier and helped to drag out the wounded and carry them back, receiving a tiny shell splinter in his leg as the German anti-tank guns continued firing. It was his only wound of the war.

Zgorzelski accused him after the engagement of losing one of his carriers. 'Well, it was your bloody orders, you know,' Stas answered furiously. They were already at daggers drawn.

Stas received a recommendation for a third Cross of Valour on 24 April 1945, two weeks before the end of the war, after a tough action in which the dragoons tried to cross a well-defended canal and force the river Leda in the small German town of Potshausen. Three squadrons of dragoons attacked at 9.30 a.m. but met such strong resistance that they only crossed the canal in darkness after ten hours' fighting. They gave up the attempt to push on and cross the river that night. Stas's citation said:

> In the attack on the bridge on the Hault Fehn canal his unit moved forward to the canal and received such heavy fire from three sides that it could neither advance nor retreat. Second Lieutenant Tarnowski, under enemy fire, went up to the forward position and then under cover of smoke grenades rushed the first house, carrying the unit with him and taking three prisoners.

But he never received the decoration, because his relations with Zgorzelski had completely collapsed before the colonel approved it. The critical incident happened just after the dragoons crossed into Germany. They bivouacked for the night beside a wood, and Stas volunteered to take out a patrol to capture prisoners and find out why supplies were not reaching the front line. He returned in the morning with three prisoners, dropped them off at squadron headquarters for interrogation, and went to his tent for a wash. He recalled later:

'As I was shaving I saw this young fellow who hated Germans, he loathed the Germans but he didn't go out and fight in the line, he stayed at squadron headquarters typing on a typewriter. I saw him leading my three prisoners, whom I'd taken personally, along a sandy track with young pines on one side and older ones on the other. And when he reached the wood I saw him turning into the trees.

'I said, "My God." I had a premonition that he was going to shoot my prisoners. So I ran. I just had my belt and revolver but no shirt, and I dashed into the wood and as I saw him he shot the first man. I heard the shot and saw him shoot the first prisoner. So I shouted at him, "You bastard, stop that." And he looked at me and shot the second one. And so, still running, I pulled out my revolver and shot him, running. And of course the third prisoner was kissing me and lying at my feet, so I gave him a kick, got him back to squadron headquarters and told the squadron commander Captain Zbigniew Bojanowski that I'd just shot this soldier.

'"Oh my God, why?" '

Stas told him.

'Well, you were quite right to do so, but you'd better report it to Colonel Zgorzelski,' the captain said.

He went back to regimental HQ and reported. Zgorzelski was furious. 'You will be court martialled,' he said.

'I saluted, turned and walked out,' Stas continued, 'banging the door as hard as I could. But on the very next day the brigade commander Colonel Skibinski issued orders that if he saw anybody shooting prisoners he would personally kill him. So that let me out . . . But if it hadn't been for that I would have been court-martialled by Zgorzelski.'

I can't help being proud of Stas for that. How many men would have risked killing one of their own men and being court-martialled to save captive Germans? The Polish troops in the West were deeply demoralised by early 1945, and killings of German prisoners did occur. The troops knew about the Nazi atrocities and death camps in Poland, and they also knew that Poland was doomed by the Yalta Agreement. The United States and Britain had agreed to leave Poland and most of eastern and central Europe under Stalin's control after the war, without consulting the Polish government-in-exile or the 250,000 Polish servicemen fighting with the Allies, and despite knowing of the bloodthirsty treatment Stalin had dealt out to Poland and the Poles at the start of the war.

The Polish troops in the West knew after Yalta that by continuing to fight the Germans they were no longer fighting for Poland's freedom but were helping Stalin to take over their country. They knew their country would be under Soviet tyranny after the war. Despite all the sacrifices they had made, and all the comrades they had lost, there would be no free Poland for them to return to after the war. They had every reason to question what they were fighting for as the war in Europe drew to a close. 'Why die for Stalin?' asked German propaganda leaflets written in Polish that troopers in Stas's regiment found. 'By dying for Stalin your soldiers are not dying for democracy, they are dying for the establishment of communism and Stalinist tyranny throughout the world . . . they are not dying to preserve the integrity of small nations but they are dying so that Poland shall be a Soviet state.' It was all true. The soldiers of the Polish Second Corps in Italy were so angry and demoralised by the betrayal of the Yalta agreement that their commander General Wladyslaw Anders asked the Allies to withdraw his men from battle. In the end he and his men soldiered on loyally. But why not kill as many Germans as they could while the war lasted?

Stas believed his shooting of the Pole and the confrontation with Zgorzelski that followed cost him the award of the *Virtuti Militari*, the highest Polish decoration for valour, which he desperately coveted, and the Cross of Valour he had won at the Hault Fehn canal. He believed he deserved to be decorated with the *Virtuti Militari* for his part in an engagement on the river Leda at Potshausen on 26 April 1945. It was to be the dragoons' last major engagement of the war, and before they went into action it was announced that General Maczek would personally decorate the officer who distinguished himself most on the battlefield with the *Virtuti Militari*.

Facing the dragoons across the river was a German criminal battalion recruited from men released from jail and sent to the most dangerous positions on the front. They were among the toughest soldiers Germany had. Stas was in the lead platoon when the attack began. The first two flimsy canvas boatloads of dragoons were sunk by machine-gun and mortar fire. When the Poles managed to win a toe-hold on the far bank, the Germans pinned them down with heavy fire from strongly entrenched positions. The situation looked hopeless until Stas suggested bringing armoured carriers with flame-throwers across the river to winkle out the Germans.

'I was told that no carriers could cross that river,' he said. 'So I said, "I'll find a crossing. I'll get them over. Tell the artillery to lay down a smokescreen beyond me so that the Germans can't see what's happening." And that's what was done. I got the carriers over, and they went into action. We cleared the Germans out and captured the position. We lost quite a few people, of course. After the action I had five men left out of my platoon, two of them slightly wounded.'

During the fighting he tended a wounded young soldier from his platoon who had a gaping hole in his chest. When he radioed for stretcher-bearers they answered that they could not get to the front line. 'So I went back across the river, saw the regimental second-in-command sitting in a ditch and said a few sharp words to him. I ran all the way back to regimental HQ, got some stretcher bearers and forced them at pistol point to come back over the river. I told them I would shoot them if they didn't come, and I bloody well would have done so. I saved the fellow's life, and he thanked me afterwards.'

He expected to receive the *Virtuti Militari* for taking the carriers across the river and turning the tide of battle. 'After the action all the other officers in the regiment and all the men in our squadron congratulated me,' Stas said. But it was a senior officer who received the coveted decoration. Stas said the officer had crossed the river at almost the same time as him but then dug a hole in the ground and stayed in it until Stas brought over the carriers and broke the German resistance. 'Then he got out of his hole and started shouting, "On, on, on." But he'd done nothing.'

Stas was furious and bitterly disappointed, and he couldn't help showing his bitterness when the officer was decorated. 'All the officers congratulated him. When it came to my turn

I said, "I congratulate you, but in your place I wouldn't have accepted it."

' "Why is that?"

' "Because I think you don't deserve it in the least", and I turned and walked away. Colonel Zgorzelski called me in after that and asked if I criticised decorations, and I said, "Yes."

' "How dare you," the colonel said. "What I do from above you destroy from below."

' "I don't understand you," I replied. "In my family we still remember today when my great-grandfather won the Golden *Virtuti Militari*. It's a decoration that you either deserve or you don't. You don't arrange things with decorations." '

Zgorzelski apparently tried to placate him by awarding him his third Cross of Valour for the 24 April action, but Stas would not have it. He lost his temper. 'You can hang your medal on my arse,' he told Zgorzelski in front of the officers, and Zgorzelski decided on the spot to dismiss him from the regiment. Stas received none of the campaign medals awarded to the dragoons.

Before leaving the regiment Stas was in the first Polish vehicle to enter the naval part of Willelmshaven just before the German surrender. He got hold of a German.

'You must get me an eight-cylinder Mercedes. Open car.'

'But sir, I don't know where to find a car like that,' the frightened German replied. 'I can get you a six-cylinder, almost new, it's very good.' Stas handed over 100 German occupation marks and drove back to the dragoons' head-quarters in a splendid Mercedes Benz open tourer. He was then sent to the rear for transfer to an infantry unit.

As he waited at the rear, he met his cousin Stefan Zamoyski.

'Good God, Stas, what are you doing here?' Stefan asked.

Stas told the story. Stefan repeated it to Jas Tarnowski who relayed it to General Maczek. The general called Stas in. 'Of course, this is nonsense,' Maczek said, 'but you must understand that Colonel Zgorzelski is in command of the regiment and you're only in command of a platoon. I can't dismiss the regimental commander, but you can pick any of the armoured regiments you wish to join.'

Stas thanked the general politely, but said: 'No sir, I'd like to be dismissed and allowed to leave. I want to go to Egypt.' He had decided not to return to Poland after the war and planned to ask Prince Youssef to lend him money to buy a farm in Kenya.

General Maczek agreed, and on 25 June Stas was transferred to the Polish artillery training centre in England, and from July 1945 he was granted leave without pay.

It was the end of his war.

CHAPTER TWENTY-TWO

The Scarlet Plague

*E*arly in 1944, while Stas was still training as a commando in England, the Soviet army advanced into pre-war Polish territory after its great victories at Stalingrad and Kursk and began driving the German army westwards across the country. But rather than being welcomed as liberators, the Red Army struck fear into the hearts of Poles. They knew that the coming of the Russians meant there would be no restoration of an independent Poland and no democracy when the war ended.

Bitterness and disillusion ran deep. A Home Army soldier captured the misery in Polish hearts in a few lines of poetry:

> We're waiting for you, O scarlet plague
> To save us from the Black Death:
> Waiting for a salvation
> To be welcomed with disgust
> By a country that's already been hanged and quartered.[1]

The fears were not misplaced. Stalinist tyranny replaced Hitlerian brutalism. Once again Poland's historic eastern territories and millions of her people were absorbed into the Soviet Union and subjected to a murderous regime. The sacrifices of hundreds of thousands of Poles who had fought the Nazis, and of millions who had died, were largely in vain. Poland's reward for being the first ally of Britain and France and the first to stand and fight Hitler, for fighting at home and abroad for six years, and for having sacrificed more of her people than any other country in proportion to her population, was abandonment to a tyrant who unleashed a bloody repression even before the war ended.

As the Red Army advanced, Home Army units rose to drive out the Germans, planning to welcome the Soviets and fight on by their side. The Red Army rounded them up and arrested them as 'fascists'. Some got a bullet in the back of the head, some were imprisoned and some sent to the Gulag. Others were forced into a new Polish Communist army. In every region the Red Army occupied, NKVD secret police troops and their Polish Communist satraps followed and hunted down Home Army fighters and independent, democratic and non-Communist Poles.

When the Home Army began the Warsaw Rising against the Nazis on 1 August 1944, the Soviet forces halted for six months on the far side of the River Vistula and watched as SS troops slaughtered 250,000 people, then levelled what remained of the city. When the Russians entered the ruins in January 1945, they found a moonscape like Hiroshima after the atom bomb, whole sectors mass tombs. For the Poles, the Communist takeover that followed was the worst possible outcome of the war, the ultimate betrayal. Anyone who could fled to the West.

Landowners and aristocrats like Hieronim and Wanda knew that what awaited them was at the very least dispossession and more likely imprisonment, deportation to Siberia or death. But neither Hieronim nor Wanda fled. They had treated their people decently and done their best to protect them, and they stayed with them as the unwelcome liberators approached.

Wanda was at Zaleze with Artur, who was now fourteen,

her companion Tadeusz Strugalski, and her French companion Madame Rolland when the Soviet Army arrived in the
neighbourhood at the end of July 1944. The sounds of battle
were already close on the morning of 31 July when a German
armoured car drove up to the house and an officer leaned out
of the window.

'Why aren't you fleeing west?' he shouted to Wanda.

She replied in her matter-of-fact tone. 'I didn't run away
when you lot came, so I am not going to flee when you leave.'

'Do you know what is coming? It's an absolute rabble,
barbarian hordes, you don't know what will happen to you.'

'Well, we coped with you people, so we shall cope with
them, too.'

The Germans drove off.

Not long afterwards Russian soldiers trotted past on a
horse-drawn cart. But the Soviet summer offensive had run its
course and was slowing to a halt after reaching central Poland.
That night there was a German counter-attack and a fierce
bombardment and a Russian infantry charge round the house.
They heard more fighting around the city of Rzeszow to the
west. After another couple of days the Soviet army drove the
Germans out and the front stabilised. The offensive halted
and Russian soldiers arrived at the estate.

The first to come was a general and his staff. Wanda invited
them in, just as she had offered German officers a cup of tea in
September 1939. It was the most sensible way to treat
dangerous newcomers. Besides, Wanda liked Russians, and she
had a way of getting on with people. Although the Poles feared
and hated Tsarist imperialism and Soviet Communism, and
looked down on the Russians as a backward people historically
incapable of freedom, they still felt an affinity with them. They
loved the Russians' warmth and humanity, their humour and

earthy vigour, and their deeply sentimental songs and wild dances. Russians and Poles were both Slavs, after all. So Wanda fed the general and his officers, poured them tea and vodka, and asked them to sing. The house resounded with wonderful old Russian songs. Beautiful voices, beautiful songs, Artur remembered, like an ancient choir.

The general slept and moved on, leaving a note for the troops who would follow that the lady of the house was friendly and was to be well treated. But the next wave of soldiers looked blankly at it as they took over the house. Exhausted men sprawled everywhere. Artur found two asleep on his bed. He saw another standing in the drawing room looking at horse whips and riding crops decorating the walls, and heard him mutter: 'Aha, that's what these Polish aristocrats use to whip the servants and the people.' Another soldier knelt down and washed his face in a toilet bowl and cursed the vicious aristocracy when he pulled the chain and got splashed with water.

Trucks parked in the farmyard and Artur filched submachine-gun magazines and took them under his shirt to Bronek the blacksmith, a former Polish army sergeant who was in the Home Army. But he realised the times were changing when village boys began digging potatoes and cutting hay without Wanda's permission. When he tried to stop them they jeered at him: 'We're in charge now. Your time is over.'

The Red Army had not been at Zaleze long when NKVD agents and Polish Communist police descended on the estate to hunt for evidence of Home Army activity. Artur was in the act of catching a revolver Madame Rolland had thrown out of a window for him to hide when a Polish policeman appeared round the corner of the house. 'Hands up,' he shouted, cocking his rifle and marching Artur inside. He was only saved from arrest by a Home Army fighter who had infiltrated the police. Arthur heard someone whisper in his ear '*Jestem Zemsta*', 'I am Vengeance' – the *nom de guerre* of an underground fighter he knew of. Zemsta had a shouting match with the policeman and Artur was released.

But not for long. It was one of the ironies of being Polish at the end of the Second World War that people who had risked their lives in the anti-Nazi resistance were flung into jail as 'enemies of the people' by the Communists. Wanda and Artur, who had been a local courier for the Home Army, were arrested after a land-reform decree in mid-October 1944 ordered the confiscation of properties over fifty hectares.

A truckload of People's Militia, as the new police were called, drove up to the house. Artur only had time to grab a sweater before he and Wanda were bundled in and driven away. Servant girls sobbed as they waved goodbye, and Madame Rolland was weeping. '*Priez Dieu*', 'Pray to God', she shouted.

Artur looked out of the back of the truck over the heads of the policemen for a last glimpse of the white walls of the house in which he had lived for six years. 'As those dear walls vanished I felt that a chapter had closed,' he wrote later. 'The chill autumn wind tore the leaves from the linden trees and I watched them pirouetting fitfully above the bleak fields and thought that the brown leaves, spinning desultorily at the whim of the wind, held a sinister message for us.'

For the crime of being landowners and aristocrats suspected of having helped the Home Army they were thrown into an underground cell at Rzeszow police headquarters where not long before the Gestapo had interrogated and tortured Home Army prisoners. The cell was dark and packed with more than a hundred people, mostly landowners and aristocrats. There was barely room to sit, let alone lie down, and they stood or squatted on the concrete floor. The rotting carcass of a skinned horse lay in a pool of blood in a corner, apparently intended to reduce them to a state of humiliation. 'Since they did not give us any food, the feeling amongst us was that they were waiting until we were so hungry that we would eat that raw, stinking flesh,' Artur recalled. Nobody did.

After three days they received a filthy bucket of watery potato soup. On the fifth day interrogations began, and afterwards Wanda and Artur were moved to a small, freezing cell with nine other people. The floor was covered with a thin layer of straw infested with vermin. Cockroaches scuttled over their faces as they lay huddled together for warmth. There was no toilet bucket, and a corner of the cell was awash with a spreading pool of urine and faeces.

After a few days, they were marched out one by one and interrogated by a ginger-haired NKVD bully flanked by photographs of Stalin and the Soviet-nominated provisional government. He demanded the names of their 'fascist' contacts, making clear that he meant Polish anti-Communists, not German Nazis. 'Our prospects remained desperately bleak,' Artur remembered. 'A million of our countrymen had been sent to Siberia by the Russians in the earlier part of the war. Plenty more were on their way to join them now. It seemed almost inevitable that we should join them.'

But they were saved by the prison cook, who had been in the underground and learned of their Home Army activity. She got them assigned to peel potatoes in the kitchen and used her pretty teenage daughter, who had captured the heart of the prison warden, to have them released. The warden was a thin, cold, sadistic bully, but the cook told the girl to smile and give him hope. When she had won his confidence she told him she and her mother knew Wanda and Artur well and could vouch that they were good people who should be released.

It was never said quite how sweetly the girl smiled, but within forty-eight hours the warden summoned Wanda and Artur and released them with a warning never to speak about their experience in prison. They emerged at the end of November after five weeks in jail with slips of paper stating that Wanda and Artur Tarnawski – their names misspelt – were returning home after being released from jail.

But as dispossessed landowners they were forbidden to return to Zaleze, and since Wanda feared they might be arrested again they hid on the outskirts of Rzeszow in the home of Pan Parecki, a butcher who had bought meat from the estate. Artur was so infested with lice when they arrived that he had to soak his head in petrol. They stayed for two weeks until they were warned one evening that the militia were coming to arrest them. They left within minutes, and carrying their possessions in bundles wrapped in cloths, they headed east through the night, walking forty kilometres past Zaleze and through the little town of Lancut until they reached Przeworsk, another small town further east.

They took refuge in a cottage owned by two young underground fighters named Jan and Helena. A Soviet officer was living in the room next to them, but he was polite and gave them no trouble. But in late December, when they had been there a couple of weeks and heavy snow lay on the ground, Jan came home one evening from his work at a brewery white faced and shaking with fright. He said militiamen had surrounded the cottage. It could only mean they were about to be arrested again.

Wanda's abiding terror was of being sent to Siberia, the vast, frozen wasteland thousands of kilometres to the east where generations of Polish patriots had been consigned by Tsarist and Soviet occupiers to a living death. When they got out of the jail in Rzeszow she had made Artur promise they would never let themselves be taken alive again. She was determined to die rather than be captured. Now that the moment had come she prepared calmly. Out of her cloth-wrapped bundle of possessions she took a British hand grenade and two glass phials of cyanide. She put the cyanide and the grenade on the table covered with an immaculate white cloth and poured two small glasses of vodka. Then they sat at the table and waited for the militia to burst in. Their plan was to bite the cyanide and swallow it, gulp down the vodka, and detonate the hand grenade.

'We waited for what seemed an eternity, without uttering a word,' Artur remembered. 'Nobody stirred, it was as though the silence of death had descended. I stared at the five objects on the spotless tablecloth.'

Nothing happened. Hours passed. Jan came back into the room and said he was going outside to check if the militia were still there. When he returned and said they had gone, Artur felt a sense of utter release he remembered all his life. Jan went out again before dawn to find out what had happened. He learned that the militia had come to arrest two young women, couriers for the underground, who lived in the next house. They had surrounded the whole district to make sure they could not escape.

That scene of the hunted mother and her teenage son seated at a table ready to swallow cyanide and vodka and blow themselves up is as chilling as any nineteenth-century painting of wretched columns of Polish insurgents trudging to Siberia after futile uprisings against Tsarist rule. Just like her daughter Sophie, defying the Germans in Alexandria, Wanda demonstrated indomitable courage and strength of will as she waited erect and motionless without a flicker of emotion for the militia to burst in.

They fled that morning, moving deep into the woods to a filthy hut packed with Home Army fugitives. Tadeusz joined them and they travelled to Krakow late in January 1945, shortly after the city was taken by the Soviet army. They stayed in Krakow ten months, living apart under assumed names, avoiding regular work and relatives, and frequently changing lodgings. Artur lived in a succession of lice-infested rooms, scratching endlessly by night and squashing blood-filled bugs by day. They ate dry bread and boiled potatoes and counted themselves lucky not to starve.

A messenger came from Madame Rolland in the spring with news that she was living in a small room at Zaleze, receiving a little food from people on the estate and giving French lessons to support herself. Although frail and in her late sixties, she walked three kilometres and back into town along a rutted, muddy road three times a week. The messenger handed Artur a small wad of money with a message.

'I received it in both hands as if it were something holy, which indeed I felt it to be,' Artur said. He considered Madame Rolland a second mother, and could not bring himself to spend her hard-earned money. Although he was often very hungry, the thought of buying food with money she had earned with such sacrifice gave him anxiety attacks.

Artur nearly died of typhoid that spring after eating unwashed fruit from a street stall. Stricken with diarrhoea and fever, he grew so weak that he could not even turn over in bed or raise an arm, and could barely speak. Unable to go to hospital for fear of discovery, he got worse and worse until finally Wanda brought a priest to give him the Last Rites. He received the sacrament. The crisis passed. But it was nearly another month before he could get out of bed and crawl to the chamber pot.

After he recovered Wanda decided to leave Poland. Somehow, she obtained French passports for herself, Artur and Tadeusz, and scraped together money to buy clandestine passages to the West. In November 1945, carrying her cloth bundle and a dilapidated suitcase, Wanda and Artur boarded a cattle wagon at Krakow railway station with sixty other Poles posing as foreigners being repatriated to France and Italy. The wagon was locked from outside and the train moved off and rolled slowly towards the Czechoslovak border. A rumour spread among the fugitives that Polish frontier guards had recently caught a similar transport and lined the escapees against a wall and shot them. But the journey was uneventful and at seven a.m. next morning they crossed into Czechoslovakia after a twenty-hour journey. At Prague they changed trains, and a week later they reached the American-occupied sector of Germany. They were free.

'Suddenly a flood of pent-up tension was released, and we went almost mad with excitement,' Artur recalled. 'Everyone danced, cried, sang and laughed. We were free at last, after more than six crazy years of crushing terror, free to walk, eat, sleep, free to live without the fear of hunted animals.'

CHAPTER TWENTY-THREE

Dispossession

ieronim also refused to leave when the Soviet army approached in July 1944. Jadzia Hass'a Mach, the daughter of the faithful old butler, saw the Germans asking him to go with them as they packed up to flee Rudnik. They pressed him, telling him the Russians were close, and as they got into their cars they asked him again to get in with them. He hesitated, nervously trying to make up his mind. He was alone. What was there to stay for at Rudnik? But finally he said, 'No, no, I will not go. I'm not leaving yet.' With that, the Germans drove off and silence fell over Rudnik.

Why should he have left with the Germans? How could he have? No matter how fearsome the Soviets might be, how could a decent Pole get into a car and flee with Germans who for five years had treated the people of Rudnik with pitiless barbarity? The shame would have been too great. He may have feared the Soviets and he may have had nothing to stay for at Rudnik, but he could not leave with the Germans.

Jadzia remembered the havoc when the Soviet Army arrived. 'They were bandits. They were savages. They didn't even know what toothpaste was, and they told the Poles, "You shall dance as we play."'

The soldiers gathered everyone at the mansion and officers brought girls and vodka and home-made alcohol and partied in Hieronim's home for days. Captains and majors took local girls and sometimes gave them bits of Hieronim's furniture as presents.

Hieronim lived on at the mansion for nearly three months amid chaos and terror as the Soviet troops behaved like primitives. I do not know how he survived. He sent a guarded letter to Sophie in Cairo describing what was happening, writing that the soldiers used the baths in the mansion as toilets and filled them to the brim with urine and excrement. 'He said there were plenty of toilets in the house, so he couldn't understand why they did it in the bath,' Stas said.

Soldiers banged on the door at the home of Antoni Podstawek, Hieronim's under-footman, demanding vodka. Antoni, who had a beautiful young daughter, knew they were raping women wherever they went. He refused to open and they fired through the door and shot him in the arm.

Hieronim had managed to do one thing just before the Soviet army arrived in an effort to protect the family's interests. Knowing that the Communists planned to confiscate properties of more than 50 hectares, he went to the notary public in the nearby town of Nisko and made out deeds giving 50 hectares of land to each of those dearest to him: to Sophie, his sister Jadzia, her husband Roman Bninski, their son Wacek and me, but not to Stas.

The end came, as it did for Wanda and Artur, on an autumn day in October 1944, when a swarm of officials and police descended on Rudnik without warning and called the employees to a meeting. There were Communist Party officials and a political commissar, UB (*Urząd Bezpieczeństwa*) security policemen, People's Militia (civil police) and district councillors. They gathered the employees in the estate office: twelve or fourteen stable boys and grooms, farm hands and servants, the butler, the housekeeper, the administrator and the gardener, more than thirty people in all. Hieronim was also summoned. He stood a little apart.

The officials told the employees there would be reforms and the land would be divided amongst them. A UB security policeman named Rodzen spoke next. 'Has this count been good to you? Is he a good man?' he asked the employees. He repeated the question to everybody, to the stable boys, the house servants, to everybody present. But nobody answered. Nobody. Not one. They were afraid to speak out.

When Rodzen finished there was silence. The officials and police made notes and whispered to each other. Then they gathered up the estate records and account books while Rodzen and the political commissar went into a back office alone to talk. When they emerged Rodzen told Hieronim that he had to leave Rudnik. Hieronim argued, until Rodzen gave him a direct order: 'You will now leave, according to the law . . . You must go from here and you are not allowed to remain in this district.'

Hieronim was distraught, wringing his hands, pulling at his moustache. He was weeping, but he went up to each of his employees to shake hands and say goodbye. 'He was very emotional, worn out, broken down,' Jadzia remembered. 'He was destroyed and very nervous. He kept twisting his moustache nervously. He said goodbye to all of us. Some of the servants kissed his hand. Most of the workers came up to say goodbye, the ones that liked him, but not everyone did. The two militiamen from Kopki village were so false in what they did. They even kissed his hand. I just said goodbye. I was choking on my tears.' Jadzia heard Hieronim tell Pan Okon, the estate administrator: 'Take the land because we will be able to get it back from you quicker. Don't let strangers take the land.'

Hieronim walked slowly out of the estate office followed by the police and officials. The silent crowd of employees came on behind. He walked down the dirt road to the ornamental lakes and up the slope towards the mansion, passing the wooden chapel among the trees where Sophie and Andrew had been married. A squadron of People's Militia in greyish-blue uniforms was drawn up in front of the mansion, and a horse and cart stood waiting at the door. Hieronim walked past them into the house to collect clothes and supplies. The employees gathered outside.

He was only allowed to take essentials. He took a few mattresses, two or three suitcases, some linen and clothing. Nothing more. The militia helped him carry them to the cart.

He climbed in. Two farm workers named Piotr and Marian got on to drive him away. The house servants, stable boys, grooms, clerks, gardeners and farmhands stood on one side. The militiamen, security police and Communist officials stood apart. Piotr shook the reins, the cart moved away on the dirt road that winds down the slope to the right of the house. The horse trotted past the chapel, past the lakes and up past the estate office and the tall wooden cross that marked the mass grave of 1914. Reaching the main road at the top of the slope, it turned south and disappeared from sight. The militia dispersed the crowd of people, telling them to go away and not gather together, and locked the mansion.

Hieronim's expulsion from Rudnik was the last of the many flights and expulsions the family suffered during the twentieth century, and it is the one from which we have never fully recovered. Wars and invasions eventually pass, peace returns, survivors come home, and what was destroyed may with time be rebuilt. But in 1944 Hieronim was cast out from Polish society. He and landowners like him all over Poland were dispossessed and branded as parasites and enemies of the people. Some were jailed or sent to the Soviet Gulag. When the war ended and reconstruction began there was no place for them in the new Communist society. Those who did not flee the country remained as impoverished relics of a different age, second-class citizens at best, they and their children discriminated against in all things.

The farm cart that carried Hieronim away like some revolutionary tumbril cut him off from the world he had known with the finality of the guillotine. He sat weeping in the bottom of the cart as the two farm workers drove him into the gathering dusk, past the forests and meadows he loved and would never see again. 'Everybody said Piotr and Marian robbed the count on the road,' Jadzia said later. 'They even took what little he had, whatever he had left with him. That's what people here said. Maybe it's just a story. Maybe it's not true. I don't know.'

Hieronim sought shelter with the Catholic Church. Piotr and Marian drove him seventy kilometres to the town of Lancut, where he asked the parish priest for a bed. The priest, Father Antoni Doszynski, knew Hieronim well. He had been the parish priest at Rudnik, and they had worked together to rebuild the parish church after the Great War. He had taught Sophie and Stas catechism on Sundays and lunched afterwards at the mansion with Hieronim and Wanda. But it was a time of revolution and emerging conflict between the Catholic Church and the Communist regimes taking over in central and eastern Europe. It would soon become dangerous for even church leaders to defy the Communists, let alone rural parish priests. Cardinals at the head of national churches would be arrested and imprisoned or confined. For less prominent people and humble parish priests it was easy to be shot or sent to the Gulag. So Father Antoni turned Hieronim away. It was an understandable decision, but even so, it is hard for members of my family to think of that sad night without a terrible sense of shock and betrayal.

The horses trotted on into the darkness. I do not know where they slept that night, but they must have headed west, because Hieronim eventually found refuge at Gora Ropczycka, the pre-war property of Sophie and Andrew. Franek Pazdan, Andrew's former gun bearer and gamekeeper, took him in, although he lived in a tiny wooden house with only two rooms. He and his wife squeezed into one room with their three sons and gave the other to Hieronim. He stayed all winter, and they nursed him for months when he caught pneumonia. After he recovered a little he began walking up the hill each morning to Mass in the church behind the manor house where Sophie and Andrew had lived. He walked past the graveyard where their son Andrew, his first grandson, was buried. The Pazdans would have been in danger if the authorities discovered that they were sheltering a former landowner, but they did not stop Hieronim from going to church. The whole village kept secret the identity of the homeless count in their midst.

He was still weak and had barely recovered from pneumonia when, probably in late February or early March 1945, he left for Krakow. When he got there he received another terrible blow: The Szlak, the splendid mansion in which he was born and lived for many years, had burned down. Hieronim's beloved nephew Wacek, who had narrowly escaped death in the Warsaw Uprising, arrived in Krakow in January 1945 to find the massive stone walls still smouldering, the only part of the building to survive.

Krakow had escaped the terrible destruction of Warsaw and many other Polish towns and cities because the Soviet Army had advanced so fast across Poland after launching its offensive in January 1945 that the Germans had no time to defend the city or carry out Hitler's orders to destroy it. But once again misfortune had sought out Hieronim. The Szlak was one of only two buildings in Krakow that were destroyed throughout the war. The other, curiously, was the *Resursa Krakowska* or Krakow Club where his father Professor Stanislaw Tarnowski had attended Thursday luncheons given in his honour by conservative intellectuals at the turn of the century.

The Szlak had caught fire by accident the day after Soviet troops captured the city. The troops commandeered an old imperial Austrian barracks across the street, and since the mansion had been the headquarters of the Hitler Youth for the *General Gouvernement,* they and the inhabitants thought its huge cellars were full of supplies. On 19 January 1945, soldiers and local people went in to look. 'The Soviet soldiers and some inhabitants started to loot,' Wacek said. 'Somebody was smoking a cigarette and threw it away, or threw away a lighted match, and so the Szlak burned down. Once the fire started it just burned. Nobody tried to save the house. It was such chaos then that there was no fire station and no fire service.'

Devastated by the news and still weak, Hieronim went to live in a small first-floor apartment with Wacek's sister and father. He shared a bedroom with his brother-in-law Roman. When Wacek saw him he was in a terrible state, exhausted and crushed by all that had happened as the war drew to a close. He spent at least a month after his arrival in Krakow slowly recovering his strength, without leaving the apartment. He did not want to see the ruins of the Szlak where he had been born.

That summer, he and Wacek arranged for his father's papers to be donated to the Jagiellonian University and the

Polish Academy of Science. He deposited the Szlak furniture and valuables, which had been in the safe keeping of relatives, at the National Museum to avoid pillaging by the Soviets. He also offered the Szlak to the University in the hope it would restore the building.

But before that was settled he fell ill with pneumonia again. All the losses and sufferings of the family seem to have settled upon his head. By the time the war ended he was sick, penniless and broken-hearted, worn out and old beyond his years, living in a cramped Krakow apartment, his properties confiscated, his childhood home destroyed. A photograph from 1945 shows him grey-haired and exhausted. For the first time he is wearing a neatly clipped beard, but it is white, and his face is long and drawn with fatigue. It has the solemn, mask-like appearance of a deeply wounded man trying to hide his sufferings.

He took to his bed in the tiny flat, cared for by his niece Jadzia, who was a nurse. He weakened rapidly, and it was already clear that the end was approaching when Wacek received a message that Wanda was in Krakow and wanted to know how he was. Wacek went to see her and when he described Hieronim's condition she asked to visit him. Wacek told Hieronim, who thought it over and said: 'Well, all right, let's get it over with.'

Hieronim was in bed when she came. She was deeply moved and shocked by what she saw. He was conscious but motionless with a look of pain and indifference on his face, evidently reluctant to see her. They had said nothing to each other when Wacek left the room. He waited in the next room for about an hour before Wanda opened the door.

Hieronim was very weak and tired after the meeting, and needed to rest. Wacek left the apartment with Wanda and walked a short way with her. She seemed extremely happy, but she was so moved that she could not speak. When Wacek got back he found Hieronim very tired, but instead of pain and indifference there was something like happiness on his face. He thanked him for bringing Wanda, and Wacek believed that the meeting had brought some sort of reconciliation between the couple. Wanda returned with Artur a day or two later. This time Hieronim could only manage a few minutes. Wanda seemed happy with the meeting, but Artur, who was fifteen, did not seem to realise what was going on nor why he had come.

Hieronim faded fast in late October and prepared for death. At one point he felt momentarily better and joked that Jadzia and her sister Roza were caring for him too well: '*Chciałem spokojnie umrzeć, ale te baby mi nie dały,*' he said. 'I wanted to die quietly and those girls wouldn't let me.'

He died on 31 October 1945, aged sixty-one. Barred from taking his body to Rudnik for burial, his old friend Karol Tarnowski, who had led Wanda to the altar on their wedding day in 1914, arranged for him to be buried in his own family's mausoleum in Krakow. Preparing the body for burial, Hieronim's niece Jadzia looked for a memento from Rudnik to put in the coffin. The only thing he had brought with him was a set of mounted wild boar tusks from Rudnik, which she buried with him.

Stas had sent Hieronim a letter after the war ended, inviting him to England, saying that although he was penniless they would at least be together, and he would earn a living somehow. It was a gesture of reconciliation after a lifetime of friction, but Hieronim died before he could reply. In late October 1945, Stas visited Downside, his former school, looking for a job. While he was there, one of the

Benedictine monks he had known when they were at the school together got him talking about his war experiences, and suggested afterwards that Stas should confess his sins and receive absolution. But Stas had enjoyed his wartime adventures and had stopped going to confession and receiving Holy Communion because he knew he was willingly going to commit the same sins again. He did not want to behave hypocritically by taking the sacraments after each affair just because he was afraid of dying in the next battle. So he refused the monk's offer.

But the monk insisted. 'He said, 'Well, you've just told me everything, so you might as well receive absolution.' So I did, and next morning, I served at Mass and went to Holy Communion, and that was the day my father died. It was quite an extraordinary thing.'

I never met my grandfather Hieronim, but I know that whenever he wrote to Stas after my birth he ended his letters with an affectionate word for me, his only living grandchild. Many years later I was given the deed of gift he made out to me in 1944. It is one of the few physical links I have with my grandfather, the only thing he left directly to me. It was signed and stamped by the Nisko notary on 25 July 1944, and the Nisko judge signed it on 4 September, when the Soviet army was already at Rudnik. It granted me six plots of land in the Kopki district of the estate. They were named as 'Fans with meadow, seven hectares; Flats, 12 hectares; Wedge with meadow, six hectares; At the Dog's House, 13 hectares; Sections six and seven, five hectares; Pastures, seven hectares'.

I never received the land, of course, and I have not tried to claim it since Poland threw off Communism in 1989 and became a democracy. The Communists were too clever in 1944. They knew perfectly well that landowners would try to get around the land reforms, so they declared invalid all gifts of land made since the start of the war. By the time I received the deed nearly fifty years later I was told that no one survived at Rudnik who could identify the plots by their pre-war names, since Hieronim had not included map references. It's a pity, perhaps, as it might have been nice to recover the land he left me and maybe build a cottage in the Rudnik forests. But the post-Communist governments have done no favours for former landowners, and it has been impossible to recover any of the confiscated land.

CHAPTER TWENTY-FOUR

Smuggler

*L*ike many others who took to the war as a great adventure, Stas was unable to settle down once it ended. There was no question in his mind of returning to Poland under Stalinism. He knew the fate that awaited former aristocrats and landowners who had fought in the West. 'I should have probably gone east to Siberia. I should think so,' he said. But he remained a Pole at heart and found it hard to accept England as his home.

Switching from a soldier's life of adventure to the hard grind of post-war civilian life, he suddenly found himself a penniless nobody in London. Britain was exhausted and impoverished. Life was grey, drab and hard. The food was bad, rationing was strict, pay was poor and jobs offered little prospect of improvement. Stas, of all people, was the least suited to settling down in post-war Britain.

If the opportunities Britain offered seemed unattractive, its welcome was also fading. The popularity the Poles had enjoyed during the early years of the war fell away when tens of thousands of Polish ex-servicemen decided to stay on, flooding the crowded job market. The political welcome the Poles had enjoyed had also been whittled away since Stalin became Britain's principal ally against Hitler in eastern Europe. By the end of the war the Polish government-in-exile in London was an inconvenience to Britain, with its awkward demands for a democratic and independent Poland, and its embarrassing protests about the Stalinist terror. Soon after the war ended, Britain withdrew diplomatic recognition from the government-in-exile and established relations with Stalin's puppets in Warsaw. At the same time, Clement Attlee, the socialist who succeeded Winston Churchill as prime minister, tried to persuade demobilised Polish troops to return home. He had caught the mood of Britain, enamoured as it was of 'Uncle Joe' Stalin. 'Poles go home' was scrawled on walls in British cities, and insults were shouted in the streets.

Stas felt the betrayal deeply and needed little encouragement to leave Britain. Having made no effort at university before the war, he lacked qualifications for an office job and had neither the enthusiasm nor the temperament to start at the bottom of the ladder and work his way up. Instead of job-hunting in London he set his heart on living somewhere with beauty, sunshine and fun, somewhere like South Africa, where he had spent happy weeks during the break on the voyage to Britain. Now demobbed, Stas wanted to go back to Egypt and ask the kindly and generous Prince Youssef Kamal ed-Dine, Sophie and Chouquette's benefactor, to lend him money to buy a farm in the White Highlands of Kenya. He began scrabbling the money together for the journey.

He was so fixed on making a new life outside Britain that when one of his aristocratic English friends, the immensely wealthy Lord FitzWilliam whom he had met at General Bernard Montgomery's headquarters in Brussels during the war, offered to make him manager of the home farm on his estate at Milton near Peterborough, with the prospect of a prosperous life for himself and his family, Stas turned him down without a thought. 'What the devil do you mean, manage a farm?' he answered curtly. 'I'd manage your whole estate, but not a damn farm.'

He admitted many years later that he had made a bad

mistake. Yes, he said, he had been a fool. But then, recovering from the moment of honesty, he said dammit, he would rather be a penniless Polish nobleman than an English country gentleman. He showed not a trace of remorse for his arrogance and rudeness to Tom FitzWilliam.

He was still in London in December 1945, with no job and no income, when Wanda reached Germany with fifteen-year-old Artur and her companion Tadeusz after their escape from Krakow. He crossed to France and met them in Paris, where he had left the Mercedes. It was their first meeting since the summer of 1939, and although deep down Stas hated Wanda, resented Artur and turned up his nose at Tadeusz, they celebrated their survival and reunion after six years of war.

They had much to be thankful for and much to tell each other. But one of the first things Stas did after greeting his mother was to demand that she hand over to him the family's Romanov jewellery, which Wanda had deposited in a London bank before the war. The precious stones, fashioned like frozen flowers, had been given by the Russian Empress Catherine II to the Branicki family in the eighteenth century and passed down to Stas's grandmother Imcia. They were the last valuable heirloom our family possessed as they began their post-war life in the West. Stas had good reasons for demanding the jewels. Imcia had bequeathed them to the wife of the eldest son of the family in each generation, and in 1945 that meant Chouquette. To Stas's way of thinking, of course, they were a way to finance his plans.

Wanda naturally refused, no matter how furiously Stas argued, and the dispute dragged on after he picked up the Mercedes and began driving them to Italy. Tadeusz was to join the Carpathian Lancers Regiment headquartered since the end of the war at Ancona, Artur would be sent to school, and Wanda hoped to receive treatment for her breast cancer.

As they began the drive in Paris, Stas pulled up beside another smart-looking Mercedes Benz parked on the Champs Elysées which had spare tyres on either side of its bonnet. He jumped out, calling for Artur to help him, and together they unscrewed one of the spare tyres, threw it into the trunk of their car, and drove off with it in broad daylight. Artur was terrified he would be sent to Siberia if he was caught stealing.

At Nice they had an emotional reunion with Madame Rolland, who had recently managed to escape from Poland. She was in poor health after the hardships she had suffered at the end of the war, and she died in the summer of 1946. Arriving in Italy, Stas delivered Wanda, Artur and Tadeusz to the headquarters of the Carpathian Lancers and had a happy reunion with Andrew, who was aide de camp to the regimental commander.

Andrew was in fine form. He had been with the Carpathian Lancers throughout the long Italian campaign of 1944–45, and had been living the high life. There were other relatives with the regiment, including young Jas Tyszkiewicz, a grandson of Count Zdzislaw Tarnowski, who had left Poland in the family convoy in September 1939. After leaving Belgrade in March 1941, Jas had spent nearly two and a half years with the family group at a Polish refugee colony at Crikvenica, a Yugoslav seaside resort. They were looked after there with great kindness by the Italian army, but after Italy pulled out of the war in September 1943 and the Italian army left Yugoslavia they were rounded up by the German army and early in 1944 they were packed off in cattle wagons to the concentration camps at Ravensbruck and Dachau. All of them, including Count Zdzislaw Tarnowski's three daughters and their children, survived for sixteen months in the camps and most of them got to England, where they settled after the war.

Jas had spent his time at Dachau as a teenager carting corpses thrown out of the huts each morning, and had twice fallen into comas due to sickness and starvation, narrowly escaping death. After Dachau was liberated at the end of the war, he got to Paris and managed to reach Ancona. But he was still weak, and Andrew took him under his wing. 'Life with Uncle Boubish [Andrew] was wonderful,' Jas wrote in his memoirs. 'That delightful man, such a dear person, began little by little to educate me in his own manner, making me drunk with litres of red wine and feeding me kilograms of Italian cheese, observing that this was the most effective way of restoring my health after life in the camp.'

Another person who fell for Andrew's charms was Martha Gellhorn, the American war reporter and then wife of the novelist Ernest Hemingway, who spent a brief but memorable time with the Carpathian Lancers in the summer of 1944. When she left she wrote a cheerful testimonial to the vitality of the regiment in the guest book of the officer's mess, saying never before had she had so many hands on her knee at one time. She called Andrew her 'dearest aide' and wrote him letters and postcards for years after the war. 'Where will I ever find you again? Venice, Warsaw, Tarnowskiville in Poland?' she wrote from London on 7 September 1944.

Who can say and who can say what we will be like then? You couldn't ever be a stranger and I never found anyone easier to laugh with and, if it hadn't been so obviously useless, I'd have fallen in love with you. Take care of yourself my dearest aide, do not get ill because there is still so much time left to live and still fine things to do, despite all the armies and all the politicians and all the bastards who ruin the world. I will see you. Marty.

Stas sold the Mercedes to the colonel of the regiment, said goodbye to Artur, Tadeusz and Wanda and took a boat to Egypt. Disappointment awaited him at Cairo. The prince politely turned down his request for a loan, explaining that he was hosting the entire former Turkish imperial family and could not help him. So, to make himself some money on the return trip, Stas began a modest career in smuggling. He got hold of a large consignment of American cigarettes in Cairo, took them to Italy on a troopship, and sold them on the black market at a big profit.

He still hoped to get the family jewels from Wanda, but since they could not resolve the disagreement they travelled together from Italy back to Cairo to see Sophie and ask her to mediate between them. Stas got another nasty surprise when, instead of mediating, Sophie demanded a share of the jewels for herself. He had wanted to take the jewellery to the United States, advertise it as Romanov treasure and sell it at a high price. He promised Wanda they would divide the money, but she replied that she knew very well that if he got hold of the jewellery, neither she nor Sophie would get a penny.

'She was probably right, incidentally,' Stas laughed. Much to his disgust, he had to agree that they would sell the jewels in England and split the proceeds three ways.

Before going to England he went back to Ancona, where he and a cousin, Ludwik Popiel, a major in the Carpathian Lancers, dreamed up a scheme which Stas hoped would enable him to buy the farm he wanted in the White Highlands of Kenya, or at least provide some money to live on.

They were still living in the heady days of 'anything goes' that followed the war, and they travelled to Lebanon to buy hashish which they hoped to sell at a profit in Cairo. In Beirut Stas called on the military attaché at the British embassy, who turned out to be a former schoolmate: 'He put us in touch with the people we needed. He knew where to get hash,' Stas said.

They made an appointment to meet a drug dealer, and a few days later drove about forty kilometres out of Beirut and waited at a rendezvous at an open-air café. A car came to pick them up and drove them to a villa where they met the most enormous man they had ever seen. 'I could have fitted into his belly, the whole of me. It was amazing,' Stas recalled. The drug baron asked them in good English what sort of hash they wanted. They didn't have a clue, so they asked him for the best hash to sell in Cairo. They agreed to buy four *okka*, about ten kilos, for £120.

Stas and Ludwik took the hashish to Cairo by train, but trying to sell it to Egyptians was useless; they had all the hash they needed. They had endless trouble before Billy Moss, Sophie's husband, who had many friends in Cairo, found a way to dispose of it, receiving barely the price they had paid.

Later that year Wanda moved to England with Artur and Tadeusz. A Polish military doctor had confirmed that she had breast cancer and that it was spreading and it might be too late to operate. Since the regiment lacked the facilities, she needed to get to England urgently. But they had to wait until early December, when the last units of the Polish Second Corps were transferred to England for demobilisation. They travelled by train to Calais and crossed the Channel in stormy weather on a ferry packed with soldiers, half of whom were being sick. It was raining when they reached Dover on

6 December 1946. England was a strange and gloomy land after the warmth and beauty of Italy. They were puzzled by notices at the port which referred to travellers arriving from Europe. If they weren't in Europe, Artur wondered, where were they? A notice in Polish warned about English habits: 'In England, we greet each other without shaking hands,' it said.

They were taken to a camp near Chester. It was cold and wet, and the black, corrugated Nissen huts shaped like half moons were so dispiriting that the Poles wryly nicknamed them 'barrels of laughter'. Wanda, Tadeusz and Artur moved quickly to London and spent Christmas Eve, that warmest and most intimate of Polish family celebrations, shivering in a cheap hotel in Queensway Gardens in a shabby district of central London. Too poor to stay on in the hotel, they moved into a rented room on Queensway soon after Christmas. It had begun to snow heavily on Christmas Eve, and snow was soon piled two metres high in the streets as the winter of 1946–47 turned into one of the worst of the century. It was bitterly cold and snow kept falling until April. They had little money to feed the gas meter and keep a fire burning and they shivered miserably through the winter months. In January 1947 Wanda and Tadeusz were married in London, and soon afterwards Wanda underwent successful surgery for cancer.

Sophie and Billy Moss also arrived from Cairo in 1947 and moved into a flat in central London. Once Sophie reached England, they sold the Romanov jewels to the London jeweller Spinks & Son for £4,300. It was a very large sum in those days, but Stas thought it was ridiculous, a fraction of the jewels' real worth. Wanda used her share to make a deposit on the purchase of a four-storey house in Bayswater, a lower-income district of central London. Tadeusz began renovating it, and they were soon renting out rooms and living off the income. Stas, of course, bought himself a long, sleek Triumph sports car.

Sophie and Billy also bought a house eventually, and Billy settled down to write *Ill Met by Moonlight*, the story of the commando kidnapping of General Kreipe on German-occupied Crete, which became a bestseller and was made into a film. Sophie overcame her trepidation about having children after the loss of her two sons by Andrew, and she and Billy started a family. To her immense relief she eventually had two healthy girls, Isabella and Gabriella, known as Pussa and Fee.

Andrew and Martha Gellhorn met once more after the war. Andrew had settled in Grimsby on the east coast of England, and Martha travelled up from London by train, but the dreariness of the journey and the grime and gloom of post-war Britain buried what flicker of romance remained between them. She found Andrew sharing a tiny brick house in a working-class district with a colleague from the regiment. They were running a small restaurant for fishermen and labourers on the ground floor of the house with the help of Wendy, the beautiful, big-hearted daughter of a local fishmonger, who was many years younger than him. Martha was appalled by what she saw, and sensing competition from Wendy, she returned to London sooner than planned to write a bitter little magazine piece about the sheer grottiness of life in Britain and the sadness of seeing a dashing former beau fallen on hard times and entangled with an unsuitable woman who lacked the worldly graces. She spared neither sarcasm nor contempt in describing Wendy, but she was wrong. Andrew married his Wendy, and she was a fine wife and mother, and in some ways a nobler person than his aristocratic siblings and cousins. They were never well off; Andrew worked for many years as a brush salesman and died in 1978.

In late 1946, Stas stopped in Rome on his way back from Cairo after selling the smuggled hashish. While he was having a drink with a friend, Prince Eugene Lubomirski, Eugene asked why he was going back to England.

'What do you mean, why am I going back?' Stas retorted. 'My wife and son are there.'

'Your wife, she's gone to America to get a divorce,' Eugene told him.

'That's the first I've heard of it,' said Stas.

He laughed when he told the story. 'Eugene was also one of Chouquette's boyfriends,' he said.

He and Chouquette had seen little of each other since the war ended. Most of her new friends were English, while his friends were Polish, and he did not really care that she had gone. 'I wasn't a faithful husband, and I can't complain about Chouquette,' he said.

Whenever he was asked about his relationship with Chouquette he would shrug. 'How could you expect the marriage to work out? Two young people, one twenty-one, the other twenty, get married, and then they're separated almost immediately, almost completely separated for years on end. How could a marriage like that work out?'

Chouquette had flown to the United States in October 1946 after telling him that Bill Stirling, whom she had met during the war in Cairo, had found her a job in the United States. In fact, Malcolm Wolfe Murray, the Black Watch officer whom she had met on the boat from South Africa to

England, had asked her to marry him. Instead of working in the United States, she spent six months with American friends in Palm Beach, Florida, waiting for a divorce.

It was easier in those days to get a divorce in the United States than in Britain. Chouquette was also afraid of Stas's reaction when he learned what she was up to, and did not want him nearby. She may well have had cause to worry. The last time Stas had visited on leave, she told me later, he had broken her nose during an argument. When I asked Stas if this was true he told me that he had turned up unexpectedly at Alathea Manton's flat in London, on a short leave from the front in Holland or Germany, and found Chouquette getting ready to go out with Malcolm. He asked her to change her plans and go out with him, but she refused. Chouquette was sitting at a dressing table putting on her make-up while Stas stood beside her. They were arguing and he said she turned sharply towards him as he gestured with his hand. Her face knocked into his hand, breaking her nose.

Whatever the truth of the incident, Chouquette had prepared the ground well for the divorce hearing. Friends such as Alathea and her sister Joyce gave sworn testimony in London about Stas's treatment of her, which she presented to the court in Palm Beach. Chouquette wrote to Malcolm from Florida on 3 April 1947, with the news that she had got the divorce:

Darling Boozle,

I went to Court this afternoon and got the divorce over. It was a little frightening as I had to answer so many questions but it seems to be all right . . . The witnessing was well done in London which is very important . . . I feel slightly limp after all this, as I went to Court like a fury determined to win my case . . . It is a funny feeling now, I am free all of a sudden and have finished with Stas.

Two months later, in June 1947, she and Malcolm were married in the Scottish town of Perth where he was based with his regiment.

Meanwhile Stas had returned to London anyway. He still wanted to buy a farm in Kenya and he tried once again to raise the money, this time with his friend Leszek Czartoryski, who came from a princely Polish family related to almost all the royal houses of Europe. Together they began smuggling currency and gold between London and Paris. But it was a dangerous trade, and when Stas met Prince Ali Khan, the son of the Aga Khan, whom he had known in Cairo, Ali Khan was appalled. 'Oh, you silly ass,' he said. 'Next time you do that, pay the money into my bank in Paris and I'll give you a cheque for Nairobi.'

But it was too late for that. Leszek was arrested on the way back from his next expedition to Paris and taken before a London magistrate who luckily turned out to be another old acquaintance of Stas's. Even so, Leszek had a hard time explaining the foreign currency that police had found sewn into his overcoat. He probably only escaped a jail sentence because the magistrate knew Stas and was prepared to turn a blind eye to the cock-and-bull story he had been told. Stas laughed: 'I remember Joyce Fitzalan-Howard and Alathea Manton testifying in court. "Prince Czartoryski, smuggling? Impossible!"'

In 1947 Stas's favourite uncle, Prince Roman Sanguszko, who was one of the few wealthy Polish aristocrats living abroad, invited him to go to Brazil to work for him. 'Sanguszko said, "Come over to Brazil, I've got a visa for you.

If you obey me and stand on your own two feet you'll be a rich man within two years,"' Stas recalled. Friends of Stas who followed Sanguszko to Brazil made fortunes.

So Stas obtained a Brazilian visa and was about to leave when he fell in love and abandoned his plans.

CHAPTER TWENTY-FIVE

An Exotic Flower

I was nearly seven when my mother married Malcolm Wolfe Murray, her tall and gentlemanly Scottish army officer, and took me to live with them in Scotland. Malcolm's small house beside a lane in the Perthshire countryside was the first family home I had ever known. It must have seemed like heaven to Chouquette, an oasis of peace and stability with the love of a naturally charming and sociable man who combined dashing good looks with the most moderate and reasonable personality. The sense of security must have been quite breathtaking after the frights and horrors she had endured for eight years.

But for me the transition from under-age world traveller and inconvenient child packed off to boarding schools and foster lodgings in Britain was not at all easy. Life as a child refugee was no preparation for joining a new family as stepson to Malcolm and stepbrother to his sons, James and Angus. Before we came to England I had never had a playmate, and since we got there I had never had a friend. Chouquette had once invited a few children to a birthday party for me in a London flat, but they were all strangers and some of them opened the bathroom door when I was sitting on the toilet and laughed at me. I just wanted them to go away.

Our arrival in the family cannot have been easy for James and Angus. It was five years since their mother had died after her ship was torpedoed, and now they were presented with a foreign stepmother and a little stepbrother with the social skills of a jungle boy. My first memory of family life is of them shouting 'dirty Pole' from behind the garden gate, while I shouted 'dirty English' back, furious that I could not get at them. Naturally, they honed Andy-baiting to a fine art, and with my Stas-like temper I was a sucker for it. I certainly had the taste for a fight. A year earlier I had chased Chouquette round a kitchen table with a bread knife. Poor Mummy, she could not deal with violence from me any better than from Stas. She shrank from it. It was gentle Boule, my beloved aunt, who took a belt to my backside that time, probably the only violent act of her life.

When we got to Scotland, Jimmy was five years older than me, and so out of reach of my furies, but skinny, asthmatic Gus was only a couple of years older and couldn't run much without wheezing and gasping. Although I was much smaller, I ran pretty fast, and I caught him once or twice at first before he started to grow and get stronger. During one memorable breakfast after I had been in the family a couple of years I sent a plateful of porridge flying through the dining room at Jimmy but missed, and seconds after it hit the wall Malcolm walked through the door from the kitchen to see porridge sliding down beside him. Once when Malcolm and us boys were playing under the trees in the garden, chucking pine cones at each other, he said, right, no more throwing at the face, and of course the next one I let fly hit him in the eye. I thought I was quick on my feet, but he was well over six feet tall and with three giant strides he picked me up and chucked me into the stream at the bottom of the garden.

Jimmy and Gus soon became fond of Chouquette, who was beautiful and friendly and affectionate, and behaved towards them more like a big sister than a stepmother. She didn't really take my side when we fought, and she shared their jokes and did her best to join in Malcolm's sporting activities. Jimmy and Gus were naturally friendly with a sense of humour and they eventually got used to me, too. They were keen sportsmen and great companions, and we had a shared youth walking and fishing and shooting among the hills and rivers and lochs of Scotland. I came to enjoy their company and admire them, and today I count myself lucky to have them as friends. It is the same with our sister Tessa who was born in 1950 and is one of the people I love and value most.

Malcolm suffered from asthma which worsened as he grew older and eventually forced him to retire from the army. He convalesced at Kelburn Castle, an ancient keep attached to a seventeenth-century mansion that looked across the sea to the islands off the west coast of Scotland. It was the childhood home of Malcolm's first wife and the residence of her parents, Lord and Lady Glasgow, whose family had lived there since the twelfth century. Granny and Papa, as we called them, were the warmest people I ever met. They took in Chouquette and treated her like a daughter. I remember with affection how beautifully they recited the Lord's Prayer each morning when we gathered for prayers in the dining room before breakfast, and how they squabbled genteelly between themselves when they played cards together in the great, draughty drawing room where we assembled after candlelit dinners for charades or bridge or Mah Jong. Every holiday there would be masses of children and young people sprinting up and down the broad front staircase and along corridors hanging with ancestral portraits, and up and down the narrow, spiralling stone staircase in the tower at the back as we played kick-a-peg all round the castle. Kelburn was how a home should be!

After Malcolm left the army in 1950 we moved down from Inverness to Peeblesshire in the Borders. It was an idyllic setting with the River Tweed in its lush valley, and rolling hills and high moors that turned purple with the blossoming heather in August, and buzzed with grouse, hare and rabbits as we walked over them, blazing away with shotguns at anything that flew, scuttled or jumped.

We lived in The Riggs of Traquair, a long, stone bungalow on a hillside above a tiny village, the home of Malcolm's mother Evelyn Pitman, or Danny as we called her. She was old and bed-bound, but her garden was one of the most beautiful in Scotland, and visitors paid to see it. She was glad to have us and extremely generous, sending us, year after year, on two-week skiing holidays in Swiss hotels. She liked us to visit her every day in her bedroom, and there was a plateful of coins beside her bed that she sometimes invited us to dig into. I was a bit afraid of her and didn't visit as often as I should have. Gus, with his comic talent, had the knack of ingratiating himself and got his hands into the plate of coins most. But he really loved Danny and she taught him a love of literature, sitting up with him and Jimmy to read to them from George Eliot's novels in the evenings.

The Riggs was pretty crowded, with Danny, the six of us and beautiful young Nanny Banks who looked after our gorgeous baby Tessa. In the summer of 1954 we moved to Glenternie, a big Victorian house in the Scottish baronial style that Danny bought for Malcolm in the Peeblesshire country-side. It was built in red granite with turrets and gables and a servants' wing complete with a gun room, and stood majestically on the side of a hill amid forty acres of bracken and pine woods teeming with rabbits, and the view over the Manor Valley spoke of perfect harmony. On a crisp day in winter, the valley white with frost, you could hear the call of a cock pheasant cracking the air from miles away.

When I think of home I think of Glenternie, of quiet evenings, Malcolm reading and Chouquette sewing beside the fire in the drawing room as they listened to Edith Piaf or Noel Coward or maybe Rachmaninov's second piano concerto on the gramophone after dinner, and of Chouquette chatting and laughing with Gus at the breakfast table as sunshine poured in through the tall, plate glass windows, lighting up the smoke curling from their cigarettes. Or of the shouts and laughter as Malcolm, James and Angus and friends up from England played tennis on the court beside the house until dusk fell. Or of walking on the hills high above the house, wrestling with teenage emotions, or fly-fishing for trout on the River Tweed or a nearby loch, or poking a .22 rifle out of my bedroom window to shoot rabbits on the bank opposite.

They were happy years and I wanted them to last forever, but James and Angus went away to school at Eton, and I went to the Benedictine monks, first at St Benet's school in Derbyshire, and then to Ampleforth in Yorkshire. I must have needed socialising badly, because for a while Father Dennis Mercer at St Benet's caned me every couple of days, thirty times in one term. 'Again Tarnowski,' he sighed. 'Bend over then.' One, two, three stripes on the bum. 'Thank you sir.' 'Close the door behind you, Tarnowski.' He had sandy hair and a kindly smile. But I can't remember a single thing I did wrong to deserve those canings. I was just difficult. And how not, with my background?

None of the other boys liked me, because I had a temper, and although I was pretty small and wore glasses for a squint I thought I was brave and tough, until I got into a fight with a boy who was bigger and heavier than me. With everyone watching in the games changing room he easily wrestled me down to the ground and sat on my chest. I was helpless and humiliated in front of them all and I never got into another fight. Why on earth did that never happen to Stas when he was a boy?

At the end of term I took the train to Edinburgh, then a local train to Peebles, and Malcolm or Chouquette would be there to drive me the four miles to Glenternie. Malcolm included me in everything, just as if I was his natural son. He taught me to shoot, fish and play tennis. He took me grouse shooting and pheasant shooting. I even shot a stag and caught a couple of salmon on the Tweed. He wasn't an intimate man, but he was extremely fair and kind to me, and he was an immeasurable blessing on my life. Better, far, to be brought up by Malcolm than by Stas. He got permission for me to wear the tartan of the Murray clan, and I wore the kilt proudly. Like Jimmy and Gus, I spat disdainfully out of the window when the train crossed the border into England on the way back to school. In a few short years I had become Andy MacTarnow, the Scottish Pole. By the time I left Ampleforth, somewhat bemused by having won a scholarship to read history at Oxford, I was well on the way to becoming British, or rather Scottish, exactly as Chouquette wanted.

But there was a darker side to our life in Scotland that I have never fully understood, though I have tried for many years to fathom it. Chouquette should have been idyllically happy in those surroundings, but after only a short while she wasn't. Sometimes she was fine and laughed a lot and was affectionate. But at other times she wasn't there. I think she had her first breakdown around the time that our sister Tessa was born, with dizziness, weeping, fear of crossing the road, depression, listlessness and inability to love her little daughter. It was all kept from me at the time, but later there was vague talk of an affair with one of Malcolm's handsome friends, or was it between Malcolm and the friend's wife?

She got worse. One summer I was sent away again, this time with family friends to the broad, white sands at Morar on the west coast of Scotland. Perhaps it was then that she first had electric shock treatment for depression. Later, she started resorting to spiritualism and faith healing, and something mysterious called the Black Box. She was tormented by the refusal of the Roman Catholic Church to let her receive the sacraments after she married Malcolm. She and I used to go to Sunday Mass together during the school holidays. When we lived with Danny at The Riggs of Traquair we sometimes walked the two or three miles to church in the nearby town of Innerleithen. She had always been a devout Catholic, and once a year she gathered up her courage and entered the confessional to ask the priest for absolution for her sins that would allow her to receive Holy Communion and resume life as a practising Catholic. But the priest always turned her away. I remember her weeping one Sunday. We were alone in the church in Peebles after Mass, and when I asked what was wrong she said the priest had refused absolution unless she promised to live with Malcolm as a sister. She said that would have been unfair to Malcolm and she could not do it.

There were other things that seem to have added to her suffering. Glenternie was miles from town and there weren't many friends in the hills. The nearest were ten miles away, and except for summertime when we were flooded with friends from England for the tennis and grouse shooting, social life consisted of perhaps an invitation to dinner and a game of bridge every couple of weeks. Life could be dour in Scotland for months on end, not much fun for a woman who had seen the world and loved gaiety and cosmopolitan society.

She and Malcolm drove to Edinburgh occasionally for a meal and a theatre. They went down to London a couple of times each year to see friends. They went to Yorkshire and stayed with Boule, who had by then divorced my Uncle Philip and married Uncle Rowland, Sophie's friend from the Villa Tara in Cairo. Rowland, still boisterous and exuberant, had inherited the title of Lord St Oswald and one of England's magnificent stately homes at Nostell Priory. He was immensely hospitable at Nostell and Las Columnas, his Andalusian retreat in the hills overlooking the Straits of Gibraltar. Even so, when Jimmy and Gus and I were away at school and university Chouquette was often lonely and bored, alone with Malcolm and Tessa in the big house in the country. The isolation deepened in winter, when they were sometimes cut off by heavy snow and Malcolm had to ski into town for supplies.

A joyful reunion dispelled Chouquette's gloom in the late 1950s when her mother came trotting down the gangplank of a steamship, clutching a bottle of Polish vodka as a gift. She had been allowed to leave Poland in the political thaw that had followed Stalin's death in 1953, and she was reunited with Chouquette and Boule at last, nearly twenty years after they had been separated by the outbreak of war. Granny, as I knew her, was short and grey and quite square and determined. She looked for all the world like Grandma Giles from the 1950s cartoons. She smiled a lot and was quite fun, and she was devoutly religious, but she spoke hardly any English. I don't think she liked me, and we didn't get on very well, probably because she had disliked Stas and bitterly regretted the marriage that produced me.

Two of her sisters came over, too. Gaunt, gravel-voiced, chain-smoking Tante Eve was a lovely, practical aunt you could always rely on. Big, strong Tante Edwige, on the other hand, was quite dotty. She had curly white hair, the profile of a Roman emperor, and a fixed, beatific smile. Boule nick-named her Big Fred and packed her away to Kolbe House, a home for genteel Polish ladies in West London, while Granny and Tante Eve became housekeepers at Nostell.

Granny and Grandfather Zygmunt had lived almost the entire war in Warsaw, surviving the most terrible battles and uprisings, always anxious about the fate of their two daughters who had left Poland without them. German bombs destroyed their home during the siege of the city in September 1939, but they survived the five-year occupation and the 1944 uprising against the Germans, and in October 1944 they were marched out of the destroyed city with the survivors. Grandfather Zygmunt soon moved on to the Silesian city of Katowice and resumed his entrepreneurial activities. When the Com-munists took over the country they enlisted his financial expertise and contacts in their dealings with the West. He travelled to western Europe, always with an official minder, and was even allowed to accept the Legion d'Honneur from the French government in Paris, awarded before the war in recognition of his services to French culture during ten years as managing director of Polish Radio, which he had founded in 1926. He died on 27 December 1948 aged sixty-six, exhausted and heart-broken after all that he and his family, his city and his country had suffered. Like Grandfather Hieronim, I never met him, and I have missed both of them deeply all my life.

Although her mother's arrival in Britain must have brought Chouquette great joy, her presence, first at Glenternie and then at Nostell, could not restore all that she and Boule had lost when they left Poland. I think there is a special warmth and intimacy about Polish families and Polish life, and there was a gaiety and liveliness about pre-war Polish society that Chouquette never found among the hunting, shooting, card-playing Scottish gentry. Although she made friends and received many kindnesses in Scotland and England, I think she never recovered from being uprooted from her own world when she was little more than a teenage girl. She often complained during her years in Scotland of missing Poland and the sound of Polish spoken around her. She remained a lovely but sad exotic flower transplanted in a foreign land.

Perhaps she had simply suffered too much, too early in life. Uprooted by war, fleeing into a refugee life with a bullying, unfaithful husband, bearing an unwanted child, she had lived for years in fear, insecurity and violence. There was a history of mental illness in her mother's family that may have made her liable to instability. I was once told that Granny's death at Nostell Priory may have been suicide.

Homesick for Poland, scarred by war and Stas's violence, bored with her isolated life, disturbed by Malcolm's flirts with younger men's wives, rejected by the Catholic Church, depressed by the prospect of losing her beauty, perhaps congenitally unstable – whatever the reasons, Chouquette died prematurely in 1968.

I remember the last time I spoke to her. Perhaps I should have recognised the signs. I had graduated from Oxford and joined Reuters news agency, and I was working in the Reuters bureau in Madrid on my first posting as a foreign correspondent. She had telephoned me occasionally before and she was fine when she visited Madrid a year earlier. But this time she wept over the telephone. I couldn't understand why. Her illnesses had been kept from me and she wouldn't open up over the telephone. When I asked what was wrong she stopped crying and said everything was all right. Then Malcolm came on the line, calm and concerned, and told me she was better now, it was nothing. I had never known her to weep over the telephone before. She must have been asking for help, I should have telephoned her again right away and flown to Scotland to find out what was wrong. But I had no idea she was ill. A month later she took an overdose in a friend's flat in London and died.

I was alone in the office when Boule telephoned to tell me Mummy was dead. Something enormous hit me, something so huge that it didn't immediately hurt. It was so impossible to understand. They say that serious wounds don't cause pain immediately, because of the shock, although you know something is terribly wrong, and that's how it was. But I ran downstairs and caught my bureau chief, John Organ, who was on his way out. When I returned to the office the tears and horror came, and John found me beating my head against a wall. He had brought his Roman missal and he took me to a church, where we climbed up into a gallery to be alone. We knelt together and turned to the prayers for the dead and I poured out my grief as we recited them. After some time I saw through my tears a happy young family cross the church floor below us with their newly christened child, and it seemed to me even then that I was being told that in death there is life. Although I did not realise it then, John's warmth and love in that terrible time were also a sign for my life. The help he gave me was just one specially intense moment in what was to be a lifetime of incessant generosity towards me that made him my truest and dearest friend.

Chouquette was only forty-eight when she died. I was twenty-seven, and I felt that the centre of my world had gone. I flew to Scotland, and after her burial in the little hillside cemetery in the Peeblesshire village of Eddlestone I wanted to throw myself on the grave and lie there weeping. I did not understand how the others could leave before her grave was filled in. Malcolm and Tessa and Boule and Rowland and I tried to comfort each other, but we were too shocked to understand what had happened. Everything, the funeral, the wake, the condolences and the mutual commiserations, passed as if it were a dream, something unreal. Later I realised that I had no idea why she had killed herself, and that this meant I had not known my mother at all. That puzzled me, and I began to wonder if she had really loved me, because if she had, surely she would not have left me without a word of explanation. Out of confusion and nightly tears and the long mourning process came a resolve that I would never repeat her mistake. I would never hide myself from my children. Better that they should know all of me, no matter how painful or embarrassing, than that I should be a stranger to them.

But even that wasn't the end of it. Poor, beloved Boule died in the same way thirteen years later. Uncle Rowland, broken by grief, lost the will to live and died three years afterwards. I suppose my gentle, delicate, lovely aunt, like her older sister, had hidden too many scars for too many years. Despite all their gaiety and humour and laughter, the joy they had often given to those around them, and the lives of plenty and comfort they had led in Britain with their second husbands, the two Polish sisters stolen from their parents in 1939 were casualties of war. Uprooted too early, too brutally, in the end they lacked the strength to live on.

CHAPTER TWENTY-SIX

The Daquise Café

Not long after Chouquette divorced Stas he fell in love with Ada Lubomirska, a sparkling, audacious girl of nineteen from a princely Polish family. They met when she visited London in 1947 from her home in Switzerland, and her warm smile, big heart and voluptuous figure captivated him.

Ada bubbled with life, but beneath her vivacious smiles she was scarred by the horrors she had seen during the war. She was eleven in September 1939 when the Red Army occupied eastern Poland and arrested her father at his home at Rowne north of Lwow, in what is now north-western Ukraine. They told him his crime was to be a Polish landowner. Before they took him away to the local jail they let Ada say goodbye. When she entered the room she was shocked to see him on his knees, weeping uncontrollably. He got to his feet and affected a fatherly air, telling her to be very brave and look after her mother, then he hugged her for the last time.

After her husband was taken away Ada's mother went to the jail every two days asking to see him, but the warden always refused. When winter came she learned he was sick. The Soviets did not treat him, but she found that she could see him through the large, un-prisonlike windows, and each day she watched over him for hour after hour. Winter tightened its grip and she stood at the window in rain, snow and freezing temperatures until she caught pneumonia. She never recovered. Ada was allowed to make a farewell visit as she lay on her death bed. Her father died a few days later. He had survived less than four months in the jail at Rowne and died between January 12 and 14, 1940. The Soviets never said exactly when.

Ada's uncle, her father's brother, was also killed. A few members of the local revolutionary committee descended on his home. On their first visit they announced the requisitioning of part of the house. Next time they walked in and just shot him in his sick bed.

The shock of losing her mother, father and uncle so suddenly in such cruel circumstances meant that for many years Ada was incapable of looking back on the past. She got out of Soviet clutches at the end of 1940 with her sister, an aunt and some cousins, thanks to her aunt Princess Bichette Radziwill in Rome, who would also help Stas, Chouquette and me get visas from Switzerland through Italy. Princess Bichette had many contacts in Germany, which was allied with the Soviet Union at the time, and she used them to persuade the Soviets to let Ada's family cross into German-held Poland under the auspices of the International Red Cross. Ada remembered a solitary goat trotting in the opposite direction into Soviet-held territory as they walked over a railway bridge into the German zone. They reached Warsaw, and by the time the war ended she was living in Lausanne, cared for by aunts and uncles.

She was studying to be an English-French interpreter when she went to visit a relative sharing the basement of Sophie and Billy Moss's flat in London. Stas was there reading St Augustine's *City of God*, a most unusual activity for him. What an interesting man, Ada thought. They fell in love, and after she returned to Lausanne they wrote to each other. Her guardians in Switzerland tried to persuade her to break off the relationship, because divorced, penniless Stas with his reputation for violence and philandering was no catch for a beautiful young woman with her life ahead of her.

But Ada shared Stas's devil-may-care attitude and ignored the warnings. He visited her in 1948 or 1949, having asked her to book a modest hotel in Montreux, but she picked the most expensive and ordered champagne and caviar on the first evening. She did not care about money, but Stas had only a small travel allowance under British foreign exchange restrictions and he told her next day his money was almost gone and he had to leave.

'Nonsense,' said Ada. 'I'll ring Aunt Jo.' Aunt Jo was Madame Fifa, wife of the owner of the Ritz hotels, a charming Jewish lady from Warsaw. But when Ada rang she was away in the United States.

'Oh, don't worry,' said Ada, 'I'll sell my fur coat.' But it only fetched eighty francs and the hotel bill was several hundred. The management was pressing them to pay.

Stas put on his aristocratic charm. 'Look, I'll ring up my uncle Alfred Potocki and ask him to lend me some money,' he told the manager. Alfred had settled in Switzerland after fleeing his immense palace at Lancut in 1944 and was living at the Beau Rivage hotel in Lausanne with Betka, his ageing mother. He had asked Wanda to marry him after the war, but she had chosen Tadeusz.

'Ah, if Count Potocki is your uncle, then of course, naturally,' the manager replied.

But Alfred would have none of it. He lectured Stas over the telephone on the need to adapt to his new situation and live within his means and said grudgingly that he would ask Betka and see what he could do to help. Next day Alfred, who had left Poland, helped by the German army, with a train and dozens of trucks packed with more than 600 cases of artistic treasures from Lancut which he took to the West, wired Stas ten Swiss francs. Furious, Stas wired back twenty. The hotel called in the police but let Stas leave after he promised to pay off the debt gradually from England. The owner even lent him a hundred francs for the journey.

He and Ada had fallen deeply in love. When she turned twenty-one in 1949 and finished interpreters' school, she took possession of a small inheritance left by her parents and went to London. She wrote to Chouquette to make sure she did not want Stas back. Chouquette replied that she was very happy with Malcolm and had no further interest in Stas. She warned Ada that he would never change. In a few years, she added, Ada would get a letter from another woman, asking her the very same things.

Ada and Stas scandalised Polish émigré society by living together. By the time they married on 20 November 1950, she was nearly six months pregnant with their first child, Sandra. They settled down in a flat at Rutland Gate in Knightsbridge, near Hyde Park, happy despite their poverty, and had a child almost every year. Stas was so much in love that for once he stopped chasing women. 'I was faithful to Ada for seven whole years, would you believe it?' he told me later. 'Seven years! Before that, I'd never been faithful to anybody for more than a couple of weeks.'

His dream of a new life under the sun in Africa or Brazil had melted away. He had lost contact with the wealthy English aristocrats Chouquette had introduced him to, and he had taken a job in London. He worked as chauffeur to a Polish factory owner, driving him around in his sports car, but was fired after a collision with a Post Office van. After that he went to the government-run Labour Exchange but the only job he could get was house painting. He began years of drudgery, scraping, plastering and painting the interiors of houses and flats. He became a skilled decorator and went freelance. 'I ended up as the best house painter in London, everyone said so,' he boasted. 'I was really bloody good.'

They were happy in their marriage. During their first years together, their oldest daughter Sandra remembered them hugging while she and her brothers and sisters held hands and danced round them singing '*Misie, misie*', 'Teddy bears, teddy bears'. Around 1956 they bought a large house in the London suburb of Ealing, where many Poles settled. Stas decorated the upper floors and rented out rooms and carried on house painting.

But the move brought their honeymoon period to an end as their lives sank into drudgery. The long hours of manual labour exhausted Stas, and although he earned good money, it was never enough to provide for their growing brood. Ada was barely able to cope with looking after five children and keeping house. Like Chouquette before her, she left dirty nappies and clothes to pile up. This time there was no Sophie to wash them, and the piles rotted on the floor. Beds were unmade, sheets and clothes unwashed, the garden wild and overgrown.

I visited them once or twice at their Ealing home, although my visits did not last long. Chouquette only let me go reluctantly because she wanted me to be British and thought it was better that I should not develop close relations with my Polish family. The children were still small the first time I visited them at Ealing in 1956, and they were beautiful, sweet and affectionate, welcoming me with great excitement, overwhelmed with awe at their big, unknown British brother. 'Boubi, Boubi,' they cried, using the nickname I had inherited from Andrew as a child, laughing, dancing around and hugging me. There were four of them then. Sandra, the oldest, was a dark, gypsy beauty with dreamy eyes and spontaneous warmth, Iza was a shining little blonde jewel, Adam was the cutest boy you ever saw with white skin and curly blonde hair, so sweet and small and shy that they called him Kotek or Kitten, and the smallest was Michal, who looked like Stas but was in nappies, so they called him *Smród* ('Stink').

The house was a mess but Ada was welcoming and wonderfully affectionate from the moment she first saw me. She seemed to lavish special care on me. Her broad, open face lit up the house with a wonderful warm smile, and she spoke English with a glorious foreign accent that mixed funny francophone Rs with broad, flat echoes of the borderlands of eastern Poland.

Stas was attentive and charming. He still walked with a lithe tread, his head held high, dark hair swept back and receding from his temples so that his forehead looked broader and higher and his profile more handsome and predatory than in his youth. Despite his lowly occupation, his vanity and nostalgia for better times extended to a superb hand-tailored Savile Row cashmere suit. 'Pope and Bradley,' he drawled. 'King Alfonso XIII of Spain's tailors, y'know.' We sat in the long grass in his overgrown garden, and I took pictures of the happy, smiling family. Stas took me to buy me a present, the only one I remember from him in my youth. I refused a bicycle and chose a beautiful long-bladed flick knife that would have made a mafioso proud. Back at Glenternie Malcolm took one look at it: 'Good God! What's that?' And he took it away.

Stas took me one Sunday to the one o'clock Polish mass at Brompton Oratory in Kensington, which in the 1950s attracted Poles in their hundreds. Every inch of space was filled, and as I knelt on the stone floor beside him I was strangely moved by the solemn passion of the Polish anthems that welled up in the enormous church. There was something immensely sad about that displaced community giving fervent voice in a foreign tongue to the desolation of dispossession, betrayal and exile, pleading with the Almighty to give them back their country. Every note they sang told of loss and love and longing, of the hopelessness of living in a strange country, and of the misery of knowing they would never go home.

Afterwards I held Stas's hand, feeling wonderfully fulfilled and complete beside my tall, handsome father, who in those days was my own tremendous hero, and we walked through the streets of Kensington to Ognisko Polskie, the Polish Hearth club in Princes Gate, to lunch among the dispossessed aristocrats and ageing generals, the stateless diplomats and ministers of the no-longer-recognised government-in-exile. Once we had tea and chocolate éclairs oozing with cream at the Daquise café beside the South Kensington Tube station amid the strangely familiar chatter of Polish voices. The Poles around me seemed to radiate warmth, familiarity, refinement and fun. It was wonderful to be a visitor to my father's world.

But his life was much tougher than I knew. He and Ada were mired in penury, and he eventually had difficulty feeding the children. Forced to borrow money from an English friend, he handed over the *proporzec,* the banner of the Swedish king from Rudnik, as surety. It had been returned to the family after the war, and although Stas managed to repay the loan, his cousin Jas Tarnowski was alarmed.

'I know how difficult life is,' Jas said. 'You will probably have to do the same thing again, and next time you won't be able to find the money to get the *proporzec* back. The only right thing to do is for the *proporzec* to go back to Poland. Don't you think it would be a good idea to present it to the nation?'

Stas was aghast at first at the idea of giving the banner to Communist Poland, but agreed to present it to the Wawel Museum in the former royal castle in Krakow, not to the government. The Polish ambassador in London was delighted. He suggested over a glass of champagne that Stas and Sophie take the banner to Poland and present it to the museum themselves.

And so in 1957 Sophie and Stas returned to Poland for the first time since the beginning of the war eighteen years before.

CHAPTER TWENTY-SEVEN

Uneasy Homecomings

Stas and Sophie's return was tinged with sadness. Much of the excitement of coming home after eighteen years fell away when they saw what war and Communism had done to Poland. It was a ravaged and blighted land, barely recognisable as the country they had known.

It was not just that forty per cent of the national wealth had been destroyed in a country that had been among the poorest in Europe, nor that the shifting of its frontiers had changed its shape and geographical position so much that it was only four-fifths of its former size, now lying 250 kilometres west of its previous position and incorporating only fifty-four per cent of its pre-war territory. Nor was it even that the population had fallen by nearly one-third from 35 million to 23.9 million, and that it had lost whole ethnic groups like the Jews, Germans and Ukrainians. All these losses and changes had been terrible and painful; but so too was life under Communism.

In 1957 Poland was a satellite state, a People's Democracy run by a Communist party loyal to Moscow that ruled with an iron fist and brooked no opposition. Soviet troops remained in the country to ensure its loyalty. Right up to the mid-1950s Soviet 'advisers' and NKVD officers had held senior positions throughout the state and the government, not least in the interior ministry and secret police. Torture and killings were common, and so was deportation to Siberia. Party censors controlled the press, literature, radio, television, cinema and theatre. Huge state-owned heavy industries weighed down the centralised economy. Private enterprise was banned or restricted. Education and healthcare were at least universal, but travel to the West was rarely permitted. Agriculture languished under a deadening system of state farms and collectives while hundreds of thousands of independent small farmers struggled under crushing taxation. There were as many horse-drawn carts as cars on the roads, and as many horse-drawn ploughs as tractors, and it seemed to Sophie and Stas that Poland was fifty years behind the West.

Poland was backward, its people were at war with their rulers, and the country lurched between economic crises and political explosions. Life was grey and hopeless and the people sullen. Every Pole sought to survive by carving out his own private niche out of reach of the party's all-embracing grasp. By swindling the state Poles took back what they could of the wealth and freedom it denied them. The Poland that greeted Sophie and Stas was physically decrepit and politically bankrupt, a land almost without hope.

Their visit was made possible by the political thaw in the Soviet bloc that had followed the death of Stalin in 1953 and a subsequent upheaval in Poland that brought at least an appearance of change. Workers had rioted in the western city of Poznan in 1956, and in the crisis that followed the Communist party took the opportunity to remove its universally hated Stalinist leaders. The new leaders embarked on a 'Polish Road to Socialism' under Wladyslaw Gomulka, a tough, home-grown Communist. When the Soviet leader Nikita Khrushchev rushed to Warsaw uttering threats, Gomulka surrounded the capital with troops and faced him down at a tense meeting at the airport. Khrushchev, who had crushed a bloody uprising in Hungary in 1956, climbed down. A deal with the new leadership left them with more independence from Moscow.

But Stas was careful to avoid any appearance of involvement with the regime when he handed over the *proporzec*. The ambassador in London had suggested that a government minister and state television should attend the ceremony. 'No television and no minister,' he replied. 'I'm not going to have any propaganda. I'm giving the *proporzec* to the nation, to the Wawel Museum, and if the television is there I won't be there.'

Yet he and Sophie were to some extent privileged visitors, since the return of émigré aristocrats to Communist Poland was a novelty, and the regime was keen to grasp at any hint, real or imagined, that it was achieving acceptance. They were able to return to the old family places despite strict laws against dispossessed landowners. The houses still stood, but they were dilapidated and drab like the rest of Poland, and they could not enter them. Agricultural students were living in the mansion at Rudnik; Second World War tanks and rocket launchers stood on the lawn at Dukla, which was a museum to the Soviet army; and the Szlak, which had been rebuilt but confiscated, was a Polish Radio broadcasting house. Sophie's home at Gora Ropczycka had been partly destroyed, and a family of peasants was living there. All that they could call their own were two Krakow apartment buildings, whose tenants paid small state-controlled rents and could not be removed.

They met relatives still living in Poland, although some had been transported to Siberia and others had been tried on trumped-up charges and jailed for years. Surviving aristocrats lived inconspicuously in small apartments, cocooned by the vestiges of their former riches. Some had managed to cling to two or three high-ceilinged rooms in their own palaces now divided into apartments. But none had a real home in the people's Poland. They lived as shadowy relics of a bygone era, often persecuted and treated as parasites with no useful social purpose. Many doors were closed to their children. The working class was given priority, and the sons and daughters of the aristocracy had to struggle against discrimination and official restrictions.

The high point of the visit for Stas and Sophie was the welcome they received at Rudnik. Despite the pain of seeing their former home in its shabby and neglected state, they were elated when dozens of former retainers and estate workers greeted them with an open-air banquet at which fifty men, women and children presented a radiant Sophie with a large bouquet as Stas looked on beaming. It was an extraordinary public demonstration of affection for the children of the former owner of the estate, and a slap in the face for the Communists that risked bringing down official anger on the participants.

Sophie received another warm welcome at Gora Ropczycka. Old farmhands told her that she had kept up their hopes in the first days of the war, when as a way of defying the Germans she had told them to keep working in the fields and carry on with the autumn ploughing. 'Various old chaps came and said, "We've never forgotten that. We felt that you still believed in the future and you gave us part of your belief. You know, it was our way of fighting an enemy without bullets,"' Sophie remembered. She went to thank Franek Pazdan and his family for sheltering Hieronim after his expulsion from Rudnik and they showed her a few meagre possessions – a book, some soup concentrate – he had left when he went to Krakow in early 1945.

But for Stas the visit to Poland turned out to be a fateful turning point that nearly ruined his life and destroyed his family. Seven grinding years in London had worn down his relationship with Ada. He was nearly forty and he had nothing to look forward to except more work and more hopelessness. But in Warsaw he began an affair with Ila Straszewska, an illegitimate daughter of Prince Eugene Lubomirski, and it rekindled his passion for life. He felt young and free again and behaved with his old arrogance and bravado. He had been allowed to recover and sell silver, porcelain and valuables that Hieronim had deposited in museums, achieving a financial freedom he had not known for years, and he and Ila lived in an uproarious style he could not have afforded in London.

When the time came to return to Britain, Sophie went back to her two daughters in London, where she remained for the rest of her long life. She, too, had a troubled second marriage. Her husband Billy had left her to move to the Caribbean by the time she went to Poland, and he lived there with a girlfriend named Twinkle until his death. Sophie raised her daughters and lived in her brick house in Putney, supporting herself by renting out rooms to lodgers. She never lost her charm and sense of fun. She was still welcome in English high society. In the late 1950s she became a friend of Lord Astor, a well-known businessman and politician, and she and her girls became frequent guests at his estate at Cliveden in Buckinghamshire. I was once told that Bill Astor might have married Sophie if Bronwen Pugh, the top model for the French fashion house Balmain, had not come along and in 1960 became his third wife instead. At forty-three, even the redoubtable Sophie could not beat competition like that. But Astor and Sophie remained friendly to the end, and he left her daughter Fee a substantial legacy when he died in 1966.

Soon after that Sophie began to play a part in my life once again. She and I had been close in the days of the *gnomek* and she had often looked after me when I was a child in Belgrade, Jerusalem and Cairo, but after my parents and I left for England in 1943 we rarely saw each other. She became friendly again with Chouquette in the 1950s and visited us at Glenternie, and we sometimes met at Nostell Priory, the stately home of Boule's husband. When Chouquette died in 1968 Sophie decided to do her best to fill the void in my life. Thanks to her, we became close once again. She wrote to me often and lovingly when I was abroad and gave me many family mementoes, such as a silver mug engraved with Andrew's signature, silver platters and serving dishes from pre-war Poland engraved with the family crest, and an extraordinary bronze crucifix that had belonged to Hieronim. It was beautifully decorated and inscribed, and opened up to show many relics of saints encased behind glass inside, including a relic of Saint Jerome, Hieronim's patron saint. Most precious of all, she gave me the signet ring my great-grandfather Professor Stanislaw Tarnowski had worn, which I treasure to this day. Sophie told me she used to argue with Stas to persuade him to treat me as his oldest son, although I lived apart from him and his family.

Stas stayed in Warsaw when Sophie left for London. After he failed to return Ada began receiving letters from relatives in Poland telling her about his affair, his heavy drinking and violent behaviour. It was a terrible time for Ada and she, too, took comfort in an affair, falling in love with Andrew Zamoyski, a cousin and friend whom Stas had rescued from an English mental institution and brought to live with them at Ealing.

By the time Stas agreed to give up Ila and returned to England after two or three years he found not only that Ada and Andrew were lovers, but that he was ostracised as a traitor in Polish *émigré* society, which judged that he had compromised himself by handing the *proporzec* to the Communist regime. There was even gossip that he had become an agent for the secret police. When he visited Ognisko, the Polish Hearth club on Princes Gate in London, even his old commander at Tobruk, General Stanislaw Kopanski, who had always stood by him, refused to shake his hand. Stas could not deny that he had received special treatment in Poland when he was allowed to take some of the family silver, porcelain and other valuables to England. He had, in fact, sold Hieronim's solid silver hunting plates in London over the telephone at a fiver apiece. He could not explain why he was allowed to take such treasures out of Poland, but he angrily denied being an agent of the Communist regime.

The domestic triangle in Ealing was now almost a replica of the fateful situation in Belgrade and Jerusalem nearly twenty years earlier. Once again a close cousin and friend was trying to take Stas's abused wife from him. Andrew was determined to marry Ada. There were raised voices in the house as the tensions became unbearable. One night Andrew climbed in through a window with a knife between his teeth and attacked Stas and cut him in the belly as they fought, but he was not badly hurt.

While all this was going on I was studying at Oxford. The first I heard about all the dramas was when big, tall, handsome Andrew burst into my rooms at University College, declaring that he was my uncle and announcing that he was in love with Ada. I had never heard of him before that moment, and I had no idea what to say or do when he told me my father was not worthy of Ada and he intended to marry her. He demanded my support. It was overwhelming, far too Polish and dramatic for me. All I wanted was for him to go away and leave me alone.

A few weeks later he barged in again, this time into the sacristy of the university's Roman Catholic Chaplaincy just as Father Michael Hollings, the chaplain, was vesting to say an evening Mass at which I was to serve at the altar. Again he harangued us about Stas's unworthiness and demanded that Father Michael and I support his efforts to marry Ada. He only left when Father Michael lost patience and put his hands on his chest and pushed him slowly out of the door.

I went to stay at Ealing in the spring of 1960 to earn some holiday money carting trays of sausages at the local Sainsbury's. The house was calm. There was no sign of Andrew, and the dramatic events bubbling away were not discussed. My only glimpse of the violence beneath the surface was when Stas turned round sharply to Ada after she said something in Polish and raised a ham-like fist to her face. I later incurred his wrath by addressing him in French by the familiar *tu*, unaware that this was disrespectful to parents in Polish society. I was shocked by his anger and the coldness he showed towards me, and wondered for the first time if the father I idealised really loved me at all.

In the end, he returned to Ila in Warsaw later in 1960. Soon afterwards Ada discovered she was pregnant. She and Andrew remained in London with the children, with no income apart from the lodgers upstairs. Andrew's behaviour in the weeks that followed was sometimes frightening. One day the children heard chilling screams in the house. When they opened the bathroom door they saw Andrew slaughtering their favourite cat over the toilet.

Ada gave birth to Marek at the end of 1961, and the family disintegrated. She sent the other children away, moved into a flat in Wanda's house in Bayswater and sold the house in Ealing. She sent four of the children to a school for the children of broken families run by Polish nuns near Ascot, where they had a happy year in beautiful surroundings. But Adam, who at nine was above the entry age for boys, was sent to a school run by English nuns. Having been to a Polish-speaking school he spoke no English, the nuns spoke no Polish, and he was intensely homesick and lonely. Traumatised by the experience, he was changed, no longer the smiling, curly-haired *Kotek*, but a bitter, angry Adam. When Ada took him to visit his siblings after a few months he was so rude and angry towards her that his brothers and sisters were shocked.

Andrew was the love of Ada's life, but with her family divided she agonised over remaining with him or returning to Stas. Eventually, Stas promised to leave Ila if she joined him in Warsaw with the children. So in 1962 she left Andrew and boarded the Polish liner *Stefan Batory* at Southampton and sailed to Poland with the six children. Poor Andrew never got over it. Soon after he died in tragic circumstances.

CHAPTER TWENTY-EIGHT

A Shipwrecked Lord

*S*tas was there to meet Ada and the children when the *Stefan Batory* docked. He had brought Jas Radziwill, his drinking companion and one of the few members of the Polish aristocracy who still associated with him. If Ada had been expecting reconciliation she was disappointed. They had a bitter row that night when Stas made it clear he had no intention of giving up Ila, and Ada was to be, in effect, no more than governess of his children.

But she had made her choice and she had to live with it because the children needed a father. With the money from the sale of the house in Ealing, they bought a spacious pre-war house in the Warsaw suburb of Saska Kepa on the right bank of the River Vistula and took a maid. Stas was earning good money as translator, interpreter and editorial assistant to the American correspondent of the *New York Times* in Warsaw. He was paid in U.S. dollars which he exchanged on the black market, and he was able to support the home and the children as well as his carousing with Ila.

Even so, Ada's life was miserable. Stas would often stay out all night, sleeping with Ila on the kitchen floor of her mother's tiny flat. They drank heavily and their boozing sessions were a major part of their relationship. Jas Radziwill also visited the family home for vodka sessions that usually ended in drunken unpleasantness. He was small and cheerful and spoke good English. He worked in one of the official labour organisations, and joked that he was the only prince trade unionist in the Communist bloc. But the children came to hate him because their father always got drunk during his visits and had violent, drunken rows with Ada after he left, abusing her in coarse language.

Stas was as helpless as Hieronim when it came to liquor, but more dangerous. Unlike Hieronim's infrequent and sometimes comical inebriations, Stas loved to drink and never stopped until the bottle was empty. He usually got blind, raging, drunk, unleashing a tirade of pent-up rage. At one moment he was hospitable and oozing charm, and next moment he was spitting venom in uncontrollable anger and looking for a fight. Unusually strong for a man of his build, he fought with a bellowing rage and used deadly tricks he had learned as a commando.

He had fights all over Warsaw. One evening he fought wildly with five militiamen who tried to restrain him in the bar of the Europejski Hotel, a Warsaw landmark, breaking a leg of one of them and an arm of another before they over-whelmed him. His behaviour scandalised Warsaw. Friends and relatives kept away. Even close cousins like moderate, restrained Uncle Tomek Zamoyski stopped visiting, disgusted by the shame he was bringing upon the family.

He had a row with the *New York Times* correspondent and lost his job, and he squandered so much of Hieronim's inheritance that they had to move out of their spacious pre-war house into a concrete box in an ugly chain of low, square Communist dwellings in a cul-de-sac in the back streets of Saska Kepa. It wasn't even a street, just a pathway of concrete slabs that passed the doorway, going nowhere.

The children lived in fear of his return home at night and the inevitable row that would follow. Some of them were so traumatised that they shouted and cried in their sleep. He trampled their egos, destroyed their wills with his bullying ways, and taught them by example that self-will and irresponsibility were the supreme rules of life. If they tried to stand up to him they were likely to get punched. Adam, his oldest boy by Ada, once took a halberd from the wall during a fearsome row and jabbed it at his father's stomach.

Stas's nemesis eventually appeared in the form of Jurek, a blond, blue-eyed forester with the square jaw and bulging muscles of a Polish Arnold Schwarzenegger. Jurek came from the wild Bieszczady hills of south-eastern Poland where bears still roamed, and where Stas took Ila, Ada and the children for summer holidays. It was Ila's family home and Jurek fell in love with her.

For the third time in Stas's life a rival was trying to take his woman, and this time he was determined to keep her. He and Jurek fought in the hills like stags in the mating season. He had no chance against a mountain of a man like Jurek, but he was nothing if not brave. Once on a dark Bieszczady night Ada, Ila and the children watched screaming as Jurek beat him so badly that blood poured from his face by the light of the camp fire.

Stas never gave up, and Ila could not give him up. She was unable to choose between the rivals. Though Stas was difficult and unpredictable, Jurek offered little but love and a life in the wild. In the end Stas and Jurek came to respect each other and they formed a volatile love triangle. When the three of them holidayed together in the wilds Stas and Jurek took turns sleeping with Ila. The children hated it and disliked Ila, but they warmed to the big burly Jurek, an honest, gentle giant.

When Ila eventually tired of it and decided to marry Jurek, Stas was spurred into action. Ada agreed to a divorce, and he bought Ila a small flat in Warsaw, decorated it himself, and proposed to her. But it was too late. She married Jurek and went to Bieszczady with him and stayed there for the rest of her life, while Ada and Stas settled into a dysfunctional compromise and grew old together in the little house in Saska Kepa.

Back in England, Wanda was dying. It was February 1965 and the cancer had spread all over her body. She was in great pain, but she hid it with iron self-control. She had never lost the extraordinary courage that marked her out in life. Throughout her illness she never took a painkiller other than aspirin until near the very end.

I went to say farewell to her in the house she had bought in Bayswater after the war with the proceeds from Catherine the Great's jewellery. She was in bed, propped up on pillows in a quiet and darkened room. Rugs and tapestries covered the wall above the bed in the Eastern European way, and Tadeusz and a little dog were fussing around the room in distress. I hardly knew her and she hardly knew me, because I had only been once or twice before, but I called her Bunia, the Polish for Granny. When I bent over to kiss her, open sores were visible at the crook of her neck and under her arms, but she was perfectly awake and alert and gave no sign of pain. She said in a low voice: 'Boubi, if you have a son, be good to him.'

That was all. I left the room. A doctor came and gave her a morphine injection for the pain, and she died quietly. It was all over in a few minutes. The doctor took her corneas for donation purposes, packed up his instruments, and left.

I wrote to Stas in Warsaw describing his mother's death and telling him of her last words to me, and he was deeply moved. He believed the words were some sort of an admission of failure, an oblique request for forgiveness. He took them to heart and remembered them for years afterward, and so did I.

I went to Poland two years later against my mother's wishes. She had always discouraged any Polish influence in my life and she was frightened by the prospect of me going to Communist Poland. She got Nicholas Henderson, a senior diplomat from the British embassy, to visit me in the Reuters bureau in Madrid in an attempt to dissuade me from going. He warned me that although I had British nationality I was Polish born and the authorities in Warsaw could choose to keep me in Poland, in which case Britain would be unable to do anything for me. I was appalled to learn that the British authorities would do nothing for me, but I thought it was ridiculous to suppose that the Polish authorities would be interested in the insignificant émigré son of an ex-aristocrat and so I went ahead with the trip.

Stas was at the dilapidated old airport in Warsaw to meet me, proudly driving a battered Jaguar saloon and all set to show me round the country. After an emotional reunion with Ada and the children he drove me to southern Poland to visit 'the old places'. He took charge of my foreign currency and changed it on the black market, and he made sure we spent the lot living like princes touring Krakow and towns founded by our ancestors like Tarnow, Tarnobrzeg, Przeworsk and Jaroslaw before we visited our pre-war family homes.

We stayed in the forest at Rudnik with Stas Poisel, a lanky, gnarled forester of about fifty with a shock of short white hair who was the son of one of Hieronim's district foresters and was himself a state forester. He lived in a wooden house with his wife Sophie, a smiling *babcia* with a flowered scarf tied round her head and knotted under her chin.

The mansion at Rudnik was a disappointment. Like everything else in 1960s Poland, it was dilapidated and shabby after twenty-five years of neglect. Compared with houses I knew in Britain, such as Rowland's magnificent eighteenth-century pile at Nostell Priory in Yorkshire, and even with Glenternie, Malcolm's home in the Scottish Borders, it was ugly and uninteresting. The driveway was untended, the gardens gone, the doors and windows unpainted, and the plasterwork was a dirty grey. Standing beside Stas in front of the house, knowing almost nothing about my family's experiences, I could not imagine what it had been like when he and Sophie grew up there. It was just a lifeless relic sunk in the forest, without a hint of beauty or charm. I looked dumbly, awkward and uncomfortable at being unmoved by my grandfather's home, not knowing what to say.

I felt an awakening of interest when Stas pointed out the window of the room that had been his bedroom, but just then windows began to open and heads poked out to look at us. The house was a dormitory for agricultural students and we should not have been there. Stas decided we had better leave before questions were asked and the militia came.

But a few minutes later I experienced the emotional revelation I had expected at Rudnik. Driving away through the countryside that had been part of Hieronim's estate, we passed a couple of skinny, fair-haired boys in a field beside the narrow country road. Smoke was rising from a wood fire beside them, and some peasants were loading potatoes onto a long wooden wagon. A horse stood nearby. Beyond were more fields and the dark line of the forest on the horizon. It was towards evening; dusk was beginning to gather, and there was mist in the air as the sunlit day dissolved into a quintessential Polish mood scene of greys, greens and dark greens under a broad, pale sky.

Stas Poisel, who was with us, turned to me in the back seat of the car, and with a smile on his face, made a sweeping gesture with his arm and said something in Polish.

'What did he say?' I asked Stas.

'Oh. He said all this is yours. All this land, the forests, he means.'

It was not mine, of course, and never would be. But it might have been, and Stas Poisel's words made a powerful impression. They brought home to me who and what I might have been if Poland's fate and my parents' lives had turned out differently. At that moment I experienced a real sense of belonging for the first time in my life, a glimpse of what it would have meant to have been fully Polish and to have lived among those fields and forests. The moment helped to nurture in me the sense of Polishness that Chouquette was so anxious to avoid.

I visited Poland again five years later. I had moved from Madrid to the Reuters bureau in Rome and drove from Italy in a Volkswagen Beetle, meeting up with Tessa, my tall and lovely Scottish half-sister, and her boyfriend Nick, and together we went with the family to Bieszczady. They were all there, Stas, Ila and Jurek with Ada, the six children and one or two Polish friends. It was the first time I had met Ila, although it was fifteen years since she and Stas had met, and I wondered what the fuss was about. She was fair-haired, but nothing special: short, and slightly sturdy with a face a little bloated from drink and a snub nose that was also reddening. She was quite jolly and tried to charm me, but she left me cold. I wasn't prepared to like her.

The sixteen of us, ranging in age from six to fifty-four, with two ponies carrying the baggage, set off to trek for five days through the hills and forests of Bieszczady. We marched in a straggling line through an empty landscape whose Orthodox Ruthenian inhabitants had been deported and their villages razed by the Polish army after a ferocious partisan war in 1945–47. There were no settlements in the hills, just the ruins of villages and rusting Ruthenian crosses leaning from old wayside shrines. Occasionally, we came across a hut of wood and thatch built by a former inhabitant who had surreptitiously returned. We were never sure if we would be welcomed and we never knew where we would find shelter for the night, nor sometimes where the next meal would come from.

I woke with the sun one morning, lying on wooden planks in a loft with pigs rooting on the ground beneath me, to see Stas asleep on his back beside me with a chicken roosting on his chest. Like Wanda he had an extraordinary affinity with animals. That morning we fed on milk and a few eggs and boiled potatoes doused in bacon fat. After the day's march we came at dusk to an old oak tree on a hilltop that was on fire from a lightning strike, flames flickering from the top of the trunk where a huge branch had been blasted off. We found a boyish-looking outlaw with long blonde hair living in a house with his girlfriend and several companions. It was an abandoned state farm. The air in the house was foul with the stench of *bimber* or home-made potato vodka they were brewing. But they welcomed us, and exhausted by the trek we drank *bimber* until we all collapsed on the hay in a huge barn.

The outlaw and his girlfriend visited us later in the village where we were staying. The reputation and hospitality of the family was at stake, and we had to drink non-stop to make them welcome. I was determined to do my bit for the family and show them that even though I was British I could drink with the rest of them, so I filled my belly with pints of milk and slices of bread in preparation. I drank steadily for two days and a night, and got through the ordeal in a permanent state of mild stupefaction without throwing up. I felt pleased that I was learning to control the vodka beast but Stas wasn't so sure. He told me that the passes I had made at the outlaw's girlfriend might easily have caused serious trouble.

There was a peasant wedding in the village after they left. The wedding party rolled past our door on a farm cart one evening and shut themselves in a house to drink for the weekend. At dawn on the Monday, as I was walking past with the milk can, the door of the house opened and a foul gale of cigarette smoke, vodka, beer and sweat engulfed me.

I returned to Poland in 1976, this time with my first wife Ysabel, my mother-in-law Liliane, our little daughter Sophie and our unborn second child who was making Ysabel's stomach swell. We rented a Polski Fiat station wagon, piled in with ten people and veered around pot-holed Polish roads, once again touring 'the old places'. Ysabel and Liliane weren't prepared for the backwardness of Eastern Europe, the poverty and lack of amenities in Poland, or for Stas's squalid little house. When we returned to Warsaw they moved into a hotel but I stayed on for a bit of family life. Of course, family life with Stas involved drinking sessions. Jas Radziwill came round. Everyone got drunk. Stas started roaring insults at Ada. I objected, and he got up in a fury and came at me. I retreated up the stairs, but he charged up and punched me. So I moved out, and it was twelve years before I returned.

When I returned to Warsaw it was January 1988 and I came as Reuters bureau chief for Poland. For twenty years I had held postings around the world, in Madrid, Havana, Rome, Buenos Aires, New York, Beirut and New Delhi. That, and a failed marriage and raising my first two children had left me little time to nurture my Polish heritage. But everything changed from the moment I landed in snowbound Warsaw on a pinched, grey January day with Wafa', my second wife, and our two young children Daisy and Stefan. As Reuters correspondent I was plunged into Polish life at a time of historic change. For four and a half years I and a team of Polish and British colleagues reported on the triumph of the Solidarity movement and the collapse of Communism as Poland led the way to the establishment of democracy and the dismantling of the Soviet empire in eastern and central Europe. It was an exhilarating time for an expatriate Pole to be in Poland, and it left me with a great liking and respect for the Polish people. I was proud of their skill and courage in peacefully leading the way to freedom.

For the first time I was living in the same city as Stas and his family. They welcomed us with great warmth and we exchanged visits and dined out together. Stas was seventy, a freelance translator for official publishers, and Ada was receptionist at the Swiss embassy. But they still drank, and so did some of the children. None of us could hold our liquor and arguments erupted and tempers flared. After a few meetings Stas and I had a ridiculous row after a Sunday lunch at my home over whether it was right to take the sacred host in one's hand at Holy Communion, and he started shouting and our relations broke down. We didn't meet again for a year.

That was the beginning of my eventual estrangement from my Polish family as we went through a cycle of rifts and reconciliations. When I wasn't seeing Stas, none of them would meet me, apart from Sandra, the oldest, who had always been specially affectionate towards me. When Communism collapsed Adam began trying to recover properties on Stas's behalf. I helped him financially at first and sometimes travelled with him. Jas Tarnowski, the heir to Dzikow, also returned to Poland from Canada on a similar mission, and the three of us visited Rudnik, which was derelict and falling into ruin. We met Jadzia Hass'a Maach, who had been a cashier in the estate office, and as she lay in bed she told us how she had witnessed Hieronim's expulsion in 1944.

Stas and I had another row before I left Poland in May 1992. I was shocked by the arrogance with which he treated the local authorities at Dukla, and stopped contributing to Adam's efforts to recover properties. In the mid-1990s Adam bought back the ruined mansion at Rudnik from the local authorities. Later, when the courts ordered the Polish Radio to hand back the Szlak, Adam, Stas and Sophie tried vainly to let it out in its dilapidated state. They refused to develop it, and the historic house stood empty and decaying for nearly ten years before they sold it.

Near the end of our time in Poland, Wafa' and I began delving into the family's past, learning from Stas, Tomek Zamoyski, Jas Tarnowski and others about life in Poland between the wars. Whenever I was back in London I visited Sophie in Putney and enjoyed her roast lamb with garlic and sweet red cabbage and a bottle of red wine, and then I would settle down to hours of listening to her extraordinary tales of childhood and youth in Poland and life during the war in the Balkans, Jerusalem and Cairo.

She loved to talk about the past, not with nostalgia for what she had lost but with immense enjoyment of her memories and the friends she had known. Thinking back on those long afternoons, when her stories transported me to the world of her youth, I remember the quiet beauty of her voice, the softness of her tone, and her wicked sense of humour and gusts of laughter. As she began reminiscing she would become still, tuck her arms into her sides, put her elbows on her knees and lean forward towards the kitchen table holding up a lighted cigarette between two fingers. She pursed her lips in concentration and began to talk. Her face was animated, her eyes were huge, a clear watery blue, and as she spoke she smiled and smiled at the memories her words brought to life. Every now and then there were moments of sheer pleasure when a particularly amusing memory ambushed the flow of her words, and with huge delight transforming her face she subsided into a torrent of almost childlike giggles.

She broke off every now and then to make tea. Even when she was eighty she would pick up a bucket and go out the back, a stooped, tiny figure, to fill it with coal and stoke up the stove, or she would take out leftovers to feed the foxes that roamed the gardens of Putney. Then she would settle down again and carry on telling her inexhaustible fund of stories. She told them without haste, in astonishing detail and with great elegance, carefully enunciating each syllable in a slightly refined English accent that spoke of the exotic world from which she came.

I remember remarking, after an afternoon of listening to her, that she seemed a very happy person for someone who had been through so much and lost so much.

'Yes,' she replied, 'My mother said that, too. She couldn't understand it, but I told her I am *Manka wstanka* ('Stand-up Mary'), one of those wooden dolls that has a weight inside it somewhere. You can lay it down and it will always stand up.'

Wafa' also asked Stas one day, just before we left Warsaw, if he regretted losing the fabulous world he had known in his youth. I had so often heard him curse the Communists that I was surprised by his answer. 'Naturally, it is to be regretted by us, yes. We had a lovely life, a wonderful life,' he replied. 'But I must say I'm not really sorry having lost it all. Nowadays, living in a park, in a big manor house or a palace like Dukla would be rather strange, wouldn't it? Those times are over, it's finished, done with. Change is bound to happen. The sort of life we used to live, pre-war, was in a way still medieval . . . We were lords almighty; not officially so, but in fact we were. It's a way of life that couldn't be resumed in this country.'

Whenever I returned to Warsaw I was struck by the contrast between the penury in which he and Ada lived and the privileged life of ease and wealth he had enjoyed in his youth. The few paintings and memorabilia that adorned their little home seemed to emphasise the indigence into which they had fallen. When they grew too old to work they lived on in the little house surrounded by grown-up children, nostalgia and family mementoes – albums of small black-and-white photographs inhabited by people in old-fashioned dress, and blurred images of the Rudnik garden criss-crossed by trenches during the 1914–18 war, visitors' books from Rudnik and Dukla containing memories of happier days and relics of the professor's glory. They lived on Ada's small pension from the Swiss embassy and meagre rents from the Krakow apartment building that belonged to Stas and Sophie.

As the years passed Stas grew white-haired and heavy. By the time of his eightieth birthday he was nearly immobile and almost blind. He sat all day in an armchair in the crowded living room in front of the television, eating where he sat and rarely heaving himself up to go upstairs or take a look outside. He alternated between sleep and consciousness as the life of the house went on around him. Sandra lived upstairs with her son Franek and gave English lessons; Marek lived downstairs in the basement. Michal and Isa were in England, Jas worked in Warsaw for the Polish news agency PAP and had a rented apartment, and Adam was in Krakow in the apartment building he managed. Ada cooked, shopped and washed and sat as close to Stas as she could. They still slept apart, but they seemed reconciled, and sometimes they prayed the rosary together. The storms of late middle age had passed. 'Stas has mellowed,' Ada would say each time I came to Warsaw. 'Papa has mellowed,' the children echoed.

Sitting in his armchair, often with his head slumped on his chest, he looked like an ancient shipwrecked lord surrounded by the last vestiges of his finery – a stained silken wall-hanging embroidered with heraldic crests woven for some nineteenth-century wedding; a tattered, once-bejewelled Turkish saddle captured in one of Poland's wars; a few oil paintings; a beautiful clock or two; swords and halberds on the walls. And lying on a cabinet, stripped of the jewel that once crowned it, lay the silver mace of the Rector Magnificus of the Jagiellonian University that his grandfather Professor Stanislaw Tarnowski had proudly carried in the days of his eminence, not so long ago.

CHAPTER TWENTY-NINE

The Last
Turn of the Wheel

*I*n August 1999, fifty-five years after the Communists expelled Hieronim from Rudnik, I travelled from England with Wafa' and three of my four children for a family holiday at the recovered mansion. Adam had made enough repairs for four generations of Hieronim's descendants to spend a few days under his roof. There were about thirty of us, reflecting the scattering of the family since 1939: about half had come from England and the rest from Poland, and among us were a sprinkling of nationalities: my Lebanese wife, my half-sister Isa's Greek ex-husband, my Canadian son Marcos, and Britons as well as Poles. Some of us spoke little or no Polish.

Stas and Sophie presided over the gathering at the childhood home they loved. They sat side-by-side in wicker armchairs under the portico, looking over the lawn towards the lakes and the stables and former estate office beyond. Sadly, the wooden chapel in which Sophie was baptised and married had been dismantled during the Communist years.

Sophie was eighty-two, bent and shrunken but sprightly, smoking incessantly and telling her wartime stories. Stas, who was eighty-one, alternated between lucidity and senility. He sat with a benign smile drinking tea or beer and smoking cheroots, and occasionally whispering loudly to anyone who would listen that Sophie was an old parrot and he did not really like her. Then his chin would fall onto his chest and he slept, sometimes waking to raise his head and recite loudly in English in a deep voice, to the delight of grandchildren and great-grandchildren:

> When I was young and seventeen
> I thought it was a sin
> To put my hand between her legs
> And put my finger in . . .

Ada hushed at him in shocked tones but he ignored her and trumpeted verse after verse. He had never grown up, but at least he was happy at Rudnik after so much loss and hardship and change in his long life.

We were all happy to be in Hieronim's house, feeling that our presence was historic in its own way. No one cared about the discomforts of queuing for the solitary toilet and bathroom, sleeping on inflatable mattresses on the floor in bare rooms, fending off squadrons of mosquitoes and tending to children stung by hornets that nested under the eaves. A cheerful old lady came in to cook, where once there had been a housekeeper, a butler, an under-butler, a pantry boy, a cook and four or five maids. The food was Polish countryside wholesome – home-made soups followed by breaded pork cutlets with cabbage and boiled potatoes, or cabbage stuffed with minced turkey, or *pierogi*, fried dumpling patties filled with cabbage and mushroom – washed down with beer or fruit *compote*. We all contributed to the expenses and took turns to lay the tables, clear and wash up.

Rudnik had seen so much, even since Hieronim's day, that it was hard to take in the enormity of all it had witnessed. After he was expelled the Soviet NKVD secret police took over the mansion and used the cellars as a jail and torture chamber for Home Army fighters. Then from December 1944 until March 1945 it was an NKVD school for leftist German prisoners who had become collaborators and were being trained as leaders of the Communist state Moscow intended to set up in eastern Germany. After the war it became a domestic management school for women, and finally it was turned into a dormitory, a bare barracks really, for the agricultural students who remained until the collapse of communism. As for the estate, Hieronim's forests had been nationalised after the war and a co-operative farm was set up on the agricultural land. The house was a wreck by the time the students left at the beginning of the 1990s. The local authorities abandoned it and for two or three years it stood open to vagrants until Adam was allowed to buy it.

It still looked old and tired when we arrived. The outside was grey with dirt, and plaster had fallen away exposing patches of brickwork. Woodwork and wattle showed under the eaves where moulding had broken off. Window frames were cracked, doors dull with age, and the plaster on the pillars of the portico was a patchwork of different shades of grey.

Adam had cleaned up much of the interior and re-covered most of the roof with shining new zinc. But daylight still came through the roof in places. There were huge, empty dormitories that had been formed by knocking away walls between the main bedrooms, and we slept instead in smaller rooms at the back. But there were gaping holes in the corridor floor and the back staircase that could break the legs of the unwary. All over the house the parquet floors were ruined, some dug away, and on the main staircase curving up from the hall parts of the balustrade were broken or missing.

Something of Rudnik's charm remained in the large salon,

the little salon and the dining room, although the wall between the dining room and the little salon had been destroyed to make a large refectory. The square, carved larch beams still spanned the ceilings of the three rooms. They were well proportioned, with high ceilings and tall doors and windows, and the darkness of the beams contrasted with the whitewashed walls to give them an austere Hispanic elegance.

We all knew that but for the small matter of twentieth-century conflicts Rudnik might have been our home. But despite the excitement of returning to our roots, it had witnessed so much that it was hard to think of it as a happy house. Sunk in the forest, deep in its memories, Rudnik did its best to welcome us but the atmosphere that pervaded the house was not happy – how could it be? – and in the end our gathering brought us no more happiness than Hieronim and Wanda had experienced there.

Being at Rudnik brought a troubling sense that Poland's recent history was nothing more than an open wound, or rather a mass of wounds, inflicted upon the nation. The bloodshed and crimes of the twentieth century were so near at hand that it felt as though one had only to scratch the surface at Rudnik and blood would ooze out. Adam occasionally found human bones and skulls, bullets and bayonets given up by the soil around the mansion. For me, they symbolised the times in which our great-grandparents, grandparents and parents had lived, which had toppled our family so far from its pedestal. Poland's history in those times was radically different from any other history I knew, particularly England's, which seems reassuring, not tragic, comforting, not cruel, a series of milestones on the road to advancement and progress.

Here at Rudnik there had been only a hopeless struggle against impossible enemies that was repeated in every generation, and the results were visible everywhere: in the mansion that was a pathetic caricature of its once-elegant self; in the park and farm, both ruined, and in the tall iron cross overgrown by bushes where Hieronim had buried the dead of 1914. The cellars that had once held neat rows of home-made cheeses and wild boar hams and Pani Sarnecka's pickles seemed to reek of an unthinkable past, as though the torturers and executioners had just left. What must have been a cell door leaned open, filthy and sinister. Only a recent anti-Semitic idiocy scrawled on a dank wall marked the passage of time since the NKVD had gone.

So much time had passed. So much had happened. I wandered in the sleeping house one night, thinking that these rooms must preserve some memory of Hieronim and Wanda and of what had happened here. I sat by an open window in the little salon, and in the hours before dawn, looking out at the silent forest under a bright August moon, I tried to imagine how the house must have been in my grandparents' time.

There, just behind me, they had sat taking aperitifs and had patted Stas and Sophie when they trotted in to kiss their hands. Over there in the big salon Hieronim had thrashed his teenage son for putting a snake into the piano teacher's bed. There they had danced to gypsy violins at Sophie's wedding. In Hieronim's study beyond the dining room Stas and Sophie took a shotgun and fired it under the estate manager's window at *maly domek*, the wooden house where they were born, still there a couple of hundred metres away through the trees. And it was there in the study that Stas had knelt on 8 September 1939, to kiss Hieronim's hand before fleeing Poland. Here, where I sat at the window, Sophie had taken leave of Hieronim that evening. The *proporzec,* the standard of the Swedish king, had hung on this wall beside me until he gave it to her for safekeeping.

In the stillness of the night I seemed to hear distant echoes of that terrible battle of 1914 when the Russian and Austro-Hungarian armies fought for three weeks around the mansion. And the silence seemed to echo the silence of Hieronim's people as they watched him being driven away in 1944.

So many of our people had come and gone since great-grandmother Imcia bought Rudnik in 1898. The professor lay in the family crypt in the Dominican church at Dzikow but Imcia herself was under a crumbling slab in the Rudnik cemetery. Count Zdzislaw, the last great lord of Dzikow, was no more than a memory from a bygone age. Hieronim lay alone in a Krakow mausoleum, and Wanda's ashes were scattered on the estate from which she came. Alfred Potocki, her lover, had died in Switzerland in the 1950s after spending his last years in a wheelchair with Parkinson's disease. Artur lived in England, also in a wheelchair since contracting polio as a young man. Chouquette's father lay in a Warsaw cemetery, but her mother was in the churchyard at Rowland's home in Yorkshire. Chouquette herself lay with Malcolm in a Scottish country churchyard, and Boule and Rowland were together, next to her mother at Nostell.

I wanted to see during our stay at Rudnik all the places and things I had learned about while exploring my family's past. I walked to the cemetery on the edge of town to find the grave of Colonel Walerian Mlyniec, the officer who shot himself on the day my parents fled Rudnik in 1939. He lay not far from Imcia, his grave lovingly maintained by the Rudnik Boy Scouts. Faded silk flowers in the red and white Polish colours adorned an iron crucifix, and a metal plaque bore the inscription: 'Embrace in your mercy, Lord, him who had not strength'. Another read: 'I walked the thorny paths of life, so do not reject me now, Christ.' How good that the colonel was pitied and honoured by his people.

He lay in a cemetery crowded with the dead of two world wars that seemed far off on a bright Saturday afternoon at the close of the century. As I stood at his grave, people were moving in ones and twos along the lines of tombs. An old man placed flowers on a grave, lit a votive candle and sat down beside it. A mother and daughter walked past carrying flowers. A woman with a bucket of water and a cloth who was swabbing down a large granite tomb stopped to chat with a passing friend. A few cars drove past outside the cemetery. The sun shone and birds sang in the summer heat, and the forest stood tall and silent beyond the cemetery wall. So many years had passed. In a small town in Poland, honouring the victims of that brutal century was a part of daily life.

Wafa' and I walked with my half-brother Michal to the town hall to buy a history of Rudnik written by a local couple. At last, Poles could write freely about their past. We stopped in the market square and chatted with older residents, whose eyes lit up when we told them we were Count Hieronim's grandchildren. They smiled and spoke of him with affection, and it made me happy that he was remembered kindly by these people. There was healing in their words and smiles.

An old man named Stanislaw Ruchaj told us his father, a prosperous farmer, had lent Hieronim money just before the war that was never repaid. He said when he was an altar boy in the Rudnik church Hieronim had helped to build, Imcia used to sit in the front pew with a lady companion and 'tut-tutted' noisily if the altar boys chatted too loudly in the sacristy.

We met a granddaughter of Karol Kulpa, who was the chief groom at Rudnik before 1914 and went to the army with Hieronim as his personal servant during the Great War and the Polish-Soviet war of 1920. She told us her mother had written down her memories of life on the estate, so we invited her to visit the mansion now that the family had returned. She came a couple of days later with a friend and gave me a copy of the Rudnik Review containing her mother's reminiscences, which were packed with anecdotes of life in Hieronim's day. We introduced the ladies to the family and offered them tea, and Michal and I showed them round.

The family were uncomfortable about us bringing strangers to the house; they usually had little contact with local people. The days of *grands seigneurs* were surely over, but when we arrived there was a 'Private Property' sign on the gate with a crude Leliwa, the family crest, painted on it.

I knew there were differences between those living in Poland, and those, like me, who lived in the West. But during our stay at Rudnik I learned how deep they went. There had been so much talk of Poland becoming democratic that I had assumed Stas, Sophie and the rest would adapt. But they had clung to pre-war ways which had been archaic even in Hieronim's time. Stas had always drummed into his children that they came from a historic family. He had taught them a lopsided, nostalgic view of history that gave them a sense of self-importance, but nothing of the self-reliance and enter-prise needed to grasp the opportunities of modern life. Their imaginations were suffocated by the past and their ambitions limited to recovering family properties and restoring Rudnik as a shrine to Hieronim and the professor.

I had come to Rudnik convinced that our family could restore its fortunes by developing the Szlak in Krakow as a hotel or office building. A seventy-room mansion in an up-and-coming city had huge potential. But the Szlak had been empty and rotting for years, while what little income the family had was being used to renovate Rudnik.

Stas's violence had bred a culture of confrontation and conflict in which serious family discussions were impossible, and so my half-brothers and half-sisters habitually avoided questioning whatever course was being taken. They had been raised to give way to Stas in all things, and now that he was senile and Adam held his power-of-attorney they would not question Adam's stewardship.

Since my generation would eventually inherit the family's assets and it would be best to manage them together I wanted to lay the groundwork for future collaboration if we were to avoid unbearable confrontations when the time came. So with Stas's permission I addressed the family on our last day at Rudnik, suggesting ways of developing and exploiting the family's assets in Hieronim's spirit for the good of all. As his oldest grandchild I wanted to show a peaceful way forward.

The auguries were not good. There had been arguments and insults on the previous evening when Adam launched a tirade against Michal in front of the family. Nobody stopped him. He went on and on. It was so vile that I began weeping quietly, bringing a barked, 'Oh, shut up' from Sophie, aimed not at Adam's virulence but at my tears. Wafa' remonstrated with Sophie, but she replied with more unpleasantness until I lost my temper and shouted at her. That was the end of our relationship.

But Sophie came to the little salon next day when everyone gathered there to hear me. They heard me out, but when I finished the room erupted in shouting and outpourings of angst and insecurity. We had no right to discuss Hieronim's inheritance before it came down to us, someone said. Better to leave decisions about the inheritance until we had inherited, said another. Someone said I was trespassing on the rights of Stas and Sophie, the present owners of the family's assets. Sophie said I was trying to poke my nose into her bank account. Someone else said I was criticising Adam's management of the family properties. Adam certainly felt he was being attacked. He shouted angry comments, yelled at Wafa' that she should learn Polish, although she spoke a creditable amount already, and walked out saying he was going back to Krakow.

The room was as rowdy as an eighteenth-century *sejmik*, a local assembly of nobles fortified with mead and beer, and a byword for fractious parliamentary dissension *à la polonaise*. Amid the hubbub, Stas snapped. Hauling himself heavily to his feet, purple with rage, eyes narrowed to a furious squint, he bellowed: 'Fuck the lot of you, bloody Tarnowskis.' Then he stood there, bewildered, as if looking for a target for his rage. When Ada tried to calm him he raised a great ham-like fist at her, threatening loudly to beat her, and bellowed insults after her as she fled the room, sobbing that she had finally had enough of Tarnowskis and would never come back.

It was my first real view of the depths of the family's wretchedness, although I realised later that I was part of the problem. While the family seemed impossibly dysfunctional to me, to most of them I was an intruder committing the unpardonable offence of questioning the dispositions of Stas and Sophie, joint owners of Hieronim's inheritance and the senior generation of the family, whose will, according to family mores passed down from generation to generation, was sacrosanct and immovable.

The legacy of the past with its archaic ways that excluded common sense and rational discussion was as cruel as it had been sixty years earlier. The gathering had exposed our crippling legacy. The personality weaknesses and short-coming passed down by Hieronim and Wanda, which had made them incompatible during their lives, had burst into the open amongst us once again and had torn us apart. They were all there in plain view: Hieronim's nervousness and inability to communicate with his children, his lack of moderation and his inability to handle any form of personal conflict, his narrowness of ideas and rigidity of argument, his insistence on stretching logic to illogical conclusions, his inability to take his liquor, and his choleric reactions; Wanda's pride and coldness, her wilfulness, self-centredness, self-righteousness and disdain for the effects of her behaviour on others. They were all there, in plain view as we shouted, swore and wept.

When the noise had died down and the sobs had died away I suggested that we could try to get something positive out of our gathering by agreeing to start working together on a project that was long overdue: the restoration of Imcia's crumbling tomb in the town cemetery. Now that we were back at Rudnik it was time to show that we honoured her, who had brought Rudnik into the family. That morning Michal had driven Sandra and me around the nearby villages and we had found a monument maker, selected a fine slab of marble and agreed a price for the job. I outlined the project to the family in the little drawing room and we all agreed gladly to share the cost. Sophie hurried out of the room and returned moments later, happily flourishing an inscription she had already composed to be put on the new tombstone.

Our departure from Rudnik later that day was sad and tinged with bitterness but my family and I were glad we had spent time with them all in Hieronim's home. We had danced in the big salon one evening, and my eleven-year-old son Stefan had given a violin recital in the little salon, and Wafa' had been warmly feted on her birthday. Before we left, we all signed the old Rudnik visitors' book with the family crest embossed on the front, its opening pages inscribed with the signatures of the guests at Hieronim's and Wanda's wedding and the wise and joyous speeches that had welcomed their union. I signed myself as Hieronim's oldest grandson on my first visit to his home, but my family and I came away uneasy, feeling that Rudnik was not a happy house and that we did not belong with those who inhabited it.

We returned a year later for the re-consecration of Imcia's restored tomb but did not stay at the mansion. A small crowd of townspeople joined the family at the Mass in the parish church and at the graveside ceremony, pleased to see that we were honouring our benefactress at last.

A few days later my family and I went to Dzikow for a three-day gathering of the extended family. There were 180 of us, and we got to know relatives from around the world, cultured and interesting people. We walked around the house and played basketball in the covered riding school. We saw the library where the family archives had been kept and looked through the window into the chapel at which Count Zdzislaw had knelt to pray and grumble at God. We visited the family museum that his grandson Jas Tarnowski had established in a seventeenth-century granary nearby. My son Stefan played a duet at the family concert with cousin Bratek Tarnowski, a fine concert pianist, whose father Karol had led Wanda to the altar on her wedding day, and on the last evening we danced in the great 'sala' or drawing room with its two-storey high ceiling and sang Polish songs and watched young people from Tarnobrzeg in eighteenth-century costumes dance the polonaise. We came away elated, and I felt that the gathering was the culmination of my search for Polish roots. Although we had not found a permanent niche among Hieronim's descendants, we felt at home among this bright and friendly gathering.

Soon after our stay at Rudnik I bought a small farmhouse beside a forest in the Mazurian lake region in the north of Poland. We go every year to swim and sail and cycle through the forest, and Wafa' and I take long evening walks among the wheat fields. Sometimes, on special occasions, we take a ride through the forest in a horse-drawn carriage driven by a toothless little local farmer with a happy, smiling face, just as my grandparents drove through the beautiful Rudnik forests long ago. During long summer days we lunch in the sunshine by one of the big wooden barns beside the house, eating the soups and pork cutlets with wild mushrooms, or baked trout or roast duck cooked by our beloved Pani Wiesia from the village with her splendid bosom and *babcia* scarf and an affectionate glint in her eye. Some nights as the moon sails over the forest we grill meat over an *ognisko* or camp fire in the field behind the house. It is beautiful unspoiled countryside, our neighbours in the village are friendly and helpful, and we are all happy to be in Poland. It has become an important part of life for Wafa' and our children as well as for me.

But it is the other end of Poland from Rudnik, which we no longer visit. We rarely see the family apart from my ever-affectionate sister Sandra and her children, and our cousin Jas Tarnowski, Count Zdzislaw's grandson, known as Jas 'Glowa' or Jas the Head, who is head of the Dzikow branch and of the extended family, with whom we share the house. So in a way my family and I are back in Poland, and in a way Dzikow and Rudnik are reunited once again, and as the twentieth century fades thankfully into memory I can feel that the wheel of history has turned its circle and we are just about back once more where we belong.

Roza's Prayer

*I*f the twentieth century had a theme, for us it was war. The greatest wars the world has seen destroyed our homes and our country and swept away the world we knew. The wars brought us foul tyrannies, one black that lasted for years that seemed like decades, the second red that lasted for decades that seemed like lifetimes. An eternity seemed to pass before the last was over. It was only fifty years, but by then everything was changed forever.

But in those nightmarish times hope always remained. There was a boundless faith bred by Poland's history of survival in adversity that we and our country would survive against all odds. 'Poland has not yet perished while we still live', as the national anthem goes.

When Stas and Chouquette fled Poland in September 1939 in a family convoy of seven cars packed with aristocrats, some of those who were with them were leaving behind husbands and fathers who had gone off to the war. Two who were leaving their husbands were Roza Tyszkiewicz and Zosia Potocka, Andrew's older sisters and daughters of Count Zdzislaw Tarnowski. Roza's husband Wladyslaw, who suffered from manic depression, had left their home at Tarnawatka to serve as a volunteer traffic controller near the eastern city of Lwow. Zosia's husband Andrzej had gone to the front with his regiment as a reserve army lieutenant.

Roza and Zosia had no news of their husbands as the family convoy carried them and their children to Belgrade. They were still agonising whether to return home to look for their husbands when in March 1941 they joined a colony of 300 Polish refugees on the Croatian coast at Crikvenica, where they stayed for two and a half years. The Italian army, which controlled the region, provided them with food free of charge.

The two sisters never stopped making enquiries about their husbands through the International Red Cross, the Swedish royal family and the Polish ambassador in London but they learned nothing. They prayed and continued to pray after the German army took over Crikvenica in late 1943 and sent them, their children and friends to Ravensbruck and Dachau. They prayed in the camps and they prayed after surviving the camps and settling in England after the war, where their children and their descendants still live.

The prayer they prayed constantly for the missing men during those years was a special prayer that Zosia composed:

O God, we commend to your heart our dear Papa,
Bless him, envelop him in your holy grace,
Help him, save him, support him and console him,
Protect him from all evil:
From accidents, sickness, injury and loss of limb,
From the hatred of men and from persecution,
And especially from that which could separate him from You.
Give him unwavering faith,
Confidence in your mercy,
Great love for You and for men.
Give him strength, courage and resistance in suffering
    and in labour.
Grant that from the suffering that You send him
He may emerge braver, better, nobler, closer and more
    faithful to You,

And in good health.
Give peace and order to all nations,
So that the whole world from end to end sounds with one
   voice:
'Blessed be the heart of God by which we were redeemed,
To Him be honour and praise for ever and ever.' Amen.

Roza's daughter Lula Markowska sent me the prayer on 5 May 1993. 'We used to add it to our daily prayer in the evening, quite often said as a family together,' Lula wrote. 'I often say it when somebody I care for is in special need. Please do the same.'

Zosia learned at the end of the war that her husband Andrzej had died bravely on 28 September 1939, fighting the Germans near the Polish city of Przemysl. Roza learned years later that Wladyslaw was arrested by the Soviets in September 1939 and was shot in the Ukraine in 1941. He had returned to their home at Tarnawatka in late September 1939 to find his family gone. When Soviet troops arrived he was in the grip of a bout of manic elation and tried to stop them entering the house. He was dragged off to jail and lingered there until he was shot. His grave was never found.

I still find it hard not to weep when I read that prayer because of its great beauty and because of the faith, hope and love of the women and children who recited it during the wartime years, not knowing that the husbands and fathers for whom they were praying were already dead.

his book would not been written or published but for the generosity and talents of four brilliant women. My wife Wafa' always had time to read and re-read endless drafts of endless chapters and always encouraged and advised me. Her insights were sometimes hard to accept, but she was always right: a guiding angel whose confidence in the outcome never faltered. Caroline Dawnay encouraged me greatly after seeing an early version of chapters that no longer exist, and later made a leap of faith by agreeing to become literary agent to a distant step-cousin on what must have seemed an amateurish venture. Her backing has been crucial, and I owe an immense debt to her professionalism and patience. Caroline Knox, then at John Murray, took the trouble to show me the way from journalese towards something like novelese, and I am deeply indebted to her. Finally, Natasha Martin at Aurum Press is proof that a fine editor can breathe new life and new direction into a book. I have been enormously fortunate that mine fell into the hands of an editor of her vision and skills. Phoebe Clapham also did a splendid job editing and copy-editing the manuscript.

Kirsten Ellis, El Marqués de Tamaroń, Stephanie Wolfe Murray and Krysia Sutherland helped greatly by reading and commenting on parts of the typescript at crucial moments. Andrzej Suchcitz, archivist at the Sikorski Institute in London, lent his expertise by reading the finished typescript for Polish spellings and factual accuracy. Any mistakes are mine, of course. Jas Tyszkiewicz generously allowed me to read and include extracts from his memoirs and writings. I am especially indebted to Wendy Tarnowska for letting me browse happily through documents and photographs passed down from her late husband Andrew Tarnowski, his brother Jas and their sister Maria 'Micia' Potocka. Artur Tarnowski and his wife Izabella allowed me to see interesting memoirs. Jan S. Tarnowski sent copies of family photographs from Warsaw and, crucially, photocopies of the visitors' book from our grandfather's home at Rudnik. Karol Laskowski did me a great service by copying photographs, and Michal Tarnowski helped with some knotty translations.

I owe special thanks to Stas Tarnowski, my father, and Aunt Sophie Tarnowska-Moss for many happy hours I spent interviewing them in Warsaw and London on life in pre-war Poland and their amazing wartime experiences.

I am deeply grateful to the following who also agreed to be interviewed for the purposes of this book:

Wacek and Julia Bninski, Bisia Carroll, Ewa Czernicka, Dana Dushmaitich, Jadwiga Hass'a Mach, Andrzej Jaxa-Chamiec, Lula Markowska, Wanda Marosanyi, Jas Pomian, Stach Sieminski, Marys Skarbek, Colonel David Smiley, Krysia Sutherland, Adam Tarnowski, Artur Tarnowski and his wife Izabella, Jas 'Glowa' Tarnowski, Michal Tarnowski, Roza Tarnowska, Sandra Tarnowska, Peter Tunnard and Tomasz Zamoyski.

Chapter 2

[1] Translated by Norman Davies in *God's Playground: A History of Poland*, vol. II, Norman Davies, Oxford University Press 1982.

[2] *A European Past: Memoirs by Prince Clary*, Weidenfeld & Nicolson, London 1978.

[3] *Historia Jednego Miasta nad Sanem*, Zofia i Zdzislaw Chmiel, Wydawca: Urzad Gminy i Miasta w Rudniku n/Sanem, Rudnik 1998. (*History of a Certain Town on the San*, Zofia and Zdzislaw Chmiel, Town and District Office at Rudnik on the San, Rudnik 1998.)

Chapter 3

[1] *The Eighteenth Decisive Battle of World History*, Lord d'Abernon (London 1931), quoted in *God's Playground* (*op. cit.*).

[2] *Przeglad Rudnicki*, No. 9, Towarzystwo Milosnikow Ziemii Rudnickiej, 37–420 Rudnik n.Sanem, Urzad Miasta i Gminy, Kwiecien 1992. (*Rudnik Review*, No. 9. Society of Lovers of the Rudnik Lands, Town and District Office, 37–420 Rudnik on the San, April 1992.)

Chapter 4

[1] *Master of Lancut: The memoirs of Count Alfred Potocki*, W.H. Allen, London 1959.

[2] *Not All Vanity*, Agnes de Stoeckl, ed. George Kinnaird, John Murray, London 1950.

Chapter 11

[1] *Ten jest z Ojczyzny mojej: Polacy z pomoca Zydom, 1939–45*, Wladyslaw Bartoszewski and Zofia Lewinowna, Wydawnictwo Znak, Kraków 1966. (*This One is from My Country: Poles giving assistance to Jews, 1939–45*, Wladyslaw Bartoszewski and Zofia Lewinowna, Wydawnictwo Znak, Krakow, 1966.)

Chapter 16

[1] *Wspomnienia Wojenne 1939–46*, Stanislaw Kopanski, Nakladem Katolickiego Osrodka Wydawniczego 'Veritas' w Londynie 1972. (*War Memoirs 1939–46*, Stanislaw Kopanski, Catholic Editorial, 'Veritas' Publishing Centre, London 1972.)

Chapter 19

[1] *Cairo in the War 1939–1945*, Artemis Cooper, Hamish Hamilton, London 1989.

[2] *Ill Met By Moonlight*, W. Stanley Moss, Buchan & Enright, London 1985.

Chapter 22

[1] 'Czekamy Ciebie' ('We Await You'), by Józef Szczepanski, translated by Norman Davies, quoted in *Rising '44: The Battle for Warsaw*, Norman Davies, Macmillan, London, 2004.